THE FUTURE OF THE ATLANTIC ALLIANCE

RUSI DEFENCE STUDIES SERIES

General Editor David Bolton, Director, Royal United Services Institute for Defence Studies

Editor Jennifer Shaw, MA, BSc(Econ)

Questions on defence give rise to emotion, sometimes to the detriment of balanced judgement. Since 1831 the Royal United Services Institute for Defence Studies has been noted for its objectivity, independence and initiative; the views of its members sharpened by responsibility and experience. In continuance of the Institute's aims, the *RUSI Defence Studies Series* seeks to provide a wider understanding and better informed debate of defence and national security issues. However, the views expressed in the books are those of the authors alone.

Published

Christopher Coker
US MILITARY POWER IN THE 1980s

Christopher Coker
THE FUTURE OF THE ATLANTIC ALLIANCE

Forthcoming

Clive Rose
CAMPAIGNS AGAINST WESTERN DEFENCE: NATO's ADVERSARIES AND CRITICS

Christopher Coker
NATO, THE WARSAW PACT AND AFRICA

David Greenwood
BRITISH DEFENCE PRIORITIES

Michael D. Hobkirk
THE POLITICS OF DEFENCE BUDGETING

Michael Leifer (editor)
THE ASIAN BALANCE OF POWER

THE FUTURE OF THE ATLANTIC ALLIANCE

Christopher Coker

Foreword by Laurence Martin

© Royal United Services Institute 1984

All rights reserved. No part of this publication may be reproduced or transmitted, in any form or by any means, without permission

First published 1984 by
THE MACMILLAN PRESS LTD
London and Basingstoke
Companies and representatives
throughout the world

ISBN 0 333 37546 7

Typeset by
Wessex Typesetters Ltd
Frome, Somerset

Printed and bound in Great Britain at
The Camelot Press Ltd, Southampton

British Library Cataloguing in Publication Data
Coker, Christopher
The future of the Atlantic alliance.—
(RUSI defence studies series)
1. North Atlantic Treaty Organization
I. Title   II. Royal United Services
Institute for Defence Studies
III. Series
355'.031'091821   UA646.3
ISBN 0-333-37546-7

Contents

Preface   David Bolton   vii
Foreword   Professor Laurence Martin   ix
Abbreviations   xvi

PART I   THE ATLANTIC ALLIANCE: ITS DEVELOPMENT AND POTENTIAL

1 Introduction   3

2 NATO Defences and the Warsaw Pact Threat   7
   NATO Doctrine   11
   Forward Stationed Forces   14
   New Conventional Defence Options   16

3 The Nuclear Dimension   25
   SALT Counted Systems   25
   Theatre Nuclear Forces   27
   Battlefield Nuclear Weapons   31
   Arms Control Negotiations   34
   Public Opinion and Nuclear Weapons   37

4 The Lilliputian Senate: The Failure of European Cooperation   50
   Western European Union   54
   Britain and a European Defence Community   64
   The European Nuclear Deterrent and Franco-German Cooperation   69
   Conclusion   71

5 Alliance Management: Defence Costs and Equipment   76
   Burden Sharing   76
   NATO Standardisation   83

Contents

6 Out of Area Operations — 95
European Contribution to the RDF — 97
European Naval Task Force in the Indian Ocean — 101
European Defence Organisation — 107
The United States and the European Commitment — 114

7 The Need for an Atlantic Community — 121

PART II PERCEPTIONS OF THE ATLANTIC ALLIANCE

8 NATO: The Next Decade *General Bernard W. Rogers* — 131

9 The United Kingdom's Strategic Interests and Priorities *The Rt Hon Michael Heseltine, MP* — 141

10 The Way Ahead: Britain's Roles *Air Marshal Sir Peter Terry* — 147

11 The Maritime Extension: The Restoration of US Naval Strength *Hon John Lehman* — 154

12 Security by Negotiation *Professor Hedley Bull* — 165

13 Changing Roles in the Alliance *John Wilkinson, MP, and Commander Michael Chichester* — 175

14 NATO's Forward Defence: New Strategy *D. R. Cotter and Dr N. F. Wikner (report)* — 188

15 New Operational Dimensions *General Dr F. M. von Senger und Etterlin* — 195

16 Dynamic Defence: The Northern Flank *General Sir Anthony Farrar-Hockley* — 207

17 The Southern Flank and Out of Area Operations *Lieutenant General James M. Thompson* — 216

Notes and References — 230

Index — 240

Preface

DAVID BOLTON

Against a background of the present strains and pressures within the Alliance, the Royal United Services Institute sought to examine its possible development and the options which might be available. In consequence, a year-long study took place which addressed the relevant issues. This book is the result of that year's work.

The study was inaugurated by General Bernard W. Rogers, the Supreme Allied Commander Europe, when he spoke of his perception of the next decade for NATO. Other subjects included an examination of flexible response and forward defence, the changing emphasis towards the conventional defence of Europe, as well as an examination of national roles within the Alliance and the impact of technology on future operational concepts. As perceptions of the strains within the Alliance vary between America and Europe, the Atlantic connection was also reviewed as was the threat within Central Europe and on the flanks, along with the possible defensive responses against it. There was a particular focus upon the military implications of arms control negotiations and in trying to develop a new approach to the whole concept of European security. The Institute was particularly fortunate in having such contributors to the study as Field Marshal Lord Carver, Admiral Sir James Eberle, Hon John Lehman, Professor Sir Ronald Mason, Sir Clive Rose, General Dr F. M. von Senger und Etterlin, Lord Soames, General Sir Anthony Farrar-Hockley and General James N. Thompson.

Dr Christopher Coker, from the Department of International Relations at the London School of Economics, had full access to all the material of the study, including that for which attribution was not possible on grounds of sensitivity. He has now produced this book which gives both an historical perspective and an overall coherence to this work on the future of the Atlantic Alliance. In so doing, Dr Coker has given emphasis to those issues of particular interest and moment. Firstly, the NATO response to the threat of the Warsaw Pact: then a discussion of the whole nuclear dimension, followed by an examination of Europe's failure to make better use of its overall resources. At the centre of the debate are the problems of defence procurement and rising defence costs, as well as a possible European contribution to areas of potential crises beyond NATO's boundaries. In Part II of the book are included the perceptions of those who by their positions of authority and responsibility, and the ideas they have to offer, are of value as source reference material.

As befits an Institute which gives priority to the military sciences, the utility of military power is at the forefront of our work. Thus, in this as in other studies, strategies, concepts of operation, force structures, as well as the provision of new weapon systems, feature large. If a proffered weakness is not to tempt a potential aggressor then military power must underpin foreign and security policies. In the free world, these issues should be understood and debated so that in the event of any crisis, the strength of public support and resolve sustains a dynamic and viable defence posture across the Alliance. This work by Dr Christopher Coker is a particularly notable contribution both to that end and to the RUSI Defence Studies Series.

Foreword

PROFESSOR LAURENCE MARTIN

Dr Coker's wide-ranging essay and the distinguished lectures that follow it in this volume take a worthy place in a vast succession of studies and reappraisals that has been proceeding unbroken since the North Atlantic Treaty was signed in 1949 and followed a year later by the founding of those standing commands and institutions which now characterise NATO. From this literature one could gain the impression that the Alliance has been in an almost permanent state of crisis. It would perhaps not be surprising if it had been, for alliances are by nature uneasy and changing bargains struck over the most fundamental of national interests: security. NATO has gone beyond precedent, however, and established a framework of standing collaboration and even integration more elaborate and enduring than any previous coalition. With its boundaries cast some 7–8000 miles apart, it would be amazing indeed if problems did not constantly arise.

That problems are endemic does not mean, of course, that they cannot be serious and those of NATO are often particularly so because there is an inherent and probably never wholly eradicable flaw at the heart of the Alliance. That flaw arises from the interaction of technology and geopolitics; from the facts that, in the nuclear age, the consequences of war can be literally fatal for a nation; that NATO's primary nuclear power, the United States, lies far from Europe, the most likely initial battlefield; and that Germany, the nation most exposed on that field is virtually barred by its past from becoming a nuclear power itself. Moreover the strategic bargain represented by the Alliance has changed radically since the Treaty was signed in 1949, for only when the Soviet Union acquired nuclear weapons and nuclear weapons were married to intercontinental missiles did the potential price demanded of the United States dawn on peoples and politicians. When it did, a reappraisal began which has proved continuous and which has reached a particularly acute phase in the 1980s.

There are indeed peculiarly noticeable parallels, as Dr Coker illustrates, between the present debate and the first serious reappraisal which accompanied the appearance of the H-bomb and the flight of the Sputnik. That crisis peaked with an uproar over American intermediate-range missiles in Europe that sounds familiar today and, after the ill-fated project for a Multilateral Force, finally reached a solution in the adoption of the 'flexible response', and the foundation of the Nuclear Planning Group. These expedients succeeded in quietening anxieties, but public reassurance probably owed more to the impression of political *détente* than to the new strategic concepts. Certainly it has now become clear that the flexible response was not a fully satisfactory answer to the flaws in the Alliance and that the subsequent guidelines worked out in the NPG did not reconcile differences of view but merely – and very usefully – made it possible to live with them.

In the past few years this *modus vivendi* has been subjected to ultimately intolerable strain. The sources of this strain are well-known and ably treated in the chapters that follow. A sustained increase in Soviet military forces, nuclear and conventional, has both reminded us of the strategic problem and made it seem less tractable. The worsening of East–West relations and more particularly of those between the United States and Soviet Union has made war seem less improbable, an impression not much less alarming to the public for being in reality probably false. Four American Presidents in a row have weakened confidence in the leadership of the United States – Mr Nixon by demeaning the office, Mr Ford by being a colourless stopgap, Mr Carter by being a vacillating and irritable failure, and Mr Reagan by managing to project an image of belligerence and recklessness, little less unsettling for being largely illusory. Meanwhile transAtlantic relations have been made more complex by the shifts in economic status since the Alliance began, so that while strategic power and leadership still inhere primarily in the United States, the European are more confident, more able to pay, but not so much more ready to do so.

The strategy of the Alliance has to carry two distinguishable burdens: it must deter the Soviet Union and it must sustain that confidence among the allies which alone renders the necessary effort forthcoming. In an age of nuclear deterrence the latter task may paradoxically be more difficult than the former, for a degree of risk that may well deter a rational opponent may create a strategic world that seems intolerably dangerous to one's friends. This is potentially fatal to deterrence itself, insofar as nations have two possible less robust responses to threat: direct appeasement or, its indirect forerunner, a wilful underestimate of the threat.

Appeasement has a strong and, to a degree, perfectly proper appeal to democracies and it is recognition of the contribution reconciliation of differences can make to security that has led the Alliance ever since the Harmel Report to espouse *détente* as well as deterrence as its purposes. The disappointment of exaggerated hopes reposed in the arm of *détente* has, however, added to the crisis of confidence that has arisen in the past few years as the deteriorating military balance forced itself on reluctant public attention.

Whatever its true military importance, the notorious SS-20 dramatised the deteriorating balance at a peculiarly sensitive point, not merely because nuclear war is the outcome most feared by all, but also because theatre nuclear war is the issue on which the shifting European–American strategic bargain has always been most troubled. However misleading the hackneyed comparisons drawn between an alleged American preference for defence or 'war fighting' and the European for deterrence, however much American and European views on the nuclear 'threshold' may overlap, there is no escaping the fact that European and American interests do diverge when it comes to contemplating the process of deliberate escalation on which the flexible response is founded. The 1969 Guidelines compromise, calling for a 'militarily meaningful demonstration of resolve' as the initial recourse, left many subsequent questions unanswered. Sensibly the Alliance has lived with ambiguous answers – an ambiguity which serves at once to reconcile allies, discourage debate and, it is hoped, leave a powerful deterrent uncertainty in the Soviet mind.

Probably ambiguity will continue to sustain an effective deterrent within the limits of mutual allied tolerance. But there are limits of ambiguity beyond which the military cannot plan and the attentive public cannot preserve its self-confidence. Moreover the task has not been made easier by what seems to have been a deliberately focused Soviet attempt to erode NATO's confidence in the theatre–nuclear link that holds the flexible response together. The Soviet combination of refurbished conventional forces capable of rapid advance, and modernised and supplemented nuclear weapons in the theatre and battlefield categories, in which hitherto the Soviet Union had not competed vigorously, is calculated both to advance the hour at which NATO would need to use such weapons and make such recourse less attractive. At the same time, in its arms control policy, the Soviet Union has sought to inhibit NATO's efforts to redress the balance by denigrating the Forward Based Systems, the European nuclear forces, the Enhanced Radiation Weapons and, most vehemently, the deployment of the Ground Launched Cruise missiles and the Pershing II. Is there, NATO must clearly ask itself, a point at which this Soviet erosion of the flexible response would render military action significantly less deterred as an option for Soviet policy?

The famous call by Helmut Schmidt in his London speech of 1977 was widely taken as a warning that this could be so and that the answer must be sought in part precisely by strengthening NATO's theatre nuclear arsenal. Henry Kissinger's equally noted warning two years later in Brussels, that deterrence could not be built on inferiority at all levels, left the prescription more open. Be that as it may, a political issue was clearly posed, the diplomatic management of which has been less than felicitious.

The case for establishing a land-based intermediate-range nuclear capability of reasonable invulnerability in Western Europe is strong. Put briefly, it reduces to making it clear to the Soviet Union that a decision to go to war in Europe is very likely a decision for a nuclear war, and one very probably embracing Soviet territory. It is not easy, however, to evaluate the actual dual-track decision of 1979 and its subsequent implementation. On the one hand, it is salutary that the Soviet Union has failed to deter NATO from taking the strategic steps it considers necessary. But if the dual-track formula was the unavoidable price of consent by some allies, it has reinforced the status of the Soviet Union as a participant in Western strategic debate. If this is the inevitable consequence of a free-thinking and nervous democratic public opinion, it nevertheless constitutes an asymmetric element in the equation that will henceforth require careful and sensitive management. It is, indeed, in the area of public opinion, that some of the heaviest prices for deployment may have been paid, for if the governments have – mostly – defied the Soviet Union, several important political parties – notably the German Social

Democrats and the British Labour Party – have moved perhaps further than ever before from the underlying strategic consensus of NATO. Possibly ideological obsolesence and the defence issue itself may prevent those parties reassuming power, but even in opposition their attitude establishes a troublesome new acerbity in the Western strategic debate.

It is, of course, the nuclear issue that so troubles the supporters of the Left and to that extent the move to reinforce the conventional element in NATO strategy may have an emollient effect; indeed there is some danger that the domestic political convenience of such a trend may lead to overestimation of its military merits.

There are undoubtedly attractive technological and doctrinal prospects in the conventional arena. NATO conventional forces could be made more effective simply by providing them with more of their existing weapons and focusing the effort more selectively on perceived weaknesses in the Soviet posture: hence the talk for years now, and even some action, to increase stocks, speed mobilisation, and sharpen the attack on Soviet armour and deployment of the Pact's 'second echelon'. Much publicised 'enhanced technology' now promises to combine better information handling, precision guidance, dispersed munitions and long-range conventional strike, to disrupt the Soviet attack and discharge with conventional means many missions hitherto practicable if at all only with nuclear weapons.

There is no doubt that these opportunities must be seized and that substantial strategic and political benefits may follow. But it is also necessary to maintain a sense of proportion as to the likely results. This is far from the first time that NATO has been promised salvation by technological wizardry; indeed we should recall that it was in just such a spirit the NATO deployed and became dependent on the tactical nuclear weapons that now arouse such anxiety. Moreover, though we can hardly doubt that we are about to witness a new and remarkable generation of weapons, experience suggests that not a few specific systems will prove a sad and expensive failure. The problem of expense is another reason for restraining optimism. Defence seems likely to enjoy less rather than more real expenditure in the next few years, barring a major crisis. The new weaponry may be cost-effective but it is unlikely to justify major retrenchment on the more familiar systems. Greater efficiency may be sought not only on the battlefield but in the processes of procurement – indeed, new initiatives in collaborative manufacture may be essential to earn political goodwill for some of the new schemes. But even if such schemes save money – they have not often done so in the past but perhaps they mobilise more resources than would otherwise be the case – we must recall that we are looking to the new strategy and devices to serve two purposes at once: to shore-up an increasingly disadvantaged initial conventional defence and to do so sufficiently decisively to reduce the existing nuclear element in our more extended operations. All this at a time when, as portions of this book illustrate, the major ally, the United States, may face increasing military demands beyond the NATO area.

NATO most obviously exploit new technology to the utmost limit of its resources, simply to do what it can to redress its present deficiencies. We should curb our wilder expectations, however, as to how rapidly new technology will come into service or how radically it will improve our situation. There is also a more fundamental question to ponder when new technology and doctrine is expected not merely to improve the conventional balance but to 'denuclearise' NATO strategy. Such a process is expected to flow from both a specific and a general effect: the specific is to replace nuclear weapons in particular tasks, especially the breaking up of tank formations, the destruction of enemy airfields and the deep interdiction of enemy logistics; the general effect is to enhance deterrence by making the overall prospect of Soviet victory without first recourse to nuclear weapons more remote.

Here there are two problems. One flows simply from the doubt surrounding the overall efficacy of the new strategies and tactics. The Soviet Union will, of course, adjust its own armament and doctrine to counteract NATO's revised strategy, just as it has worked to undermine our former nuclear plans and thereby produced our present dilemma. More fundamentally, some of the Soviet vulnerabilities we are planning to exploit with new technology have arisen in part from Soviet efforts to deal with the threat of NATO first use of nuclear weapons. It is therefore important either to satisfy ourselves that the new conventional weapons can fulfil their role in a denuclearised NATO strategy or to be quite clear that the principle of 'first use if absolutely necessary' that has always underlain the flexible response remains intact.

There is an even more basic question as to whether any non-nuclear strategy can equal the deterrent aura of possible nuclear escalation. The stereotyped 'European' or 'German' fear that reducing the danger of nuclear war may increase that of war itself cannot be shrugged off just because it is familiar and inconvenient. Certainly there are many distinguished voices raised to urge NATO in the direction of 'no first use' and this volume will form a valuable source for those who wish to make up their own minds on this vital point. As it seems unlikely that the danger of nuclear action can ever be wholly eradicated from the prospect of war in Europe, there are probably limits beyond which we should not try to do so if the price is undue strain on the political-economy of the West or its capacity to cope with much more probable military exigencies elsewhere. Indeed it can be argued that it is only the nuclear aura that makes the position of fragmented democracies so closely bordered by a totalitarian military Superpower tolerable and that in a world that reverted to the pre-nuclear state, Western Europe's place in the Soviet sphere of influence would become geopolitically unmistakeable. Nor should we underestimate the political opposition Soviet propaganda might stir up against even new conventional armament, especially if this included elements that could be depicted as 'offensive'.

Real strategic needs and public anxiety do undoubtedly call for improving NATO's conventional capability but a well-presented effort to do this and stress its place in Western security can probably relieve popular concern well short of an explicitly and wholly non-nuclear strategy. Similarly, though there is probably much to be gained both directly and by way of public reassurance by continued pursuit of arms control, perhaps particularly 'confidence building measures', we should try not to take this to the point at which Western policy becomes a series of disjointed responses to Soviet pressure. Rather we need to return the Western debate to a coherent review of NATO's strategic requirements, calmly identified and reasonably addressed. To such a review the pages that follow make a substantial contribution.

Abbreviations

AVF	All Volunteer Force
BAOR	British Army of the Rhine
CNAD	Conference of National Armaments Directors
CND	Campaign for Nuclear Disarmament
EDC	European Defence Community
EURCOM	European Command (Heidelberg)
ICBM	Inter-Continental Ballistic Missile
IEPG	Independent European Programme Group
INF	Intermediate Nuclear Forces
LTDP	Long Term Defence Programme
MIDEASTFOR	American Middle East Task Force
MIRV	Multiple, Independently Targetable Vehicle
MRLS	Multiple Rocket Launcher Systems
NAPR	NATO Armaments Planning Review
NPG	Nuclear Planning Group
PAPS	Periodic Armaments Planning System
POMCUS	Prepositioned Overseas Material Configured to Unit Sets
PPP	Purchasing Power Parity
RDF	Rapid Deployment Force
SAC	Standing Armaments Committee (WEU)
SACEUR	Supreme Allied Commander, Europe
SACLANT	Supreme Allied Commander, Atlantic
SALT	Strategic Arms Limitation Talks
SLBM	Submarine Launched Ballistic Missile
STANAVFORLANT	Standing Naval Force, Atlantic
TOW	Tracked wire guided missile
WEU	Western European Union

Part I

The Atlantic Alliance: Its Development and Potential

1 Introduction

The past years have seen the emergence of serious debate within the Atlantic Alliance concerning the policies NATO should follow in order to ensure its future security. American and European thinking has appeared to diverge in a number of important areas – the level of defence effort required, the responsibility of the organisation for developments outside its formal boundaries and the precise role of military power in influencing these developments, as well as the balance between military efficiency and diplomatic negotiation, particularly the role of arms control. None of these differences is new. They have existed in varying degrees of intensity within the Alliance almost since its inception. The divergences between the United States and Europe have rarely been so potentially serious, or divisive, particularly with the nature and scale of the threat facing NATO and the measures needed to deal with it.

The most immediate differences between the United States and Europe originate from the emergence of a more assertive mood in Washington concerning America's role in the world – a mood which has manifested itself most clearly in a marked increase in public support for higher defence spending, though not at a level which the Reagan Administration would like to sustain. This mood is due to the general perception that the United States had fallen behind the Soviet Union in the 1970s, and also at the apparent (and consequent) decline in American power and influence – a perception dramatically underlined in the last years of the Carter Administration, most of all by the seizure of the American hostages in Iran. The mid-1970s appear in retrospect critical years for the United States – a time of major reverse in Vietnam, the high water mark of *détente* which failed to 'tame' the Soviet Union, the dramatic rise in East–West trade which brought a greater return for Europe than for America. These setbacks and frustrated hopes struck a society which had been conditioned to success for a generation. Clearly, many Americans have increasingly felt the need to explain to themselves what has happened and how best to redress the losses that have been suffered. The need has become all the more urgent since the Reagan Administration came to power because recent events have contrasted so strikingly with the expectations it created before coming into office, a fact with which most administrations have had to live in the last 25 years.

It has become quite common to blame the Europeans for the predicament in which the United States now finds itself – for failing to stand on their own feet, for consistently criticising American policy in the world at large while doing little themselves to maintain Western interests beyond Europe.

In 1982 in *The Wall St Journal* Paul Seabury suggested that the mere possibility of a US withdrawal would compel the Europeans to decide 'where they stand'. In *The Washington Post* Jeffrey Record found it 'impossible to justify the deployment of (US ground forces) on behalf of rich, indolent allies . . .', a position from which he rapidly backtracked in the light of the rather simplistic and ill-informed remarks which accompanied the discussion of the Stevens Amendment.[1] The picture of rich and indolent allies conjured up by Irving Kristol three years earlier – the picture of a 'risk aversive' society far more interested in marginal increments in social welfare than in playing a significant role in world affairs,[2] has become a potent image in the United States.

The criticism is made not only by conservatives. There are many liberal democrats including the former Presidential candidate Eugene Macarthy who are of the opinion that the United States in the strictest sense has 'few if any true allies', only clients that it maintains at great cost to itself in a dependency relationship.[3] It has become fashionable to believe, contrary to the received wisdom of the past 35 years, that even if America's allies could help to defend her own national interests as opposed to their own, their help would be so general as to afford little or no assistance. Amid so many voices of dissent, NATO is beginning to look somewhat anachronistic 'conceived in another time and designed for another state of affairs'.[4] From this conclusion it is but a small step to assert that without a fundamental restructuring of the Atlantic Alliance the United States would be better off on its own.

What is important about the present crisis is not these complaints or even the concerns which underlie them. It is rather the response they have elicited from the European critics of NATO who in the past have not been particularly voluble or especially responsive to such concerns. A new generation of European revisionists now find themselves in sympathy with their American counterparts although their own diagnosis of the malaise from which the Alliance is suffering is, of course, rather different.

In Europe these complaints are perhaps symptoms rather than causes of a general change in the political climate of the Atlantic community. In the United States, the respect for the Atlantic Alliance has begun to be replaced by the feeling that it is quite unable to deal with the real threats to security and that what is needed is not a specious reaffirmation of unanimity but escape into a realignment of forces. The thoughts of many Americans are increasingly preoccupied with the techniques of individual salvation – some relying on a division of labour, with the Europeans looking after the defence of Europe and the United States the rest of the Free World;[5] others seeking a complete pull-out of US forces from Europe, among them Maxwell Taylor who originally opposed the Radford Plan;[6] others again looking for a totally independent option, deriding the Europeans as 'free riders' who have not only lost confidence in the United States but also in themselves.[7]

Among the European revisionists there are those who are quite prepared to pay a higher price for defence if it means greater control over their own future.[8] Most recognise that, at the very least, this would demand an effective European deterrent, and at least, the prior creation of a European Defence Community.[9]

Both sides suspect that the Alliance has begun to trade in used images and shallow gestures, and that NATO's apologists all too easily appeal to the memories and preoccupations which lie along the undersurface of history rather than to the real national interests which inspired Marshall in his dialogue with Senator Gillette over the stationing of the Seventh Army in Europe.[10] The great age of cooperation which forged the Atlantic Alliance appears to lie behind us. What is left is potential disarray.

These criticisms of the Alliance, however, have not necessarily brought with them serious analysis of the problem. The climate of opinion ten years ago was, of course, far too optimistic. The absence of critical comment rightly annoyed many Americans and Europeans alike. But today much of the criticism is too overtly didactic, too introspective, and much too unreal.

Europe's aspirations may lie in the direction of independence, but the day-to-day business of affairs is that of a partner that may complain but must accept American leadership. The United States may wish to escape 'entangling alliances', but it is compelled to recognise for the moment that Europe would not long withstand the Soviet threat without its protection. Both parties are compelled to cast their discourse about the Alliance in the rhetoric of independence even though the rhetoric sometimes obscures popular understanding of the complexity of the Atlantic partnership.

It may be tempting to advocate a decisive break with the past, if only to escape the tactical problems which confront policy makers most of their lives. It is not difficult to understand the recurrent yearning for a single strategic solution to the problems of partnership with an inconsistent and often unreliable partner, the United States; and an often ungenerous and introspective Europe. But despite this yearning in 30 years no such solution has emerged, and none is in sight. Doubtless, it is inherent in all coalitions to defeat grand strategies. For better or worse there is no alternative to NATO. The allies must make the best of it they can.

2 NATO Defences and the Warsaw Pact Threat

The standing forces of the NATO nations total 4.4m personnel of which some 2.6m are stationed in Europe. There are also about half a million other military trained men, many in paramilitary units. Altogether the total armed forces belonging to its members, but not all committed to the Alliance, include 76 active divisions plus 123 brigades, with about 22 670 main battle tanks, and air forces equipped with approximately 11 270 combat aircraft. NATO like the Warsaw Pact relies heavily on the mobilisation of reserves to bring existing divisions up to strength as well as to mobilise new formations.

NATO land forces stationed in Europe number some 84 divisions many of which are also ready to fight at very short notice. There are in addition 13 active US divisions and a Canadian brigade in North America which could be made available in Europe in the event of hostilities.

The land based air forces available for Allied Command Europe consist of 1950 ground attack fighter aircraft, 740 interceptors and 285 reconnaissance aircraft. The few remaining United Kingdom Vulcan bombers no longer have a conventional role. The United States and Canada could reinforce rapidly with some 1900 more combat aircraft, although ground crew and equipment would have to be airlifted to Europe. NATO has made considerable progress in improving the ability of its air forces to operate and survive in a hostile environment. The introduction of the F-16 and Tornado have given its aircraft a much greater all-weather capability than the previous generation of NATO aircraft (although the range and payload improvement is not as great as that gained recently by the Warsaw Pact).

Since the late 1960s, questions have begun to mount as to

whether the current posture of NATO's conventional forces in the Central Region is capable of dealing with a dramatically altered Soviet threat. The Warsaw Pact forces which confront NATO today represent more than simply an enlarged threat. It is a threat whose character has been deliberately re-tailored to exploit the very weaknesses in NATO's conventional posture. This threat challenges not only the viability of NATO's conventional deterrent but also the capability of NATO's political machinery to mobilise that deterrent in time to meet the likely demands of a future military crisis.

References are often made to a continuing shift in the balance of power to the advantage of the Warsaw Pact. Until recently, in contrast to Soviet naval forces, the quantitative strength of the Pact's land and air forces had not increased appreciably. Now this is no longer the case, while their quality is continuing to improve. In some areas, for example, air defence systems, certain armoured vehicles and artillery, Soviet weapon systems are, at least, equal to, if not better than those of the West; and while the Pact's tactical air forces are behind the West, the gap is narrowing all the time.[1] Although NATO armaments too, are being modernised, the rate of modernisation within NATO is slower than that within the Warsaw Pact, so that the balance of military power continues to count against it.

Following a quantitative expansion, the Soviet Union has pursued a programme of modernisation designed to provide its ground forces with the capacity to wage successfully the *blitzkrieg* strategy called for in Soviet doctrine. The T-72 main battle tank has been introduced into the Group of Soviet Forces in East Germany. This improvement in tank design has been coupled with an increase of 60 to 80 tanks in its standard inventory.[2] Together these improvements have greatly strengthened the Warsaw Pact's armour which today outnumbers NATO's by almost 3:1, the margin considered necessary for a successful offensive.

The replacement of armoured personnel carriers with the BMP-60 mechanised infantry combat vehicle has enabled Soviet infantry to fight without dismounting – a capacity denied whether by choice or design to every NATO mechanised infantry division except those attached to the *Bundeswehr*. For the most part NATO is still tied to technologically obsolescent armoured personnel carriers.

Two other developments should also be mentioned. The shift from towed to self-propelled artillery which permits artillery to keep pace with advancing armour, thus significantly enhancing the tank's survivability, has been accompanied by an estimated expansion of at least 50 per cent of Soviet artillery tubes in recent years. Finally, the proliferation of a formidable array of tactical air defence systems offers the Warsaw Pact the prospect of a much better air defence system which could result in a severe loss of NATO aircraft in the opening stages of hostilities. The Pact is also becoming ever more capable of carrying out sorties accurately and deep inside NATO territory with aircraft operating at low altitudes. Aircraft which initially had a purely air defensive task are also being used increasingly for offensive action.[3]

Perhaps, nothing speaks more for the increased superiority of Soviet forces than the transformation of Soviet tactical air power. In 1968 Soviet tactical air forces were orientated primarily towards the defence of their own airspace. Accordingly, they were composed largely of short-range, low payload aircraft possessing only incidental ground attack capabilities. Since then they have been fundamentally restructured with the apparent objective of acquiring a close air support capability along the entire breadth of the battle area and deep interdiction of NATO airspace against fixed site targets such as nuclear weapon facilities, supply bases and airfields.

The rapid introduction of a host of longer range heavier payload aircraft and strike helicopters – the MiG-21 and 23 the SU-17 and 19, the Backfire bomber and the MiG-24 – greatly reduces NATO's traditional advantage in tactical air power. In the mid-1970s and particularly between 1975–77, the Soviet Union increased its deployment of new fighter-bomber aircraft in eastern Europe by over 200 per cent.

NATO air forces still have more staying power and are technologically superior though the margin is getting smaller. The Alliance also has an advantage in pilot training and experience. But the air war has significantly shifted westward and, although the ultimate mission of its air power remains that of providing fire power for forces on the ground, it must now save itself before it can save the land forces. There would still be too few military airfields available under wartime conditions to operate all the aircraft at its disposal and to provide for adequate dispersal of aircraft for survival. The new character of Soviet tactical aviation has deprived NATO's own air power of its traditional role as the great 'equaliser' of Warsaw Pact predominance on the ground.

The precise consequences for NATO of each of these numerous improvements in Soviet conventional forces remain speculative. Taken together, however, they have almost certainly altered the character of the threat to NATO in the Central Region.

The principal analytical difficulty of making sense of these statistics arises from the fact that the goal of NATO's military organisation is expressed largely in terms of deterrence. While a variety of different formulas are often used to describe the balance of forces on the Central Front, they are all based on a number of assumptions and judgments about factors that are either unknowable or incalculable. The methods most frequently used compare quantitative data involving manpower totals, equipment levels and number of combat units. Purely quantitative assessments provide a rough measure of the 'static' capability of both sides but give very little indication of the dynamics of the modern battlefield and are, therefore, of limited value in weighing the relative force strengths under conditions of conflict.[5]

Comparisons of manpower totals can be presented at a variety of levels each of which poses problems of relevance. The total active manpower of either side NATO: 4.4m and the Warsaw Pact 5.7m gives an indication of total military potential; the total active ground manpower, NATO 2 778 000 and the Warsaw Pact 2 634 000 provides a slightly narrower focus and indicates the total combat manpower that could be brought to bear. A more selective focus still, on the active ground forces in central Europe, NATO 732 000 and Warsaw Pact 935 000, provides a more relevant view of the immediate situation and shows a marked Warsaw Pact superiority, a position which many believe is compounded by the close proximity of Soviet units in the western military districts of the Soviet Union.[6] In all such comparisons the inclusion of France and a number of East European nations, particularly Romania, is a questionable assumption.

Instead of manpower totals, calculations of the number of combat units or so-called divisional equivalents are frequently used to indicate how ground force totals translate into fighting power. According to one estimate the immediate forces available to NATO and the Warsaw Pact on the first day of mobilisation (M+1) are 27 and 47 divisions respectively. These figures are used to indicate the time of greatest advantage for the Pact and of danger to NATO. The same estimate suggests that the overall force ratio on the first day of a Warsaw Pact mobilisation would be 1.7:1 in the Pact's favour. The significance of these force ratios is that most defence analysts believe that an attacker needs an advantage of 3:1 to be certain of success. Given the initiative and localised strength, however, a theatre ratio of 1.5:1 might be sufficient to facilitate a breakthrough at points of the Warsaw Pact's own choosing.[7]

Force ratios, however, depend on a number of incalculable factors, the most important of which depend on when NATO decides to mobilise its own forces, and how long US reinforcements will take to arrive. It is impossible to calculate with precision how fast either side could mobilise or augment its forces or anticipate the difficulties each is likely to experience thereafter.

The third unit of measurement – equipment totals – is also of limited value since it implies a direct one-on-one matching of identical units, a relationshp which in the modern battlefield would be only a single part of a very complex picture. Such simple comparisons ignore the fact that the different strategies and tactics of the two alliances have produced very different requirements. The offensive doctrine of the Warsaw Pact calls for an emphasis on armour; while NATO's essentially defensive doctrine calls for an emphasis on anti-tank capabilities of which the tank itself is only one element. The only real test of a weapon system is how well it performs the missions for which it is developed and how well it copes with the systems on the other side developed to counter it.

After all, the capability of any armed force to accomplish its mission is far more important than any symmetry or parity with the potential enemy. By tonnage and type of vessel the German Navy under Tirpitz was indeed a counter weight to the Royal Navy. By 1913 it was no longer possible to predict the outcome of a major engagement between the two fleets. This did not inhibit Britain, however, from going to war the following year. In the event, the German Navy failed dismally to break the British blockade, a task for which it had actually been built.

NATO DOCTRINE

Strategy for the defence of Europe has changed markedly since the formation of NATO. Until the mid-1960s, America's overwhelming strategic and theatre nuclear superiority was believed almost sufficient to deter any form of Soviet aggression. Although the Soviet Union and its Warsaw Pact allies maintained as they do today a preponderance of conventional forces on the continent, the threat of massive nuclear retaliation against the Soviet Union itself was adequate to deter the use of those forces by a country that was incapable of responding in kind. The function of NATO's conventional forces, such as they were, was primarily that of a trip-wire designed to establish the fact of aggression and ensure an immediate nuclear response.

By the mid-1960s, confidence that nuclear weapons alone could continue to deter a Soviet attack across the whole spectrum of threats ranging from nuclear attack to limited conventional aggression had markedly declined. The emergence of formidable Soviet strategic nuclear retaliatory capabilities, although still inferior to those of the United States, had rendered the continental United States itself a potential target. Doubts arose in Europe, voiced most strongly by de Gaulle, whether any American President would bring upon himself a nuclear exchange.

The Americans themselves made no secret of their own concern. At the height of the Berlin crisis the Acting Secretary of State Christian Herter admitted that he could not conceive of the President initiating a nuclear war unless the United States itself was under attack.[8] In April 1961, Robert McNamara was even more explicit when he told the Senate Subcommittee on Defence Appropriations that 'the decision to employ tactical nuclear weapons in limited conflicts should not be forced on the United States simply because there is no other means to cope with them'.[9]

The result of these concerns was the formal decision by NATO in 1967 to adopt what is still the current strategy: the doctrine of flexible response. Flexible response called for the development of strategic nuclear, theatre and conventional capabilities to provide NATO with the ability to deter, and if necessary, defeat a Warsaw Pact attack. The essence of the doctrine was the altered role of the Alliance's conventional forces: no longer simply a trigger to nuclear war, they were charged with the task of halting a conventional attack without an immediate resort to a nuclear response, at whatever level.

Flexible response still remains NATO's declared doctrine. Initially a Soviet attack would be met by a NATO 'covering force' consisting largely of armoured cavalry formations deployed well forward along the German border. The covering force would seek to identify the main attack and try to trade space for time although its options here would be limited. These covering forces today represent approximately one quarter of all active NATO ground forces deployed in central Europe.[10]

The second phase of the defence calls for waging the main defensive battle by a combination of major NATO combat formations in Europe and reinforcements brought in from the United States, Canada and the United Kingdom. The third and final phase would depend upon the outcome of the main defensive battle. Should NATO succeed in stopping a Soviet advance, a counter-attack would in theory be possible. Should NATO forces be threatened with destruction, immediate consideration would be given to using theatre nuclear weapons. Thus, even if unsuccessful, NATO's conventional forces would, at least, be able to buy time to decide whether to press ahead with a nuclear retaliation.

Flexible response has come under criticism in recent years on several counts. First, inherent in the concept of a 'covering force' operation is the loss of German territory. Currently, this risk is compounded by equipment deficiencies which threaten both the ability of the covering force to provide the time needed to mount a main defence and the capacity of the covering force to hold forward positions. Together these conditions could result in the loss of territory so substantial as to prompt Germany to consider whether it is worth fighting on. The Alliance has always had to face the prospect that once deterrence breaks down the Germans may not wish to be defended.

The second proposition is that whatever chances NATO's forces might have for success may depend upon the amount of warning time preceding hostilities. The problem is a complex one. Although a surprise attack would encounter relatively thin defences, the attacking force would be necessarily limited in number as well. Despite heightened fears about a sudden unprovoked attack SACEUR remains convinced that intelligence sources would be able to provide a minimum of 96 hours warning which would be sufficient to mobilise forces in time to blunt a quick 'run to the Rhine'.[11]

All things being equal, of course, the rapid reinforcement of forward defences by US squadrons and divisions would hopefully proceed at a rate that would dissuade the Warsaw Pact from carrying its own mobilisation further. But such a reinforcement might be so threatening that it might bring on itself the attack it hoped to prevent, and there are many who argue that such a fear would itself deter the deterrer – that it might inhibit political decision-making and, perhaps, even prompt the smaller NATO members, notably the BENELUX countries, to prohibit the influx of British and American forces during a crisis in what might only later be seen as the run-up to a Warsaw Pact invasion. If an attack were to be launched the adequacy of reinforced NATO defences would depend largely on the amount of time between NATO's political decision to react and the initiation of hostilities.

Finally, recent developments in the Soviet conventional and theatre nuclear posture suggest that the Soviet Union is hoping to neutralise NATO's battlefield nuclear options. Since the mid-1970s the Soviet Union has expanded its nuclear forces in Europe to the point where they may now credibly deter NATO's first-use of tactical nuclear weapons. A *blitzkrieg* strategy with a rapid conventional breakthrough and seizure of NATO's theatre nuclear assets might also be in prospect. It is this perception which accounts for the Alliance's unwillingness to engage the general public in a discussion of why the first use doctrine should still apply. Very few political leaders have any faith in it.

Each of these caveats has an immediate consequence for NATO's tactical doctrine. If current trends continue, the credibility of the Alliance's present conventional force posture will be increasingly subject to question. The implications of these developments warrant further discussion.

FORWARD STATIONED FORCES

Decreased warning time severely limits the reinforcements that could be moved from North America and the United Kingdom. It greatly magnifies the importance of forces already in place on the continent, the bulk of which are and, of necessity, must be European. Yet the present pace at which they could be deployed is clearly inadequate. The problem for the United States is compounded by a limited strategic airlift capability and by an acute shortage of arms and equipment prepositioned on the continent. In the face of decreased warning, the demand for existing strategic airlift might well exceed its availability.

The plan at the moment is to airlift American troops to Europe in the first 30 days of an engagement. Inevitably there would be bottlenecks, difficulties in integrating the reserves with forces in the front line, and the all too likely breakdown in communications between units which previously may never have served together. The airlift capacity the United States intends putting at NATO's disposal would largely be provided by 70 C-5 and 234 C-141 transports of Military Airlift Command and 227 commercial jet airliners which would be made available in an emergency through the Civil Reserve Airfleet. Following the decision to reinforce, it would take ten days to transport the first division even with most of the unit's heavy equipment stockpiled in Germany. Transporting three more divisions could take three weeks.[12]

These and other figures must bring into doubt the United States reserve commitment. It would take at present 14 days to airlift one infantry division to Europe. The transport of a mechanised infantry division would take even longer. A C-5 transport plane can airlift only one tank at a time; a division has about 250. The time required to transport the tanks of an armoured division would take much longer, probably nine round trips using the USAF's existing fleet of 70 C-5s, always assuming that the airfields in Germany would be available.[13]

There are two other problems of the American reinforcements. The hope that its frontline forces will hold in the initial days of an attack has meant that the United States has neither had to make, nor take seriously, proposals for improving the deployment of its forces in Europe. It makes doubtful sense to station substantial equipment west of the Rhine when the Seventh Army in the south is not even in the area most likely to come under attack. Within the first hours of a war the bridges across the Rhine might well be destroyed making it difficult for allied reserves to get to the front in time. Strange though it may seem it was not until 1978 that the United States published a report on the tactical aircraft capability for shuttling American troops from the Netherlands and the United Kingdom.[14]

The second problem of airlifting American troops is the size of the existing stockpiles and war reserves in Europe. The immediate application of immense fire power may be the only means of halting an invasion well forward, yet there is a general shortage of armoured fighting vehicles, artillery, missiles and other supplies. Ammunition stocks may well be inadequate in the light of expanded consumption rates projected for modern combat in Europe.

War reserve stocks are general stocks maintained to replace equipment expenditures or losses in combat; prepositioned equipment or POMCUS (Prepositioned Overseas Material Configured to Unit Sets) is equipment specifically held for use of reinforcing units flown in from the United States. In 1977 the United States embarked on a major expansion of POMCUS stores with the object of stockpiling enough material for three additional divisions by 1983 and six by the end of the 1980s. Yet the expansion has been made up at the cost of the reserve forces in the United States itself where all but three and two-thirds divisions have been stripped of most of their front line equipment.

In short, the separation of the Seventh Army from immediate access to its ammunition dumps; the concentration of ammunition sites in a manner which represents a standing temptation to pre-emptive air and sabotage attack; and the disposition of much of its other equipment west of the Rhine (including the United Kingdom) must raise serious questions about its true readiness for combat. Commenting on the problem Kenneth Coffey concludes:

> In summary, the limitations on POMCUS and war reserve stocks in Germany raises serious doubts about the army's ability to equip and then support a large number of additional reinforcements. The planned improvements in POMCUS stocks and war reserves if fully implemented will ease but not eliminate the problem. They would allow some reinforcements to be quickly added to the battlefield. Yet the bulk of US forces, particularly the units required for an extended conflict would still be faced with equipment and support problems.[15]

NEW CONVENTIONAL DEFENCE OPTIONS

Some defence analysts now believe that a credible conventional defence is possible for the first time since the mid-1960s. The introduction of new technologies; the adoption of new operational doctrines, and the more effective utilisation of Europe's substantial reserves of manpower all suggest that the initiative may have passed to the defence, not the attack.

Until recently the most promising development was thought to be the introduction of Precision Guided Munitions (PGM). The US Army has already committed itself to purchasing 360 000 Multiple Rocket Launcher Systems (MRLS) over the next few years. Although the Warsaw Pact may have a 2:1 advantage in tanks, the acquisition of precision guided munitions could offset the balance quite significantly. It is also much less expensive than producing tanks. The United States' new M-1 tank is 400 times more expensive than the tube launched optically tracked wire guided missile (TOW) which was developed in the 1960s and first tested in battle in Vietnam in 1972. Presently procured at the rate of 12 000 a year, each costs $7000 compared with $3m for the M-1 tank. On the battlefield of the future the large battle tank, already expensive in terms of men and money, seems to be threatened with obsolescence. MRLS fired in volleys of 12 are capable of releasing 600 submunitions. Position coordinates of the target are transmitted to mobile control centres which later release the missiles over their targets. Terminal guidance systems, scanning with infra-red sensors, are capable of homing in on individual tanks or following the shape of a tank column and releasing their submunitions in appropriate sequence.

The introduction of MRLS may enable the West to reduce its costs – allowing its armies to match Soviet capabilities without drawing upon other resources; to raise the financial costs to the Soviet Union of its own *blitzkrieg* strategy; and to raise the military costs as well by making it difficult for the Russians to meet the trade-off between armour and mobility without which a *blitzkrieg* strategy is unlikely to be very convincing.

To a limited extent reliance on precision guided munitions could help satisfy three objectives. First, as munitions are divided into submunitions each with its own guidance systems which home in on their target, the cost per anti-tank round will be substantially reduced. The cost of an anti-tank weapon is already much less than that of a tank. In the future the disparity will almost certainly become greater.

Secondly, to provide protection against armour piercing warheads, the Russians will have to replace the existing tanks with steel armour of the type already used by the American M-1. The cost will be phenomenal. Finally, a missile defence which allows NATO forces to attack tanks from behind as well as in front of the enemy will force the Soviet Union to increase the armour weight of its tanks which at 60 tons is already prohibitively heavy. This could well reduce the mobility of its tank divisions as well as make the side that strikes first more vulnerable. Despite the advantages of surprise its armed forces will be exposed from the moment they attack.

The precision guided munition is invariably if not accurately described as a defensive weapon which could well restore the advantage to the defence and reduce the tank to its old role as an infantry support vehicle. The reasoning behind this claim is that missile launchers can be easily concealed; and if employed in quantity could offset an enemy's advantage in tanks and, if not turn back a *blitzkrieg* attack, certainly blunt it. The only problem with the concept is that a dispersed defence would leave the Russians with the initiative. A weapons system can often form its own rationale. Defence alone is not a substitute for defence and counter-attack; it may indeed, be an invitation to attack by an enemy quite confident in its advantage in numbers.

To rely exclusively on PGMs would be foolish. During the war in Vietnam air-to-air guided missiles which had replaced the air cannon on American planes in the 1950s failed so frequently that they were found by many pilots to be as much a hindrance as a help in combat. The cannon eventually had to be reintroduced. A mix of systems is better than over-reliance on any one, given the chequered history of technological innovation.

The cost factor of technological change also militates against relying on PGMs. While the cost of a single munition may be low compared with the cost of its target, unit costs are still high: $4000 for one TOW missile against $3m for the Main Battle Tank, but $130 000 to field a complete system with ten missiles each.[16] The new systems with their inevitable technological modifications and improvements will be significantly more expensive than those currently deployed. Nor must one forget the cost of protection for the missile systems themselves – not to mention the platforms such as the M-113 armoured personnel carriers which are currently being modified for this purpose.

Technological improvements offer one way out of NATO's present predicament; a new conventional doctrine known as the 'air-land battle' offers another. The essence of this new doctrine is a more effective utilisation of existing forces which would enable the allies to attack the follow on (reinforcing) echelons of Warsaw

Pact forces before they have a chance to cross the frontier into West Germany. The success of a massive Soviet *blitzkrieg* against Europe would be critically dependent upon maintaining the momentum of attack to breakthrough NATO's forward defence at points of Soviet choosing. In effect, the Soviet Union would need to deploy successive echelons at a rate that would permit rapid replacement of losses and insure a swift defeat of NATO forces. If NATO, however, could isolate the attacking first echelon from its reinforcements by eliminating the latter, the momentum of the attack would be destroyed and, with it, any reasonable prospect of an irreparable and strategically decisive Soviet penetration of Western Europe.

This new doctrine, if adopted and implemented by the Alliance, might enhance conventional deterrence, raise the nuclear threshold and add new meaning to the strategy of forward defence. It seeks to capitalise on three major advances in weapons technology which have already taken place: the substantially improved effectiveness of conventional weapons carrying improved munitions that can be delivered from existing platforms; the great potential of micro-electronics to enhance the front line units' ability to collect, distribute and act on information about the opposing force; and improvements in the ability to target improved conventional fire power against enemy force concentrations.

The economics of the modern battlefield are all important. Diverting funds to defence from public investment weakens economies. There is an optimum level of current military expenditure arguably higher than that of some NATO countries, but finite nevertheless. Certainly, economic stringency does not argue for conceding numerical superiority, or for accepting without any adequate response the present imbalance. It does demand more effective procurement policies.

Pyrrhus pointed to the principle after the battle of Asculum 'One more victory, and we are lost'. Pyrrhic defence is not winning directly, but exacting an unjustifiable price for any concession; it means forcing an adversary to pay more for countering a system than it costs to deploy it oneself. It avails a country nothing to destroy an inexpensive unmanned vehicle for the expenditure of several mobile surface to air missiles; a fact which remains true even in that rare condition called air supremacy. If the costs of deploying these new systems can be kept down they may become the most natural expression of a Pyrrhic defence.

It is neither possible, nor necessary to match Soviet ground and tactical air forces on a one-for-one basis. The political and fiscal impossibility of attempting to compete with the Warsaw Pact numerically, was demonstrated at the 1952 Lisbon Conference which recommended 96 divisions and 9000 planes for the conventional defence of Western Europe. This recommendation was unacceptable to member nations and obviously remains so today given current NATO central theatre levels of 26 divisions and 1800 combat aircraft.

Instead NATO should procure conventional weapons that can be delivered by existing aircraft and surface-to-surface missiles against both fixed and mobile forces. Long range conventional weapons are being developed that, because of their greatly improved accuracy, now begin to approach the destructive potential of small yield (2 to 3kt) battlefield nuclear weapons. Conventional weapons systems such as the Corps support weapon system can now destroy perhaps 60 per cent or more of an entire company of tanks or motorised infantry per aircraft sortie or missile fired.

These new weapons now offer NATO a completely new option which would do much to offset the third advantage the Soviet Union enjoys: theatre nuclear superiority. For if the Alliance agreed to quite modest improvements in conventional forces, Western Europe could be defended without threatening the use of nuclear weapons at all. The NATO high command is not suggesting, in putting forward this strategy, that nuclear weapons can be dispensed with altogether, nor renouncing the first use policy; it is however, making out a case for not being the first to use them. SACEUR has already begun reassessing the need for the Alliance's existing nuclear stockpile which includes everything from atomic mines to anti-aircraft missiles with a view to making a large part a subject for political negotiation or even unilateral withdrawal as has been proposed concurrently with the introduction of Pershing II and Cruise missiles. If his strategy were to be implemented this would only leave nuclear weapons which could still be justified as a retaliatory deterrent, plus several hundred Cruise and Pershing missiles.

Implicit in this new defensive plan is the prospect of a higher nuclear threshold – as near to a non first-use policy as the Alliance could get without actually saying so. SACEUR has put the cost at an extra 1 per cent on NATO defence budgets for the rest of the 1980s in addition to the 3 per cent growth agreed upon in 1977.[17] The key to this non-nuclear strategy is a combination of the latest reconnaissance technology including the new TR-1 aircraft, AWACS radar planes and satellites, with a range of highly accurate missiles including Pershing II fitted with specialised non-nuclear warheads.

The aim would be to target the Warsaw Pact's second echelon forces while they are still concentrated behind front lines – lined up on main roads or at 'choke points' waiting to cross rivers for instance – and destroy them before they can join the battle. NATO is already testing a series of intelligence fusion centres fed with information from TR-1s which would feed NATO commanders with the necessary information to make rapid decisions on which targets to hit. These developments have already been included in the NATO force goals that have been prepared for the six year period 1984–90.

One of the principal targets may well be the main operational air bases in Poland, East Germany and Czechoslovakia (perhaps 30–40 in number) from which massive Warsaw Pact air attacks would be launched. During the first wave attacks, aircraft destined for the second and third waves would be moving up to the main bases, leaving the dispersed operating bases for the refuelling and rearming of returning aircraft. It is these operations that could be seriously disrupted, if aircraft were denied the use of runways at the main bases and were forced to rely instead on the less well-protected dispersed bases which could themselves come under attack from NATO ground-attack aircraft. Long range ballistic missiles with hard-structure submunitions accurately delivered might well knock out the main bases within 15 to 30 minutes of a first wave attack, while low-level strafing and stand-off attacks might deny the secondary airfields to Warsaw Pact aircraft.

The same pattern could be repeated on the second echelon ground forces. Accurate guided missile attacks could destroy bridges, railheads and road junctions within the first few hours of a Soviet offensive, tying reserve divisions to choke points behind the enemy lines where they would present dense and vulnerable targets to air attack. The main attraction of this strategy is that it would provide NATO with the option of containing the offensive on Warsaw Pact territory, while executing the missions with non-nuclear forces.

The other attractions speak for themselves. The targets of NATO strikes would be few in number: initially some 100 interdiction points and 40 air force bases. Non-nuclear missions of the missile forces would allow launch on warning, or launch under attack. An attack on fixed hardened bases by missiles would enable the Alliance to conserve its ground-attack aircraft for mobile ground forces and aircraft on the ground, a more logical role for manned aircraft with their present fire power capabilities.

These new conventional options, if implemented successfully, could substantially reduce some of the conventional disparities between NATO and Warsaw Pact forces, particularly those involving their respective air forces. The introduction of modern tactical aircraft has considerably increased the Warsaw Pact's offensive capability. Its latest aircraft are capable of carrying up to twice the payload, can travel three times the range, at higher speeds, and can conduct operations at lower altitudes than the aircraft they are replacing. These and other substantial improvements may render them much less vulnerable to NATO air defences. An increasing proportion of these modern aircraft can operate in adverse weather conditions by day or night.

It has been estimated that the target array for a single breakthrough (out of a possible range of six separate attacks) would require NATO to operate 5500 successful sorties expending in the course of operations 33 000 metric tonnes of unguided gravity bombs. Substantially smaller NATO air forces, however, would matter much less if SACEUR were able to rely less on air sorties, and more on Precision Guided Munitions. Some estimates suggest that NATO would only need to execute 50 to 100 sorties against a Warsaw Pact breakthrough in one sector of the battle zone using terminally guided anti-armour submunitions (500 metric tonnes).[18]

The effectiveness of these attacks would be such that they would in all essential respects produce the same target-kill ratio as the use of battlefield nuclear weapons. The report of the European Security Study in 1983 cited one particularly convincing example which is worth repeating at length. Contrasting the number of weapons required to destroy 60 per cent of a Soviet armoured division, the Soviet criterion for 'annihilation', it concluded:

This target would contain about 400 armoured vehicles about 2500 trucks, air defence vehicles and artillery tubes. If aircraft armed with conventional 250-kilogram unguided bombs were used, it would require 2200 successful sorties to achieve the 60 per cent destruction level. If available unguided submunitions were used on this target array, similar to those in the West German MW-1/Tornado System, approximately 300 successful sorties would be required. If these aircraft were equipped with dispensers having terminally guided submunitions similar to the Skeet munitions, ... it would require only 50 to 60 successful sorties. On the basis of the SACEUR collateral damage constraints for nuclear weapons, it would require 20 to 25 nuclear attack sorties using 10 kilotonne weapons to achieve 'annihilation' levels.

Therefore, combining the advances in target acquisition, tracking and engagement with terminally guided submunitions, one can see that NATO could approach a credible conventional defence having 'nuclear equivalence' for the mission of attacking mobile ground forces'.[19]

The cost of the new strategy according to the European Security Group would be about $2.3bn, the cost of 900 suppression missiles which would be needed for counter-air and interdiction missions, plus basing and manning needs; 30 and 40 per cent respectively might be borne by the United States and West Germany.

Yet as with all doctrines, there are objections to it that need to be stated, if not taken to heart. The first is that there is little sign of popular support for the kind of increase in conventional arms spending which General Rogers (SACEUR) and others have demanded. Indeed, the longer the recession continues, the greater the financial strains on government budgets and the greater the pressure for resources to be found to tackle industrial decline and mass unemployment, and the less enthusiasm there is likely to be for ever higher defence spending. An acceleration of arms expenditure on the scale suggested is most unlikely to be politically feasible in the absence of a political consensus, and this seems improbable in a period when the left is being pushed into opposition. This political polarisation within the Alliance is something that has not been seen since the early days of the Cold War when NATO was created. Coinciding as it does with a split in European public opinion about nuclear defence policy, it is not difficult to understand why there is some concern that a swing back of the European political pendulum could put NATO and many of its member states at variance with each other.

Secondly, the danger as many Germans see it is that if NATO starts to talk about a new strategy then members of the public may begin to ask what is wrong with the present one. They may question the underlying validity of nuclear deterrence and the credibility of the American nuclear guarantee. It is because of such fears that the German government originally wanted the new Pershing II missile based on its territory – the American commitment in its most visible form – rather than make do with Cruise missiles launched from US submarines off shore.

Where nuclear deterrence is concerned, the Germans until recently were prominent among NATO hardliners, believing that it was better to deter a Warsaw Pact attack by a convincing threat to use battlefield nuclear weapons at an early stage – even if that sounded like a strategy of national suicide – than to accept that a long conventional attack might be fought over German soil. The geographical compactness of Western Europe makes any defence difficult enough to contemplate with equanimity. One quarter of West Germany's industrial production and 30 per cent of its population are located less than 60 miles from the border between NATO and the Warsaw Pact. The geographical realities of the Federal Republic make forward defence as imperative as ever. The second echelon strategy has much to recommend it; but as the next chapter will argue, NATO will still need to rely for the foreseeable future on nuclear weapons as a strategic reserve.

3 The Nuclear Dimension

The concept of a nuclear balance can only be viewed as a whole; any attempt to assess it in separate categories for strategic and theatre forces raises a number of objections. So called theatre nuclear forces, for one, are strategic as far as Europe is concerned because they can be targeted against European cities. 400 of the 5200 US Poseidon SLBM warheads, which are classed as strategic in the SALT context, are in fact, assigned to SACEUR as part of his theatre forces.

Similarly, many Soviet strategic systems could be employed against Europe as well as the United States. The SS-11 and SS-19 ICBMs are both dual role, targeted on Europe as well as America. In military terms one probable consequence of the deployment of the SS-20 has been the retargeting of the SS-11 and SS-19s on the United States.

The optimum military response to a threat from a particular weapon is not necessarily to deploy a weapon of comparable range. NATO has always relied in part on American strategic systems to counter the threat from Soviet theatre systems and any attempt to achieve a separate theatre balance would seriously risk decoupling the United States deterrent from the European theatre. With the advent of serious arms control talks, however, a distinction between categories of weapons systems was made for the purpose of the negotiations. These can now be divided into three: SALT counted systems; European theatre systems; and battlefield nuclear weapons.

SALT COUNTED SYSTEMS

Put very simply, the Soviet Union has a 31 per cent lead in numbers of launchers and aircraft (2500 against 1900); the

United States has a 24 per cent lead in numbers of warheads (8700 against 7000) – a measure of the number of targets that can be attacked simultaneously. These crude totals represent the maximum number of deployed systems – not all on either side would be available for use. The submarine launched missiles in particular depend on the submarines being at sea. Probably an absolute maximum of two-thirds of the United States force are at sea at any one time; the Soviet pattern of deployment is much lower. Perhaps, only a third of its submarine force is on patrol. Both of these proportions, of course, could be raised in a period of tension.

These crude totals disguise significant asymmetries in the forces of the two sides. The Soviet Union has 400 more ICBMs than the United States. These are both more accurate and more vulnerable than submarine launched missiles. One of the Soviet ICBMs – the SS-18 – is very large with a throw-weight in excess of 7000 kg compared with less than 1000 for the Minuteman 111. The SS-18 is reported to exist in various models with warheads ranging from 2 to 50 megatons, and one model with an accuracy supposedly as good as 200 metres Circular Error Probable (CEP). These figures have given rise to speculation about the possible vulnerability of the Minuteman force to a Soviet first strike.

In fact, the other asymmetry in the forces of both sides is in favour of the United States. With 5000 warheads on submarine launched missiles compared with only 1300 for the Soviet Union, the United States is in a far better position to deliver a devastating second strike from its highly-survivable submarine force.

The understandable anxieties in Washington about the state of the balance arise from three factors. First, the overwhelming nuclear superiority enjoyed by America after completion of the Minuteman and Polaris systems in the early 1960s and which it enjoyed again (briefly) when it became the first to deploy Multiple Independently targetable Re-entry Vehicles (MIRVs) which increased four or five-fold the total number of warheads in its forces, has been eroded by the Soviet Union. The latter has overtaken the United States in the number of missiles deployed and reduced the gap considerably in the total number of warheads.

Secondly, the United States is understandably concerned at the characteristics of some of the very heavy Soviet ICBMs, in particular the SS-18 with its enormous throw-weight. The need for and the characteristics of this missile cannot be explained except on the assumption that it was designed as a counter-force weapon to destroy Minuteman missiles in their silos. It is also concerned at the relative age of its own weapon systems: 450 of the Minuteman missiles date from 1966; the remaining 550 from 1970. The Polaris dates from 1964, the Poseidon from 1971. Against this the Soviet ICBMs, SS-17, SS-18 and SS-19 all date from 1975 and two of its SLBM models from 1977–78.

The fear that the technology of deployed systems might be overtaken by the momentum of the recent Soviet programmes has been the spur for the United States strategic modernisation programmes. The programme to fit a heavier Mark 12A re-entry vehicle with a higher yield warhead to 300 of the 550 Minuteman 111 is nearing completion – a total of 900 warheads. A new, heavier and more accurate ICBM – the MX – has been under development for some years. Congress has recently endorsed the production of the missile, after much hesitation, and the government after considerable confusion has now agreed on the final basing mode for the MX system itself.

In addition to the MX, the Trident C-4 with eight warheads has been progressively entering service in 12 out of the 31 Poseidon submarines which are being refitted. The larger Trident class submarine with 24 instead of 16 missiles was first delivered in October 1981. An improved Trident 11 (D-5) is now to be developed with increased range and 14 warheads. It is due to enter service in December 1989.

There are three programmes for improving the existing force of B-52 strategic bomber aircraft, many of which date back to the 1950s. In the first instance, air launched Cruise missiles are to be fitted to existing B-52G and B-52H aircraft. Secondly, 100 of an improved version of the B-1 bomber, cancelled by President Carter, are to be produced, the first entering service in 1986. Finally, an advanced technology bomber incorporating Stealth characteristics will enter service in the early 1990s.[1] If the latter prove satisfactory, then only 50 improved B-1s will be required, effort being concentrated upon Stealth bombers.

THEATRE NUCLEAR FORCES

In the latter half of the 1970s the United States and its NATO allies became increasingly concerned over the growing imbalance in Intermediate-range Nuclear Forces (INF) in Europe. The large and growing advantage held by the Soviet Union appeared to threaten security by calling into question the credibility of NATO's deterrent strategy. The Alliance's answer was the December 1979 dual-track decision in which NATO agreed to deploy long range INF missiles while simultaneously offering arms control negotiations on INF.

The Soviet Union has long deployed missiles with sufficient range to strike targets in Europe, but not in the United States. In the late 1950s it deployed some 600 SS-4 and SS-5 missiles against Europe. The United States deployed roughly equivalent types of missiles in Western Europe in the early 1960s, although in lesser numbers – the Thor and Jupiter based in the United Kingdom, Italy and Turkey. These systems were under dual operation and SACEUR's command, but the warheads remained under American control. In 1963 they were phased out as new technologies facilitated the adoption of more distant and survivable basing strategies.[2]

Thus from the 1960s to the present, the Soviet Union has held a monopoly of INF. This lead was acceptable in an era when American strategic nuclear superiority permitted an imbalance of intermediate range systems; it became unacceptable with the deployment of the SS-20.

The SS-20 is more accurate and has a much greater range than the SS-4 and SS-5 missiles it is replacing. From the Soviet Union it can strike targets in Europe, the Middle East and much of Asia. Its mobility allows it to be redeployed from present locations to any site in the Soviet Union. As opposed to the single warhead of the earlier missiles, it carries three independently targetable warheads. Its launchers also have a reload capability.

As a result of continuing SS-20 deployments at the rate of one a week the Soviet INF force has been substantially improved both qualitatively and quantitatively. As of March 1983, the Soviet Union had deployed 351 SS-20 missiles with 1053 warheads as well as retaining several hundred older SS-4 and SS-5 missiles. In short, it had increased from 600 to 1300 the total number of warheads deployed on longer range INF missile launchers. Construction of new SS-20 bases in the eastern USSR continues.

By 1977 political leaders in Europe became concerned that these trends, if unchecked, might lead Soviet leaders to conclude, however mistakenly, that the evolving military balance made aggression feasible, or intimidation worthwhile. The American commitment to the defence of its allies had not changed, but it was feared that the Soviet Union might perceive the linkage between European and North American security as less than credible. Such a Soviet perception could undermine deterrence on which that linkage was based.

These concerns led to intensive NATO consultations, as a result of which the Alliance decided to redress the INF imbalance through deployment in Western Europe of 108 single warhead Pershing 11 missiles and 464 ground launched Cruise missiles. This was the modernisation track of the decision, as part of which the United States also withdrew 1000 nuclear warheads and pledged that for every Pershing and Cruise warhead deployed, an additional older weapon would be withdrawn.

The second element of the 1979 decision was the arms control track. While agreeing to modernise its nuclear forces NATO concurrently offered arms control negotiations on INF. The criteria for these talks was developed within NATO's Special Consultative Group, a body specifically established to discuss INF arms control matters. That group met on five occasions between the May 1981 NATO ministerial meeting at which it was announced that the United States would open formal negotiations with the Soviet Union and the 30 November opening of those negotiations in Geneva. A second NATO body, the High Level Group of NATO's Nuclear Planning Group, also met to address questions raised by the prospective deployment of US longer range INF missiles. Taken as a whole these meetings represented one of the most intensive intra-alliance consultations in NATO's history.

The modernisation of theatre nuclear forces has nonetheless drawn the fire of two separate groups: those who believe that the 572 warheads are a totally inadequate response to the SS-20 threat; and those who contend that the costs let alone the validity of the programme will far outweigh any marginal gains. Criticism of the two track decision has become increasingly marked in the United States.

The first group has criticised the NATO proposal as a totally inadequate response to a serious deficiency. They argue that the NATO decision of 1979 has focused on a single element of the theatre nuclear spectrum and thus distracted attention from the real problem facing the Alliance – the across the board modernisation of Soviet theatre nuclear forces. This case has been argued most persuasively by Richard Burt, a former *New York Times* defence correspondent; now Assistant Secretary of State for European Affairs:

> Moscow's nuclear modernisation programme is not centred around a single system but consists of several new weapons, including the SS-21, SS-22 and SS-23 battlefield nuclear support missiles, the Backfire medium range bomber and the SU-19 attack aircraft ... a comprehensive approach to theatre nuclear modernisation must be taken in replacing the Alliance's increasingly obsolete nuclear posture rather than taking the piecemeal and *ad hoc* steps now underway.[3]

Burt and others contend that NATO can no longer choose between defence and deterrence. Because of the wide range of military options that the Soviet Union now has available NATO must possess credible capabilities at all levels. In this sense the 572 warheads should be seen as the beginning of a thorough reshaping of the Alliance's theatre nuclear forces.

At the other extreme there are a number of critics who believe that the 572 warheads are unnecessary. They do not accept the principle that strategic parity neutralises the deterrent effect of central strategic systems for all situations except a direct attack on the homeland. They believe that the current capabilities of the United States, plus its pronounced willingness to defend Western Europe, are sufficient to deter the Soviet Union from any initiative which would invite a nuclear exchange. For those Europeans who doubt the American commitment, it is difficult to see why they should trust any more to the Americans launching a nuclear strike on the Soviet Union from Europe than from the continental United States. If this is not the case such deployments, rather than strengthening the ladder of escalation, would probably weaken it by making possible the containment or limitation of a nuclear exchange to European territory.

With regard to the more precise question of the SS-20 the critics point out that the West has lived under the threat of 600 intermediate range missiles and hundreds of medium range bombers for 20 years. They question whether the SS-20 represents a quantum leap in capability that justifies the modernisation of NATO's own theatre nuclear forces. As for the 'selective' capability afforded by the increased accuracy and reduced yield of the SS-20, they argue that the term 'selective' is difficult to appreciate when used to describe the use of 150KT warheads (each ten times the yield of the bomb used against Hiroshima) on a heavily urbanised and densely populated Europe. Any attempt by the Soviet Union to pre-empt the first use of nuclear weapons by NATO would comprise, to all intents and purposes, a strategic strike of the most devastating nature. If the situation is, in fact, politically and militarily incredible, why erect a hypothesis of escalation dominance which, in reality, does not exist? The critics such as Paul Warnke (President Carter's chief arms control negotiator), believe that as with 'the window of vulnerability', the 'escalation gap' in theatre forces is visible only to those preoccupied with the narrow and selective world of targeting criteria.

BATTLEFIELD NUCLEAR WEAPONS

The relatively short-range battlefield (or tactical) nuclear weapons comprise tube artillery and surface-to-surface missiles with ranges up to 100 or 150km. The artillery, of course, has a conventional capability as well. A NATO study on force comparisons published in May 1982 shows an overall NATO superiority of short-range nuclear forces in Europe with 1100 compared with 950 for the Warsaw Pact. It is possible to add 42 French Pluton missiles to the NATO total. These overall totals, however, are built on large asymmetries with NATO superiority in tube artillery of 1000 compared with 300 for the Warsaw Pact, and Pact superiority in surface-to-surface missiles of 650 compared with only 100 for the Alliance. The artillery pieces, of course, are capable of firing more than one round although it is unlikely that all of them would ever be assigned to the nuclear role simultaneously. A better measure of the balance of nuclear-capable artillery would be the number of nuclear rounds available to each side – information which, if known, has not been published.

From the outset of their deployment, perceptions concerning the use of tactical nuclear weapons were never very clear and the passage of time has not produced greater clarity. A clear conflict of interest exists between the United States and its European allies. The latter have traditionally viewed tactical nuclear weapons as obviating the necessity of providing conventional forces sufficient for a credible conventional defence. They have favoured an early use of battlefield nuclear weapons and, therefore, a relatively low nuclear threshold in order to signal their political resolve to escalate to all out nuclear war, and to minimise collateral damage to German territory. American officials, on the other hand, would obviously prefer to delay any decision which could lead to escalation to the strategic level. As William van Cleave noted over ten years ago:

> On the one hand, we had tactical nuclear weapons deployed for deterrence of attacks on allies; on the other hand, avoidance of nuclear usage always had at least as high a priority or value as deterrence. Western thought became again focused on the avoidance of nuclear war and this became translated into avoidance of usable weapons, usable doctrines, usable strategies, avoidance of what would make war 'thinkable' since to avoid nuclear war required that it be kept unthinkable and the way to keep it unthinkable is to base nuclear strategy not on military effectiveness and limiting damage but on propositions of the utmost destructiveness and on threats of escalation.[4]

NATO has absorbed these deep rooted differences by making the precise terms of the employment of battlefield nuclear weapons deliberately obscure.

Most of NATO's battlefield nuclear weapons are more than 20 years old. The most recent addition to its inventory, the Lance missile, was deployed in 1972. With their relatively limited ranges (under 100km in most cases) ·they would have to be targeted against enemy units on allied, not enemy territory. The process of nuclear release and command has taken in some exercises up to 60 hours, not the 24 often claimed by SHAPE, by which time re-targeting would in all probability be necessary in the light of an enemy advance, and a repetition of the release procedures. In these circumstances it is difficult to envisage a German government sanctioning their use. In the event of a Warsaw Pact attack, NATO stockpiles of battlefield weapons will probably come under two forms of attack: terrorist/fifth column operations and ground attack including supporting aircraft. Most of the stockpiles are located in the American sector of the 5th and 7th US Corps. In 1978 a CIA report identified them as the most likely target for terrorist attack. In 1982 during the public campaign against nuclear bases incidents increased by 30 per cent.

The employment of aircraft to deliver a battlefield nuclear mission would also render strike aircraft especially vulnerable to attack. Other than those pre-destined for a nuclear role, it has been estimated that even in good conditions, dual purpose aircraft could take up to eight hours to change from conventional operations to nuclear missions. The present command and communications system linked to nuclear operations, entails lengthy time delays. It involves grounding aircraft that could be used more effectively and at less immediate risk to themselves on other missions, and holding them prepared for a nuclear role.

These limitations have led many NATO commanders, especially in the United States, to question the wisdom of modernising the present generation of battlefield nuclear weapons. The use of tactical nuclear weapons could actually increase the problems local commanders would face. They are largely a political weapon. Modernisation will not give commanders on the spot the decision-making power. Their use would, in addition, commit NATO to the first crossing of the nuclear threshold, thereby throwing away a trump card for little return. Such arguments suggest that the weapons should best be used as bargaining chips in future arms control negotiations. It might be best not to use them as political weapons at all, but to look to the operational concepts which would render them militarily redundant.

Yet it is perhaps, worth noting that the advocates of the air-land battle plan do not themselves believe it desirable or possible to eliminate tactical nuclear forces. They are on the whole, unanimous in their opinion that the deployment of such forces complicates Soviet planning in the same way as the use of INF for conventional roles. The elimination of these weapons would raise the nuclear threshold on the battlefield and confront the Alliance with the unenviable choice of not responding with nuclear forces at all, or of using theatre nuclear forces at a much higher (non-battlefield) level of escalation.

The effect of battlefield nuclear weapons on Soviet doctrine and tactics when those weapons were first introduced in the 1950s has been remarkable. The Soviet Union was forced to disperse and echelon its forces, avoiding the heavy post-war densities of 500 troops per square kilometre. These were further reduced to 10 per square kilometre when NATO forces were equipped with nuclear artillery and short-range rockets in the mid-1960s. This was true even though Soviet division troop sizes grew by about 70 per cent. This was an eloquent testimony to the seriousness with which the Soviet army took the challenge of battlefield nuclear weapons until quite recently.

The problem since the mid-1970s has been NATO's redundant inventory of short range weapons. One reason for the redundancy has already been noted: the perception that NATO can only fight a battlefield nuclear conflict on its own territory. But a far more important drawback has been their vulnerability to Soviet rapid-fire long range conventional artillery which has been deployed in ever increasing numbers since the mid-1970s.

If tactical nuclear weapons are to remain in NATO's inventory, the Alliance will need to deploy long range missiles which can be stationed further away from the front line where they will be able to threaten Soviet forces in the second and third front organisations deep in Warsaw Pact territory, and even the Western military districts of the Soviet Union. A Warsaw Pact *blitzkrieg* could effectively be blunted simply by the threat of a nuclear attack if Pact commanders are compelled to disperse their forces, with all the related complexities and vulnerabilities this would entail, with many more bases and depots less well defended against ground-attack aircraft during the first phase of a Pact offensive.

ARMS CONTROL NEGOTIATIONS

The arms control negotiations on INF forces opened on 30 November 1981. From the first, the Soviet Union put forward proposals which the West could not possibly meet. The first was a renewed call for a complete moratorium on so called medium range theatre missiles and aircraft in Europe. Its second proposal was a plan for the four nuclear powers – the United States, the USSR, Britain and France – to reduce to 300 medium range missiles and aircraft in, or 'intended for use' in, Europe. The Soviet proposal, while permitting the Russians to retain a substantial number of SS-20s in the European USSR and to continue its build-up in Asia, would have prohibited the deployment of Pershing II and Cruise missiles in Europe.

As the negotiations progressed, several areas of disagreement emerged. The Soviet Union based its proposal on the assertion that a balance in medium range forces in Europe already existed. This claim was based on a highly selective use of data. In fact, the Russians held an advantage in every category of INF systems. They included in their 'balance' independent British and French systems and American aircraft not located in Europe. At the same time they ignored missiles in the eastern USSR that could strike NATO targets and excluded thousands of their own nuclear capable aircraft with characteristics similar to the American aircraft they included.

The Soviet Union first claimed there was a balance in October 1979 when there were only 100 SS-20s deployed. They repeated this claim in 1981 when there were 250 SS-20s and continued to assert it in early 1983 when there were 351 in place. As of March 1983 the Soviet Union had deployed some 1300 warheads on Long Range INF with the numbers still growing; the United States had deployed none.

The geographical scope of the missiles also divided the two sides. The United States argued for limitations on the basis of capability regardless of the missiles' location. This position reflected the range, mobility and transportability of modern LRINF systems. The Soviet Union proposed limits only on systems in or 'intended for use' in Europe, leaving an increasing number of systems in the east which posed a growing threat to America's allies in Asia, in particular Japan.

But perhaps the most divisive issue was the Soviet proposal to include aircraft. If aircraft are to be included which type should be counted? If 1000km radius is taken as the criterion, all tactical aircraft would have to be excluded except the Soviet SU-24 and the US A-6. If the threshold were to be lowered to 500km then the Soviet MiG-27 and SU-7 and -17 would have to be included as well, together with NATO's F-104, F-4, Jaguar and Mirage aircraft.

The next question is how many of each type should be counted as nuclear weapon systems? Out of 219 Anglo-French Jaguar aircraft only 80 are thought to have been constructed as nuclear delivery aircraft; and only 40 of these are believed to have been assigned a nuclear role. From the standpoint of external verification, 219 aircraft would have to be counted; from the standpoint of intention only 40.

Counting carrier-borne aircraft is another problem to which

there are no easy solutions. The nominal strength of the Sixth Fleet's carriers in the Mediterranean is two. In the Atlantic the Second Fleet has five. Each carries a total of 30 A-6 and A-7 aircraft which could be employed in a nuclear strike. Today, however, most of these carriers in the Atlantic are assigned to sea control roles; at times there have been no carriers in the Mediterranean. Thus the perceived threat to the Soviet Union could vary from 238 aircraft to none at all (238 with 476 nuclear bombs). In short, introducing aircraft into the talks could delay and perhaps, even prevent agreement on the systems of greatest concern to both sides – Long Range INF missiles.

The United States' position on strategic arms talks with the Soviet Union has been much more positive than its discussions on INF. President Reagan's approach is quite different from that of previous administrations. SALT 1 and 2 had been based on the notion that deployed launchers could be measured readily by satellite photography. Today the United States is trying to devise a new method of counting. The proposals for reductions and ceilings have focused on the numbers of warheads, rather than the number of missiles. The United States has expressed a wish to reduce significantly the most destabilising systems – ballistic missiles – and the number of warheads they carry. In the first phase, warheads would be reduced to equal ceilings at least a third below current levels with no more than half to be land based. Phase two will aim at a ceiling on other elements of strategic nuclear forces including limits on throw-weight at less than current American levels. President Reagan has also indicated a willingness to negotiate reductions in bombers and Cruise missiles. What all this may mean in actual figures is not absolutely clear. It seems possible, however, that a common ceiling of 850 SLBMs and ICBMs could be achieved with a total of not more than 5000 warheads of which only 500 would be land based. This would involve a reduction of 1500 Soviet missiles and 1300 warheads compared with a reduction of 850 US missiles and 2200 warheads, the reductions being carried out over ten years.

Yet the proposals would actually involve overall greater reductions for the Soviet Union. Against a reduction of 2200 warheads by the United States would have to be set a ceiling of 2500 warheads on ICBMs which would involve a reduction of 3000 Soviet warheads but would permit an increase of 350 US. Phase two limits on throw-weight below present US levels would affect five Soviet models all of which exceed the heaviest American system – the Trident D-5.[5]

Whether the START talks will succeed is another question entirely. The Reagan Administration is facing the Soviet Union with much tougher demands for arms control than have previous administrations. Yet the Soviet Union is already on record as rejecting President Carter's 'deep cuts' in 1977 which came as a surprising departure from the outline agreement reached with the previous administration at Vladivostok in 1974. The Soviet Union also has confusing experience in dealing with successive Presidents who have changed every four years and sometimes more frequently.

There are now three outstanding arms control agreements that the United States has signed – the threshold test ban treaty signed by Richard Nixon in 1974; the peaceful nuclear explosions treaty signed by Gerald Ford in 1976; and the SALT 2 Treaty signed by President Carter in 1979. All three have been ratified by the Soviet Union, but not yet by the United States, despite the urging of its allies. The trilateral negotiations on a comprehensive Test Ban which nearly reached agreement in 1980 have been suspended. The shifts in US policy have not always been the responsibility of the administration in office; changing attitudes in the Senate have been an important factor. The picture is nonetheless a confusing one from the Soviet Union's point of view, and cannot inspire the Kremlin with much confidence that arms control is a realistic option.

PUBLIC OPINION AND NUCLEAR WEAPONS

Three years ago it was possible for Fritz Stern to write that however attached the Germans might be to *Ostpolitik* or *détente*, they knew that neither could be successful on the terms they would prefer without their continued dependence on the American nuclear guarantee.

> For all the temptations of *détente* and for all the apprehensions of an eastward drift, the Germans know that the Western Alliance and the American nuclear shield are the sole guarantee of German security ... Doubts about the credibility of the

American shield are not going to tempt the Germans to abandon it. They are not likely to commit suicide out of fear of death.[6]

The extraordinary rise of the Peace Movement in recent years has brought such certainties into question, not only in the Federal Republic, but in Western Europe as a whole.

It is worth reminding ourselves, however, that the present crisis of confidence in deterrence has a long history. The special intractability of extended deterrence confounded even the sober hopes initially placed in the American nuclear umbrella in the 1950s when its nuclear superiority was not in doubt. When in 1957 the Americans confronted their allies with the deployment of IRBMs, they found them distinctly lukewarm. Norway and Denmark were unequivocal in their opposition. Germany and France insisted on reserving their positions. Most NATO members with the exception of Britain were distinctly unenthusiastic about lowering the nuclear threshold until they had been given an opportunity to take up Bulganin's offer of a dialogue with the Soviet Union.

Although the new generation of missiles were deployed in 1959, precipitating the emergence of the first serious peace movement in Britain – the Campaign for Nuclear Disarmament (CND) – the United States and its European allies found it convenient to fudge the doctrine which governed their deployment. The Europeans wanted a theatre nuclear posture which would leave the Soviet Union in no doubt that the weapons would be used in their own defence and NATO's members with no worry that they would be used at all.

European public opinion was not so reassured as the growth of the first peace movements soon revealed, particularly in Britain. It now appeared possible for America to pre-empt an attack upon the continental United States by 'a diversified means of delivery' – the deployment of nuclear weapons in Europe. Even a pro-NATO journal like *The Economist* believed that the United States could only defend itself by confining a nuclear exchange to Europe:

> Once the Americans possessed a decisive superiority then they had, at least, a half-share in the balance of mutual terror; now they can avoid a period of perilous inferiority only if they can achieve a wide enough dispersal of the weapons they have.[7]

The Economist was arguing about the specific period which it would take the United States to catch up with the Soviet Union in the development of the ICBM. But it was clear that the passing of what the Europeans took for American nuclear superiority would have lasting consequences for European security. Indeed, the Americans quickly reformulated massive retaliation to 'measured retaliation' and later more ominously still for their allies 'graduated deterrence', an idea which was originally put forward by the British.

How sobering this change was likely to strike those Europeans whose commitment to NATO was less unequivocal than *The Economist's*, was revealed in an article in *The New Statesman* which was cited by Dean Acheson to illustrate how the association with the United States could appear more dangerous as its military position became weaker:

> ... the missile agreement is one of the most extraordinary and complete surrenders of sovereignty ever to be made by one country for the exclusive benefit of another. For the missiles are not intended to defend Britain; on the contrary, they decisively increase its vulnerability. Their prime purpose is to reduce the likelihood of a Soviet ICBM onslaught on America during the crucial three year period which must elapse before America possesses ICBMs herself. The sole beneficiary will be America.[8]

Although the United States soon caught up with the Soviet Union the first generation of intermediate range missiles – the Thors and Pershing Is remained. Given the Soviet Union's immense superiority in theatre nuclear weapons the readers of *The New Statesman* and journals like it were not reassured. They perhaps had even more reason to be concerned in the early 1960s than they do at present. At the time of the Cuban missile crisis the Soviet Union could only have launched 40 ICBMs and 200 long range bombers against the United States. Against Europe, however, it could have targeted more than 1200 medium range bombers of various types and almost 600 SS-4 and SS-5 intermediate range missiles. Today their intermediate forces, although more powerful, represent only a fraction of their strategic forces.

Even fervent NATO supporters saw the deployment of American missiles as militarily questionable, and worse, politically inept. As Walter Lippman pointed out at the time it contrived to provoke the Russians without offering any extra protection for the Europeans.[9]

Twenty years later Helmut Schmidt's offer to freeze the deployment of Cruise missiles after the United States had refused to ratify the SALT 2 Treaty was seen in the United States as German reluctance to press ahead with deployment while relations with the Soviet Union remained in a state of crisis. Chancellor Schmidt's subsequent visit to Moscow was taken to be a sign that the Europeans were not prepared to rectify their own weakness if in the process the Soviet Union was likely to be provoked.

The 1957 decision, therefore, precipitated a crisis of confidence in the Alliance which manifested itself in grave doubts on the part of many Europeans about the credibility of deterrence, and a reluctance on the part of European governments to take public opinion for granted. Although the Cuban missile crisis and the signing of the Test Ban Treaty the following year reassured the majority of Europeans, the doubts that had surfaced in 1957 always threatened to re-emerge, this time more decisively, once America's nuclear superiority could no longer be taken for granted. In the event the passing of its superiority proved so rapid that it caught the Alliance off-guard. Henry Kissinger may well have asked what anyone meant by superiority but the speed with which it passed into history was disturbing. Until 1969 it was still possible to talk of superiority; until 1972 of 'marginal superiority'; by 1974 the phrase Dr Kissinger himself used was 'essential equivalence'.

Robert McNamara's decision to maintain an ICBM ceiling (at 1054) invited the Soviet Union first to match that figure and then overtake it. In a series of articles published in 1974 Albert Wohlstetter demonstrated not only that Soviet military spending had exceeded that of the United States on strategic weapons for the past decade, but that US projections had consistently underestimated the Soviet build-up.[10]

It could be argued, of course, and was, that although the Interim Agreement to SALT 1 (1972) had frozen Soviet missile strength at a point considerably higher than that of the United States (1330 versus 1054 ICBMs; 950 versus 656 SLBMs) American missiles were more accurate and, in large part, MIRVed. But these distinctions, though valid, were not always uppermost in the public mind. In discussing the strategic arms race even Dr Kissinger admitted that 'while a decisive advantage is hard to calculate, the appearance of inferiority – whatever its actual significance – can have serious political consequences'.[11]

Dr Kissinger tried to match the Soviet build-up after the signing of SALT 1 by pressing ahead with qualitative improvements in America's existing force, including the Trident and Cruise missile systems. Yet it was the development of Cruise and its future deployment in Europe in the demonstrable absence of a clear American strategic superiority that triggered off the resurgence of the European Peace Movement, now inspired by the fear that, unable to engage with any confidence in a strategic nuclear exchange, the United States might prefer to confine a nuclear confrontation to Europe.

The United States' failure to press ahead with the development of programmes which were permitted under the Interim Agreement, including the B-1 and Trident, appeared to make the imbalance between Soviet and American forces that much greater. By October 1977 when the Agreement expired none of these systems were in place, or near deployment. The B-1 was actually cancelled by President Carter, and then resurrected by the Reagan Administration.

By not competing the United States lost the confidence of its allies. They could no longer shelter comfortably beneath the nuclear umbrella. The credibility of the nuclear guarantee became increasingly transparent. And this had two unfortunate consequences. First, it forced the Europeans to confront the nuclear balance in Europe itself; it was they not the United States who requested the deployment of Cruise missiles in 1977. Secondly it exposed how little confidence the Europeans had in deterrence itself. As Henry Kissinger perceived five years after leaving office, the Alliance had embarked on a disastrous course: the Europeans had accepted the deployment of weapons in which they no longer believed; the United States continued to pay lip service to a defence doctrine which was often hard to distinguish from massive retaliation.[12]

The Cruise debate left the allies in some disquiet and the Europeans in a dilemma largely of their own making. Above all it brought into question whether Europe could take any nuclear decisions, a problem which had first surfaced during the debate over flexible response, and which had prompted France's withdrawal from the integrated military command. Yet it was not Cruise, but an earlier discussion over the neutron bomb in April 1978 which first brought this into the open. The deployment of the enhanced radiation weapon was the first time that the United States had shifted responsibility for NATO's nuclear policy from its own shoulders to the Alliance as a whole. In Richard Burt's opinion the episode revealed:

> that many allied countries have yet to create the political and societal underpinnings to make difficult nuclear decisions. Asking them to stand up to be counted on nuclear deployment decisions . . . is a prescription for alliance *immobilisme*.[13]

In retrospect, it seems extraordinary that the first peace movement fizzled out when it did; that the European governments did not find themselves under siege much earlier. The debate over flexible response after all, had been the first indication that the Alliance might no longer be able to sustain a public consensus on nuclear policy, or that such a consensus could only be sustained by distancing oneself from NATO. The 1979 crisis brought the problem sharply into focus; it did not create it. It was hardly the case that the crisis unleashed new aspirations in European politics. European politics had been developing in this direction for some time. The INF debate merely accelerated the trend.

That the consensus survived for so long is quite remarkable. It is extraordinary that the NATO decisions of 1977–79 – the 3 per cent increase in defence expenditure, the Long Term Defence Programme and the introduction, subsequently deferred, of the enhanced radiation warhead – achieved a consensus that for the most part represented the views of left of centre, not right of centre, political parties who found themselves in government in this period. In Britain, Labour Party conferences have considered 72 resolutions on defence since 1965 and thrown out about a third of them. Yet, Labour governments have pursued a policy on nuclear defence identical almost entirely to that of the Conservative Party which has considered only 30 resolutions on defence at its party conferences and carried all of them. It was even more remarkable that European governments of every political persuasion actually increased their defence budgets in the period of *détente* and arms control that preceded it. Europe's share of

NATO defence expenditure rose by almost 20 per cent in the ten years after 1969.

All these decisions were taken against the background of the massive growth in Soviet military power. But because governments never successfully communicated to their own citizens the conclusions NATO had drawn from the build-up, and because in the case of the Callaghan Government in Britain it rarely communicated those conclusions to the majority of the British Cabinet, they were caught off guard by the Peace Movement and its plausible if mendacious claim, that NATO's response in the nuclear field was both unwarranted and destabilising to the nuclear balance; that the very increase in conventional forces in the 1970s made the first use of nuclear weapons unnecessary. Many years ago one of the most perceptive analysts of nuclear thinking, William Kaufmann predicted that:

> A policy of nuclear deterrence will seem credible only to the extent that important segments of public opinion support it . . . a policy of deterrence which does not fulfil this requirement is likely to result only in deterring the deterrer.[14]

To the extent that European governments have lost public confidence, the Peace Movement represents not only a challenge to the Atlantic Alliance, but also to European society. Its comparative success means far more than the traditional expression of left-wing alienation from the United States which first surfaced in a decisive way at the time of the Vietnam War. It represents an expression of all the forces that have left Europe divided and restless within itself – the *angst* which remains as ever a permanent part of the German psyche, the alienation from the materialistic society to which the Marshall Plan acted as wet nurse if not midwife, an inevitable historical epilogue to a period of affluence and economic growth, a desire hitherto unarticulated by those outside the political arena to take a direct part in their own future.

Beneath the purely political slogans of the movement can be found the psychological discomfort felt by the young outside the world of political parties. In this respect, if no other, the growth of the Peace Movement may mark a decisive turning point in the history of the Atlantic Alliance whether or not it succeeds in changing the direction of nuclear policy. For it may well have put an end, perhaps permanently, to political bi-partisanship on defence matters, without which deterrence would never have been credible at any time in the Alliance's history.

European governments must bear the main responsibility for losing public confidence in their judgment. In part, they were responsible for simple tactical mistakes which have had grave repercussions. The neutron bomb might have been introduced before the Peace Movement had time to adopt it as a symbol of what Egon Bahr has described as 'the perversion of human thinking'. Helmut Schmidt later confessed the folly of announcing the deployment of Cruise missiles five years before their emplacement and in a subsequent interview with *The Economist* in 1979 agreed that it would have been better to have modernised the 7000 missiles already deployed than to have introduced a completely new generation.

At the same time, Europe misled the Americans into thinking that the demand for greater public participation in the nuclear debate could be defused by broadening the basis of consultation in nuclear planning, instead of accepting, for example, the dual key arrangements that President Carter actually offered in 1978. In the mid-1960s the Nuclear Planning Group (NPG) was, at least, successful in giving the Europeans access to nuclear planning. NATO imagined that the creation of a High Level group (HLG) in the Nuclear Planning Group parallel to the Special Consultative Group (SCG) responsible for arms control, would defuse public anxiety.

Unfortunately, the public support for the Peace Movement revealed that many people derived no confidence at all from the new consultative procedures and believed that they would have little or no effect in restraining the United States from engaging in a limited nuclear war at Europe's expense. The machinery might have been adequate in an era of *détente*; it was quite inadequate in a period that had witnessed the onset of Cold War II. Indeed, one may question whether the NPG itself would have silenced public criticism in the 1960s if European youth had not spent much of its energy demonstrating against American operations in Vietnam. If one can have little respect for those who allow themselves to be blinded by hindsight, there is little to be said for those who are reluctant to answer the questions hindsight suggests. The creation of the NPG may have removed tactical nuclear weapons from the public arena, but it left unresolved the rationale of deterrence, as well as the actual deployment of the missiles.

The upshot of all this should be of great concern to all European governments. The problem of Alliance management has been made difficult enough by the fact that since 1964 the British, French and Germans have never all had governments of a similar persuasion at the same time. In the past this was not a major problem because of the bi-partisan consensus to which the main political parties in all three countries subscribed. Now that the left of centre parties have been forced to respond to dissentient voices within their own ranks, that consensus has largely been eroded.

The problem is twofold. In the first place, some political parties have begun to play politics with NATO membership. Norway's Labour Party has already broken the consensus by refusing to approve payment of the country's five yearly share of the NATO 'infrastructure bill' in protest against the costs of Cruise and Pershing missiles. It certainly does not help the Alliance to have Norway's traditional commitment undercut by the party that established it in the first place. In Britain the Social Democratic Party has threatened to use the continued presence of the British Army of the Rhine (BAOR) as a bargaining chip to force the Alliance to rethink its nuclear strategy. The policy is not advocated by a militant anti-NATO group but by a former Labour party Foreign Secretary, David Owen, who left the Labour Party several years ago partly because of its attitude towards Western security. Even so, Dr Owen continues to support the initial deployment of Cruise and Pershing II missiles in the interests of Alliance cohesion. However, NATO cannot survive if politicians advocate partisan prescriptions. Without a basic measure of bi-partisanship a pluralistic alliance cannot survive for very long.

Secondly, and perhaps more alarming, political re-alignments within left of centre parties have threatened to make it impossible for the party leadership to command party support for defence policies. In Germany, the victory of the Green Party in obtaining representation in the *Bundestag* has removed for the moment the dangerous proposal advanced by Willy Brandt to coopt the movement into the SPD itself. What this might have led to is clear from the experience of the Netherlands where the Labour Party spent six months in opposition occupying the ground hitherto monopolised by radical unilateralist parties such as the Socialists.

By so doing it was able to win the election of September 1982 to emerge as the largest party of all, but at the cost of being unable to sustain a pro-NATO consensus within its own ranks.

Since resigning from power the Danish Social Democrats – still the largest single party in the country – have swung quite significantly to the left. Many of its members want it to move even further left and to take the lead in rebuilding a powerful grass roots movement outside Parliament among those who remain doubtful of the ability of political parties and the political system to deal with defence issues, and who accord extra-Parliamentary protest a much higher priority than Parliamentarianism. The situation in Denmark is more serious still because one of the coalition parties that supports the present government is so pacifist on foreign policy matters that the Prime Minister actually needs Social Democratic support to prevail on national security questions. Yet he does so at a time when the Social Democrats have broken the cross-party consensus that has existed for almost the entire post-war period by pushing through Parliament a motion suspending 'until further notice' any new Danish payments towards developing support bases for Cruise missiles, the first NATO country to do so. The Social Democrats have also forced through small cuts in the 1983 and 1984 military budgets, cuts which largely undo its own decision when in government to boost defence spending in real terms by 2 per cent over three years. Although they continue to insist on Danish membership of NATO, they are no longer prepared to pay the price.

Since Denmark has never been prepared to deploy nuclear weapons on its own soil, the extent of bi-partisan support may not prove decisive. But this is hardly the case in Britain. The Labour Party's commitment to unilateral nuclear disarmament, the renunciation of the first use of nuclear weapons, and the withdrawal of American nuclear bases from Britain has made it unnecessary for the Peace Movement represented by the Campaign for Nuclear Disarmament to set up an independent party, or to contest elections on the ticket of unilateralism. The situation today is a far cry from that of 1963 when not a single Labour MP would accept nomination for the CND National Council.

While it is true that the moderates in the party, represented by its front bench defence spokesmen, have succeeded in obtaining a commitment to nuclear disarm within existing NATO decision-making machinery, the commitment is so alien to the spirit if not the letter of the party's manifesto, and so removed from the spirit of the conference decision of 1982 that the negotiations would almost certainly have reduced the massive vote to remain in NATO that was recorded at the party's 1982 conference.

The existing NATO machinery is extremely cumbersome. It takes on the whole up to five years, often longer, for any specific proposal to be adopted. Any broader defence initiative such as General Bernard Rogers' (present SACEUR) second echelon attack which NATO would need to adopt *in lieu* of a first use policy, would have taken up to ten years, which is well beyond the most optimistic life expectancy of a British government. And General Rogers' 4 per cent increase in conventional expenditure which would have made a second echelon strategy possible went well beyond the Labour leadership's plans to increase conventional expenditure at the expense of Britain's own nuclear deterrent, and its wish to increase spending on the Navy at the expense of spending on the Army of the Rhine.

The Labour leadership was always bound to seek shelter behind a policy which embraced unilateralism without calling for Britain's withdrawal from NATO even at the very real risk of reducing the majority for NATO by delaying the implementation of the party manifesto once it was returned to office. The paradox of the party's policy was that the more fundamental its opposition to nuclear weapons, the more circumspect it needed to be about the timing and presentation of the British initiative. Yet the pledge to introduce a non-nuclear defence within five years was quite simply incompatible with its promise to consult its NATO allies given the length of time the Alliance has taken in the past to reach collective decisions. Even if the leadership had been willing and able to fudge the issue, the price of frustrating its rank and file members would have been high. It would have reduced support within the party for NATO membership, and almost certainly made it more difficult for any future Labour government to implement NATO policies, even on non-nuclear matters.

In short, the advent of the Peace Movement since 1979 has gone a long way in undermining the decision-making process in the Alliance which for all the mention of participational democracy in the Atlantic Charter has always been the responsibility of a very narrow *élite*. That this is bound to raise doubts about the European commitment in the United States is inevitable. The problem is not the simple one of anti-Americanism. Although the

Peace Movement has provided an opportunity for discussion in a dramatic context of those more general doubts about the Atlantic partnership which continue to haunt the European left, the peace marchers are by no means all anti-American. The Reagan Administration appears to have accepted that the European people do not sympathise with the Soviet Union. It is merely that the more readily they believe that the United States is a threat to peace, the more readily they will believe that the Soviet Union is not: the more frightened they will be by American re-armament than the armament programmes implemented by the Soviet Union since the mid-1960s. That is why it is not Soviet actions which have fuelled the Peace Movement, whether the invasion of Afghanistan or the adoption of martial law in Poland, but America's attempts to make security more credible. The Alliance's response to those crises has brought the demonstrators onto the streets.

The problem as President Reagan well knows is not an erosion of popular support for NATO, or even the size of the Peace Movement which in both Britain and Germany is still very small. The opinion polls continue to show popular support for the Alliance, if a distrust of American leadership. The real problem is that a future administration may decide from a reading of America's own experience during the Vietnam War that the majority, however silent or vociferous, is likely to count for very little politically if it fails to make its voice heard; or if civil disobedience on an extensive scale undermines the confidence of political parties in or out of power.

In this respect the perceptions of the United States may be as important as the success or failure of the European political system to govern. Dr Kissinger's exaggerated fear of Eurocommunism in the mid-1970s was no less real for being exaggerated. This was the first time in the Alliance's history that the Americans publicly questioned the ability of their European allies to arrive at decisions without taking excessive note of opinions inherently antagonistic to its survival. In the event only Portugal was denied full access to NATO channels after the brief drift of the military *junta* to the left in 1975. And no one could have predicted that an Italian government supported by the Communist Party, would be among the most willing NATO countries to agree to the deployment of Cruise missiles, or that a socialist government in

France with Communist support would also be more outspoken than its predecessor in support for INF modernisation.

Unfortunately that is not the point. It does not really matter whether or not a bi-partisan consensus is restored by the end of this decade if in the interim anti-American sentiment erodes support for Europe in the United States. In demanding the recall of 1000 soldiers of the Seventh Army for every 100 000 peace marchers who took to the streets, Daniel Moynihan expressed the same lack of confidence that Europe would resolve its political difficulties that Henry Kissinger had first expressed six years earlier. Even if the Peace Movement is finally disarmed and the major political parties of the left manage to exorcise the spirit of anti-Americanism, European governments may find themselves in possession of a battlefield from which their American allies may have long since withdrawn.

4 The Lilliputian Senate: The Failure of European Cooperation

In a philosophy which postulates a clear cut relationship between US military strength and the lack of European self-reliance the patent disarray within NATO nations over the modernisation of theatre nuclear weapons, and American suspicions and Europe's failure to meet the 1977 targets in war reserve stocks of fuel and equipment both suggest that the United States is still assuming an unduly high burden.

But if the American revisionists operate within a narrow frame of reference, their European counterparts operate within a more narrow framework still which implies another interpretation: that Europe would be much better off without exclusive reliance on the United States. It was Dr Kissinger who reminded the Europeans 20 years ago that Atlantic partnership is something of a misnomer, that 'real partnership is only possible between equals'.[1] It was a point taken up more recently by Professor Hedley Bull who maintained that only a European defence community would enable the old world to recover the sense of purpose and vitality which it has so conspicuously lost.[2] As one of NATO's younger critics contends: the relationship of protector and protected evokes arrogance and condescension from one side; resentment and irresponsibility from the other. The Alliance, is not one of equals. The two sides can only reach agreement if they engage in a proper division of labour.[3]

This presupposes a picture of an Alliance whose present difficulties have sprung from an unequal partnership which in turn has justified a disproportionate American commitment and an inadequate European role. Unfortunately, the reasons for a demonstrably inadequate European contribution have very little to do with shielding under the American nuclear umbrella, but much to do with the internal divisions among the Europeans themselves which the creation of NATO did little to resolve. One explanation for Europe's reluctance to ask the questions posed by Hedley Bull and others is not that they are the wrong questions, or that there is no answer, but that the answer is not a very realistic one. There is, in fact, an unspoken fear that the question will only serve to undermine the confidence of the questioner.

All the crises in the past over Europe's failure to build up an adequate defence force have been occasioned by intra-European suspicions. French opposition to German re-armament in the early 1950s; the opposition of the BENELUX countries to de Gaulle's 1958 scheme for a special NATO Directorate of the three most important powers; similar objections to the exclusion of Britain which prompted the same countries to reject the Fouquet Plan; French objections to German participation in the MLF; French and German suspicions of Britain's attempts in the 1950s to open up a proper dialogue with the Soviet Union.

These crises reflect a crisis within Europe, not a crisis within the Alliance. On all important questions the United States has been able to bring the Europeans into line without inviting the prospect of a united Europe. Any crisis within the Alliance would have to reflect what Claude Cheysson has termed 'a progressive divorce' between the United States and Europe, and in particular, since the United States is still the senior partner, a demonstrable challenge to American leadership. It is precisely because European cooperation in the defence field has proved so very disappointing that the United States is still NATO's most important member.

In the early 1950s the United States was able to bring France into line over Germany's membership of NATO even though France refused to join the projected European Defence Community. In 1958 Eisenhower chose to side with the BENELUX countries in order to pre-empt de Gaulle's plans for an equal partnership with France and Britain which would have given both powers the right to veto American operations outside Europe. The collapse of the MLF was not unwelcome to the United States – it had never really believed in an independent European nuclear deterrent as shown by its lack-lustre endorsement of General Norstad's proposal for making NATO a fourth nuclear power.

Looked at from this perspective it is difficult to detect any crisis within NATO which has ever worked to America's disadvantage. Yet it is equally difficult to detect a crisis which has really disadvantaged Europe. The Europeans have been able to mask their own differences by claiming that any greater cooperation in defence would alienate the United States. When the Europeans did cooperate they often did so to reassure America that they were willing to assume greater burdens. As NATO's Secretary-General Manlio Brosio admitted to Richard Nixon in 1970, the Eurogroup had been set up not to create a European force, but to defeat American unilateralism, to reassure Congress that the Europeans were pulling their weight.[4]

The fact that Europe cannot even agree to the discussion of defence within the one organisation which expresses European unity – the European Community – is all the more lamentable because it comes at a time when the need for greater defence cooperation has been put by among others the German and Italian Foreign Ministers – the Genscher-Colombo Plan which is now over three years old. The protests which have arisen from President Mitterrand's proposal to work more closely with the Federal Republic in defence have served to reveal at a critical time how ugly such divisions could become if they are ever flushed into the open.

In short, if there is a crisis within the Alliance it would be wrong to see it entirely in an Atlantic context. The Europeans have been forced to confront their own failure to extend political cooperation. The fears which were so often expressed in America in 1973 about the 'threat' of European unity have in one sense been resolved. European unity is now less real than at any time since 1973. The picture of the European Community is one of 'fragments floating in the here and now' in the words of Stanley Hoffmann's sombre analysis of Europe.[5]

It is Europe's self-evident disunity – its failure to come to grips with unemployment and its failure to solve the problems of its dying traditional industries such as steel which explains its rift with the United States. The emergence of national antagonisms within a community that cannot even solve its budget deficit provide little encouragement that a European security policy could ever get off the ground.

The solutions put forward to resolve NATO's problems are quite unrealistic if they ignore the more general crisis through which Europe is passing. The skilful dissection of the Alliance by revisionists each anxious to offer the patient his own private nostrum serves only one useful purpose: to draw attention to the very real problems it faces. It does not confirm the thesis that the Alliance would be more convincing if the Europeans worked together more closely.

Affirmations of support, for example, for a European defence community are really little more than propositions derived from the experience of a widening rift between the United States and Europe. With few exceptions they reflect an *ad hoc* response to the present troubles which reveal little, if any, careful consideration of the long term requirements of European defence cooperation. This can be seen clearly from the indifferent support for two quite different organisations: the Eurogroup and the Western European Union (WEU).

France's absence from the Eurogroup makes it a particularly redundant body, despite the agreement in May 1982 by the defence ministers of the member countries to develop it as a forum for 'substantial politico-strategic discussion'.[6] Ever since the German Defence Minister Georg Leber first engaged Michel Jobert in a debate in 1973, the path towards greater European defence cooperation has appeared to lie with the WEU or the Eurogroup, and only for some in the European Community. Willy Brandt once described the Eurogroup as the clear expression of a European identity.[7] Yet a European identity without France is a curious conceit.

Recognising the problem, the Eurogroup proposed to change itself in 1975 into an independent forum open to all NATO members including France who were members of the European Community, or members of the Community who were not members of NATO. Although later that year the British Defence Secretary confirmed that France had responded favourably to the proposal nothing more was ever heard of it.[8] France's continued absence makes it inconceivable that the Eurogroup's initiatives will achieve very much. More likely they will represent brief excursions into cooperation followed by long periods of little or no progress.

It is the Western European Union (WEU) which has attracted the most support, largely because of France's membership and its periodic enthusiasm for revamping the organisation. It is worth examining this option further.

WESTERN EUROPEAN UNION

Since coming to power the Mitterrand government has put forward suggestions for revamping the WEU, an almost forgotten institution comprising Britain and the original six Common Market members who came together in 1954 to coordinate their defence policies following the collapse of the European Defence Community. Schemes for reconstituting the WEU have changed very little since they were first put forward in the early 1960s. On the whole, the organisation has inspired no more than idle scholarly curiosity. French support, however, has attracted a great deal of attention, perhaps because European unity in recent years has made but little progress and has produced consistent views on no more than a few mainly economic matters.

Support for revitalising the WEU raises a number of questions about the relationship between European security and the development of European cooperation. In its simplest form it assumes that one depends upon the other. This assumption is highly debatable and could not be made on the analysis of Western defence policies to date. It is increasingly made, however, by many defence analysts who have drawn from the present transatlantic crisis the lesson that Europe's security will increasingly depend on its resolve to defend itself with markedly less reliance on American support.

It is, perhaps, not surprising that in the quest for greater European cooperation the focus of attention has once again fallen on the WEU. To what extent, if any, however can the WEU contribute to European security? It would be well to admit at the outset that it is probably unrealistic to expect the organisation to succeed in the future where it has failed in the past. This is not to cast doubt on the value of its discussions both in the Assembly and the Council. But the WEU must go beyond merely debating the issues if it is to promote greater cooperation. For policy is the outcome, not of debate, but of the immensely complex political and bureaucratic processes of European politics of which those debates form only a part.

Since the support the French have given the WEU is so

important it is useful to place it in its historical context. In response to an American request that Germany and Italy be admitted to NATO the French proposed a European army which would include all the forces of Western Europe. Once it became clear that the scheme had little support the French put forward an alternative: that of a European Defence Community. When this too was thrown out by the French Assembly the putative members salvaged what they could by the Paris Agreements of 23 October 1954 which associated Italy and Germany with the signatories of the Brussels Treaty of 1948. The new scheme was devised, signed and ratified by France within four months.

From the beginning, the WEU was a somewhat anomalous organisation. Article 8 which set up a Council with unlimited responsibilities was, in turn, governed by Article 4 which required it to rely on the appropriate NATO authorities for information and advice on military matters. Article 9 which set up the Assembly required it to submit an annual report on its activities to the Consultative Assembly of the Council of Europe. The signatories were clearly concerned that the WEU should not duplicate the work of other international organisations. The exercise of the Council's strictly military responsibilities was transferred to NATO from the outset.

The full meaning of the restrictions was not confronted fully until the early 1960s when the WEU's social and cultural activities under Articles 2 and 3 were transferred to the Council of Europe with the exception of those already undertaken by the Public Administration Committee. Its activities in the economic sphere defined in Articles 1 and 8 of the treaty were entirely overshadowed by the conduct of business within the European Community. Even before Britain's accession the agreement of July 1963, which provided for an exchange of ideas between Britain and the EEC, largely made the WEU's economic responsibilities redundant.[9]

By the mid-1970s the WEU appeared to be largely, if not entirely, moribund. The Assembly complained that the Council took no note of its deliberations. For two years the Council itself did not meet. Between 1974–7 the post of Secretary-General was left vacant. With the significant increase in momentum towards EEC unity after the 1969 summit at the Hague, the Council reduced the scale of its own activities.[10] Even in the specific case of defence it often refused to answer the Assembly's questions on the grounds that European defence cooperation had not yet reached the point at which the European Community could present a collective view. The Council seemed unwilling to speak on behalf of its own members.[11]

It was the EEC's failure to discuss defence matters and the growing crisis of confidence in America's leadership of the Atlantic Alliance which prompted France in 1973 to suggest reactivating the WEU as a framework for defence consultations. From the outset, the French Foreign Minister Michel Jobert, made it clear that he was not interested in using it as a forum for a European nuclear planning group despite support for the idea from the French Parliamentarians in the Assembly. He was much more interested in using the Standing Committee on Armaments as 'a privileged framework for European cooperation in arms manufacture' at a time when French manufacturers felt particularly threatened by American competition.

An explanation of Jobert's proposal in terms of French Europeanism would obscure the real significance of the changes that had recently taken place within NATO of which the creation of the Eurogroup was, perhaps, the most important. Concerned about unilateral American moves to reduce the strength of the Seventh Army, the British with German support, had set up the Eurogroup to persuade an increasingly sceptical Congress of Europe's resolve to do more in its own defence. After publication of the May 1972 guidelines which expressly gave the Eurogroup precedence over other NATO bodies the French became concerned that their absence from the Group, which was in keeping with their decision to leave NATO's integrated military command, might prejudice them in the future.

Obviously for France the WEU, as an alternative to the Eurogroup, had certain advantages, not least the fact that cooperation on weapons standardisation, one of the Eurogroup's main responsibilities, had been under discussion in the Standing Armaments Committee (SAC) for several years. Nonetheless, the French had to accept that until the Germans or the British pulled out of the Eurogroup neither would have much time for the WEU. Jobert concentrated on Germany. His initiative did indeed, appear to confront Bonn with the key institutional and political question of enjoying or foregoing French cooperation. For a brief moment in November 1973 following Brandt's visit to Paris the Germans appeared to waiver.[12]

In the event, however, they showed the same scepticism of the WEU as their British partners. In principle, neither objected to using it as a debating forum but, as so often in the organisation's history, support for the principle was not always evidence of support for its work. Britain's preference for the Eurogroup was voiced by Roy Hattersley, the Minister of State at the Foreign Office, as 'the best available means for developing greater practical European defence cooperation'. He even underlined the point by asking the WEU Assembly to give full support to the Eurogroup's attempt to coordinate defence procurement despite the fact that it had a Standing Armaments Committee of its own.[13]

France's mistake in 1973 was to imagine that progress in the area of arms cooperation, in which the WEU had made some headway, would automatically extend to that of political understanding, in which it had not. It was by no means self-evident that institutional changes would enable the WEU to succeed where NATO itself had made but little progress. Uwe Nerlich even doubted whether it would have provided a useful debating chamber. 'The West European Union', he wrote at the time, 'should be viewed as no more than an extra-territorial meeting place to be replaced by a different forum according to the success of its consultations.'[14] Jobert's arguments might have been more persuasive if he had agreed to discuss European cooperation on an *ad hoc* basis outside the Eurogroup, if necessary, but outside the WEU as well.

Renewed doubts about the American commitment, at a time when the United States itself is more anxious than ever to share its defence burdens, has once again prompted the French to throw their support behind the WEU. In an address to the Assembly in December 1981 Georges Lemoine, the Secretary of State to the Ministry of Defence, reminded its members that:

> . . . A military balance at the lowest possible level and effective and verifiable disarmament are France's goals. And it wishes to discuss them within the only European organisation which stems from a specific treaty still in force . . . That organisation is the West European Union.[15]

Lemoine reaffirmed French support at a WEU Colloquy two months later. Later still the French Minister of Defence told a German newspaper that the WEU was the only organisation in which the Europeans could discuss common defence problems outside the framework of NATO.

Verbal support for the organisation has not been confined to France. At the December session Britain's Minister of State for the Armed Forces agreed that the WEU had the only Parliamentary Assembly empowered to debate defence matters. Italy's Defence Minister remarked that it was 'the only real European point of contact for problems of defence and arms control'. In essence, however, these affirmations of support are really little more than propositions derived from the experience of a widening rift between the United States and Europe. With few exceptions, they reflect a short-term response to the present difficulties within the Atlantic Alliance which reflects little, if any, careful consideration of the long-term requirements of European defence cooperation. Support for the WEU hardly matches the proposals put forward by the Foreign Ministers of Italy and Germany for a defence dialogue within the European Community, the so-called Colombo-Genscher plan, which was last elaborated in their joint appearance before the European Parliament in November 1982. Even France's support appears somewhat suspect when one looks into Lemoine's proposals more closely, particularly his desire to reactivate the Assembly rather than the Council where all substantive decisions are made.

Support for the WEU is not new; nor is French sponsorship. What is new is the extent to which support for a European defence organisation is heard more often and more loudly. Whether the WEU offers any real scope for greater European cooperation is another question entirely.

The WEU will never be able to make an important contribution to European security as long as its own Council members continue to treat it with little respect. At the moment, its critics may be excused for the belief that their apparent disregard of the organisation speaks more for the absence of a clear understanding of the Council's role than any inherent limitations on the WEU's field of action.

This was not always the case. One of its original founders, Mendès-France, believed that nothing in the Treaty excluded the Council of Ministers from discussing defence matters whether or not they were already under discussion in NATO.[16] Nothing, in fact, prevents it from exercising its full responsibility today except the narrow frame of reference from which its more NATO-minded members continue to derive an understanding of its role.

Today the Council is undoubtedly more important than it was in the early 1970s when the German Foreign Minister, Walter Scheel, suggested that its meetings be discontinued on the grounds that ministers already had an opportunity to consult with one another within the framework of the EEC.[17] But the Council's deliberations still command little attention. Until Britain joined the European Community it used to meet quarterly. Today it only meets once a year. Governments are represented at a level they wish, although only very rarely by a Minister of Foreign Affairs, or even a Secretary of State except where it finds itself in the chair. The great majority are represented by ambassadors. Even during informal meetings the chairman usually speaks on behalf of everyone else.

Joint meetings between the Council and the Assembly committees occupy only a single day. The Council's Chairman in Office and the Chairman of the Assembly's General Affairs Committee did not even meet in 1981. For the last five years the Council has continued to contend that informal meetings provide a much better vehicle for communicating answers to the Assembly's questions on the somewhat questionable understanding that the procedure is more likely to guarantee freedom of expression.

Yet it is the Council's lack of accountability that has given rise to the popular belief that the organisation itself is a political anomaly. In 1981 the number of written questions put by Assembly members fell to five, the lowest number ever. Few members have any real confidence that their questions will be answered. Some governments, notably France and Belgium, have made a mockery of the whole procedure by repeating the Council's previous answers in reply to questions, a practice which could only be justified if their own policies corresponded exactly to the Council's unanimously expressed opinions. The Council's report in 1976 explicitly stated that the individual opinions of each government were best communicated, not in the Assembly, but in the national Parliaments of its respective members. Were this procedure to be generally adopted the Council would be able to bypass the Assembly altogether.[18]

The main reason why the Council has adopted such a restrictive view of its commitments is entirely one of self-interest. The debates in the Assembly and the recommendations to which they have given rise have occasionally disturbed governments who are anxious to keep their foreign policy options beyond the reach of public opinion or Parliamentary scrutiny. It has long been a standing tradition that relations between the Council and the Assembly are confidential, but the tradition is also essential if the Council is to deprive the organisation of substance, if it is to deny it precisely that element of Parliamentary supervision which the Assembly is supposed to exercise. Certain foreign policy issues that have aroused public interest at home, often to the embarrassment of the countries concerned, have not been discussed at all.

In recent years, for example, the Council has refused to answer questions on relations between the WEU members and Eastern Europe. Since 1975 it has also devoted less space in its reports to relations between the United States and the European Community despite the present hiatus in their relations. By refusing to take up the crisis in Poland, or the Soviet invasion of Afghanistan with the NATO Council, or the pipeline dispute with the EEC heads of state, the Council failed to discharge its obligations under Article 7 of the Paris Treaty which requires it to act '... with regard to any situation which may constitute a threat to peace in whatever area that threat should arise', whether economic or political.[19] It also compounded the omission by refusing to allow its chairman to communicate the substance of its discussions to the three members of the European Community and the nine members of NATO who are not members of the WEU.

In the light of such attitudes it seems most unlikely that the WEU will ever form the basis of a European defence community. Its silence on so many issues bears too close a relation to the explicit and implicit policies of the EEC for the coincidence to be explained away as merely fortuitous. The Council's inaction accurately reflects Europe's continuing disingenuousness on political matters to which it is reluctant to apply, or even admit to, a military solution. The EEC has preferred to use its resources not to invest in a defence community but to prevent the onset of the type of crises with which such a community would in all probability be unable or unwilling to deal. In December 1980 it preferred to provide food aid as well as further financial assistance to Poland in an attempt to pre-empt a Soviet invasion, rather than discuss the security measures that might have been required if an invasion had gone ahead.

But the problems of defence cooperation are much more

profound. Even the Federal Republic seems unwilling to discuss in any greater detail what it might be able to contribute to European security notwithstanding Genscher's original Stuttgart address. There appears to be a profound lack of political will to move nearer European integration at a time when the course of European unity has been set back, perhaps permanently, by the delay to Spain's accession to the European Community, the persistent threat of Britain's secession and the ambiguous position of Greece, its most recent member. The people of Europe have begun to look inwards not out. In this respect, the real crisis which the Atlantic Alliance faces is not a 'progressive divorce' between the United States and Europe, but the latter's failure to develop institutions which would help realise Monnet's vision. The Community, far from maturing, looks every year more and more like a case of arrested development.

During a tour of the Middle East in January 1981, Dr Henry Kissinger raised the question whether Europe would be able to act alone in certain foreign policy areas without lessening its dependence upon the United States in the sphere of defence. He might also have asked in the absence of any evidence that the Europeans could take their cooperation in defence much further, whether their foreign policy initiatives were likely to prove very effective. Their traditional sensitivity to the danger that too great a degree of cooperation in defence might alienate the United States has, in one respect, been resolved; European unity is now less real than at any time since 1973.

If the Council had patently failed to fulfil its promise, what of the Assembly? In the confident world of the early 1950s Mendès-France imagined that the WEU would be compelled to extend, not merely expedite, its responsibilities under pressure from a democratic Assembly. He always hoped that the Assembly would have a role commensurate with its status as a Parliamentary forum, despite the fact that it had no legislative powers.[20] Responding to the momentum towards European unity he hoped that the Assembly would soon generate the enthusiasm that would allow it to transcend its own consultative status.

The Assembly's potential is still impressive. It is distinct from other European assemblies not only by virtue of its mandate but also its membership. Until recently, the North Atlantic Assembly only partially represented the member countries since it had no Communist representatives. Its committees are still accountable only to themselves and speak in their own name rather than the Assembly's, which is why their reports are rarely, if ever, discussed in plenary session. To a large extent, the Assembly's discussions go largely unheeded. They are not discussed in NATO Council meetings despite Article 18 of its own Rules of Procedure which allows it to address its recommendations directly to the Council of Ministers. They are not even discussed in the Parliaments of the individual members.[21]

The same limitations also apply to the European Parliament at Strasbourg. As a result of direct suffrage it no longer can claim a permanent link with national legislatures. It has less opportunity than ever to discuss matters outside the scope of the Paris or Rome Treaties. In the past meetings were held between the bureaux of the WEU Assembly and the European Parliament (1957), between their respective clerks (1956/7) and between their respective Presidents (1971/8). But since the MEPs ceased being members of their own Parliaments they are no longer kept informed of the Assembly's work, except upon request. The Assembly's right to discuss European security is, therefore, not only politically and legally indisputable, but also unique. It still remains the only European assembly with the express statutory power to consider the interlinked problems of policy and strategy.[22]

Three years ago an attempt was made by a group of European Christian Democrats and Conservative MEPs to establish direct links with the Assembly. Both parties felt that the European Parliament should be more demonstrably concerned with Europe's defence. The attempt was successfully defeated by the French government in the person of the Minister for Foreign Affairs, Francois-Poncet, who reminded the Assembly that there was no provision in the Brussels Treaty or its own Rules of Procedure for inviting observers to its discussions.[23]

This does not mean, however, that the French, for one, have taken the Assembly very seriously. They have, in fact, remained uncompromising in their insistence on the Council's right of silence. The Assembly was reminded by its Chairman Pierre Werner that its tenth annual report could 'only consist of a summary of the Council's activities. Anything constituting a political assessment of these activities is ruled out'.[24] The almost permanent state of tension between the Council and Assembly reached its climax in June 1967 when the annual report was referred back for not being sufficiently informative. As a German Christian Democrat remarked, the Council's derisory replies to the Assembly's questions revealed its refusal to accept the principle of accountability.[25] Seven years later a German Social Democratic member who happened also to be Chairman of the Assembly's Political Committee, accused the Council of 'persistent neglect' of its deliberations.[26] Whenever the Council has responded to the Assembly's recommendations the content of its responses has always been determined by national preferences and contexts.

Repeated attempts to improve the Assembly's standing have failed for lack of support within the Council, principally from France. In 1980 Dr von Hassel, a former President of the Assembly, recommended that Ministers of Defence or their representatives should take part in its discussions. He also suggested that the Council should meet before the NATO Council meetings to discuss the reports of the Assembly committees.[27] In the event, his report for all its worth, received little attention. The matter was not even raised in the European Parliament despite von Hassel's own membership. So far the Council has shown little willingness to rise to the challenge or investigate the merits and demerits of allowing the Assembly a much wider role. Too much intellectual energy has been expended in discussing its reports, too little in exploring whether the scope of its discussions could be extended.

It is not surprising, therefore, that all the reports about reforming the Assembly which have been put forward by General Affairs Committee members – De Bruin, Leynen, von Hassel and de Poi – have met with a muted response. In advocating a joint standing committee with the European Parliament, de Poi recognised the need for a working group on European security, a concept which the Council has always opposed.[28] Despite widespread recognition of the need for closer European cooperation in defence it is clear that the Council's lack of enthusiasm reflects a general failure to press ahead with European unity in spheres other than defence.

In short, the Assembly has no real powers of sanctioning the Council. It has neither a permanent majority nor a permanent opposition and no legislative powers. Its authority derives solely from a consensus which must reflect the unanimous opinion of its members. As a result, its recommendations all too often appear bland and anodyne. If they did not, the Council and Assembly would never find themselves in agreement.

BRITAIN AND A EUROPEAN DEFENCE COMMUNITY

What does seem clear is that Britain would never be reconciled to a European defence community on such a basis. The collapse of the consensus on defence has had two consequences already: it has reinforced the nationalist sentiment of the left which has compounded its distaste for Britain's existing membership of the European community; and it has given rise to a much more serious, because more plausible, creed of neo-Gaullism on the right which has strong support among some members of the present government.

The steady erosion of British power since 1945 appears to its allies so irrevocable and absolute that it is hard to regard it as other than inevitable. That is not how it is always seen in Britain. It is not the decline of Britain's power overseas that is often the focus of discussion, but the extent of its commitment to the defence of Europe which many now claim has militated against a variable defence posture for the past 30 years. For the force commitments now are the largest Britain has ever made as a percentage of forces assigned exclusively to NATO, a fact which was brought home by the Defence Review of 1981. This attempted to bring to an end the parade of overseas commitments that the country could no longer meet and change the balance of the services by cutting the Navy twice as much as the Army and seven times as much as the RAF.

The extent of Britain's continental commitment needs to be underlined. By the Paris Treaty of 1954 Britain undertook to maintain four divisions and the 2nd Tactical Air Force on the mainland. When that commitment was made the Rhine Army was 14 per cent of the British Army; today it is 34 per cent. The Air Force in Germany was 4 per cent of its total force; it is now 10 per cent. In the 1950s Britain had conscripts and massive reserves; now it has neither. Britain has to spend more per head of population than any other NATO member except the United States in order to sustain a separate army on the continent and the largest naval force after that of the United States. The cost is already becoming difficult to support.

The continental commitment has come under increasing attack for three main reasons. First, the navy lobby, supported in part by the Labour Party and the right-wing of the Conservative Party, no longer believes it possible or justifiable to maintain the BAOR at its present size. Two defence spokesmen in the present government have both stated in print the case for a substantial reduction in the Rhine Army.²⁹ At a time when the collapse of confidence in NATO has served to heighten Labour Party nationalism it is not surprising that it has become the Navy party, deeply critical of the fact that but for the Falklands War the Royal Navy would have been left smaller in terms of personnel than the BAOR. If it is surprising at first glance that the left wing party in British political life has become the Navy party this is largely because the Navy is the service now associated with independent action both within Europe, and NATO itself.³⁰

Secondly, despite the level of Britain's commitment to Europe it is clear that it is no more convincing than it was ten years ago. It is difficult to see how three armoured divisions and 12 aircraft squadrons in Germany could restore an imbalance in conventional forces which on SACEUR's own admission is now 2:1 in the Soviet Union's favour. In the light of such depressing statistics the European people have tended to find some reassurance in the reassertion of national control over their own forces. In some instances, notably the BENELUX countries and Denmark, this has manifest itself in a refusal to deploy Cruise missiles on national territory; in others in a reluctance to station conventional forces in the front line. Five of the six Dutch brigades committed to the defence of the First Dutch Corps along the Elbe are now stationed in the Netherlands.

In Britain those opposed to the presence of the Rhine Army argue that it is a palpable illusion to suppose that any money saved by the reduction in NATO's maritime defences (upon which any successful land and air operations in Europe may largely depend) could be usefully employed in the defence of north-west Europe. No less than 40 per cent of Britain's defence budget provides only 10 per cent of allied forces in Germany. Any increment which would have been paid for by half the projected cuts in the Navy would have increased those forces by only one armoured division and one squadron of Tornado aircraft. In the opinion of many only a drastic reduction in the strength of the Rhine Army and its redeployment west of the Rhine would enable it to be re-equipped with Challenger tanks without denying the Navy its Trident submarines and a new generation of Invincible class aircraft carriers.

Yet even that would mean limiting the Rhine Army to protecting the airfields of the 2nd Tactical Air Force at Wildenrath, Laarbruch and Bruggen.[31] Whether the Germans would gain any reassurance from the redeployment of the BAOR is an open question. Finally, the British have only adhered to the Paris Treaty to date because of the political influence it has given them within NATO, and within the EEC. It was long a French complaint in the 1950s that the British and Americans between them held all three of the main commands, and all but two of the secondary posts.[32] The British still hold more positions than strictly justified by their contribution because of France's absence from the integrated military command. In a European defence community this would no longer be the case. Nor would it be within NATO if the Rhine Army is reduced. If the British Corps were cut back to say a single division, NATO's Northern Army Group could hardly continue under British command. Whether a future Labour government would find the prospect discouraging is doubtful. If Britain left the European Community there would be much less to influence German opinion; if it remained in and the British economy continued to decline the Germans would in any case be much less inclined to listen. Either way the case for maintaining the BAOR up to strength for political reasons is no longer as compelling as it once was.

That Britain will have to make some quite serious defence choices is no longer in question. With a relatively low rate of economic growth and an unusually large number of commitments, Britain has been struggling to make ends meet since the 1950s. A once imperial power has been left with residual overseas responsibilities; a country that was once in the forefront of the development of atomic weapons naturally wishes to keep them; a country which more than any other created the Atlantic Alliance is obviously unwilling to play second fiddle to France or Germany. Yet a Think Tank paper presented at a Cabinet meeting in September 1982 maintained that the country could not maintain an independent deterrent, a naval force second only to the United States and an army on the continent beyond 1986.[33] One of the roles would have to be abandoned. If the commitment to Trident holds good, the Rhine Army may well be the first to go. Even if Trident is abandoned, increased expenditure on the Navy will suggest the same choice.

The conflict in the south Atlantic, the first major naval engagement since the Second World War, has once again re-opened the debate about a British role east of Suez. In its aftermath some pundits have put forward arguments for revising the Atlantic Treaty to take account of the fact that Britain's primary responsibility should be to defend the overseas sea lanes and to keep enough forces in reserve to patrol the eastern Atlantic.[34] Increasingly they see themselves as revisionists because of their belief that unless the Alliance is drastically revised it will continue to shape rather than be shaped by national commitments.

The most alarming feature of all, however, is that in calling for a national division of responsibilities in NATO which may or may not be demanded by public opinion, the neo-Gaullists of both political parties are peculiarly insensitive to the genuine concerns of Britain's allies. As one of the most perceptive of them has recognised the Germans above all would find such policies very difficult to live with. Any shift in British defence thinking which amounted to a *de facto* revision of the Atlantic Treaty might well leave Bonn with the feeling of being ill-served or neglected in allied discussions.[35]

A number of neo-Gaullists have contended that the Berlin garrison and the Rhine Army are the last vestiges of Britain's past as a great power, at one with its previous role East of Suez.[36] This in itself is worrying enough. For the case for withdrawing the Rhine Army altogether (although not often heard) or reducing it substantially (which is heard increasingly often) goes far beyond the case for improving the cost effectiveness of Britain's NATO contribution. It amounts to claiming in effect that the BAOR is the main area in which British forces are over-extended – the east of Suez of the 1980s. Such a conclusion would not reassure Germany that Britain would come to its assistance in time of a crisis, any more than the strategic airlift of British forces in the early 1960s reassured Britain's allies in the Far East or the Persian Gulf. It would leave as it did East of Suez not so much a vacuum of power, as a vacuum of purpose, which no commitment on paper could ever dispel. The Rhine Army's permanent presence on the

Central Front is part of NATO's 'forward defence' by which the Germans set so much store because the alternative is to regard their own countryside as an expendable battlefield.

The effect on the United States and its 320 000 troops stationed in Germany would also be significant, possibly profound. British politicians should not overlook the political importance which the Americans continue to attach to the fact that another non-continental power for whom the membership of NATO was also a dramatic break with tradition maintains 40 per cent of its armed forces on the continent. Unilateral withdrawal on the part of Britain more than that of any other country could precipitate a substantial reduction in the front line strength of the Seventh Army.

In this lies the main distinction between British neo-Gaullism and the policies pursued by de Gaulle. Although de Gaulle found scope for reaffirming his belief in the nation state as the principal reality of political life, his eventual disengagement from NATO was undertaken on the clear understanding that it would help to make Europe more independent of the United States. The French cast their discourse about the Atlantic Alliance in the rhetoric of European unity, even though it sometimes rendered popular understanding of the Atlantic partnership somewhat opaque.

British neo-Gaullism is inspired by no such vision. As has already been stated, it appears to be part and parcel of a general disillusionment with Europe, a profound lack of political will to move nearer European integration at a time when its course seems to have been set back perhaps permanently by the persistent threat of Britain's own secession and the ambiguous and unresolved position of Greece, its most recent member. The people of Europe have begun to look inwards not out.

In that respect the real crisis which the Alliance faces is not a 'progressive divorce' between the United States and Europe, but Europe's failure to develop institutions which would help to realise Monnet's vision. Britain's membership has contributed a large part to this state of affairs. It has served to set back European unity as de Gaulle always predicted; it has not marked a step on the road to confederation as Pompidou originally hoped. Political life in the European Community is beginning to look like the state of nature described by one of the characters in a novel by Paul Theroux, as 'nasty, British and short'.

In spite of the fact that Europe is now more powerful than it was 20 years ago the European countries are clearly no more capable of undertaking their own defence without substantial American support. If the United States wishes to ignore this, or sacrifice Europe for vital interests elsewhere, that must be its decision. It has every cause to be irritated by Europe's unwillingness or inability to cooperate more extensively; French *amour propre* which finds its manifestation in Gaullism; British colonial nostalgia which finds its most absurd expression not so much in Fortress Falklands, but the desire of those who should know better to retreat into Fortress Britain by spending more on the Navy at the expense of everything else.

The United States has cause to be irritated but no cause to deceive itself. Its NATO commitment is still a cheap option; its European allies still its most important friends; even as Senator Fulbright recognised 20 years ago, the most important check on the arbitrary exercise of power. As allies of the United States the Europeans do no service to themselves to expect too much of it, or encourage America to expect too much of themselves. They do themselves even less service, however, to expect too much of each other.

THE EUROPEAN NUCLEAR DETERRENT AND FRANCO-GERMAN COOPERATION

Last November in an interview with the Swiss magazine *Weltwoche*, Dr Kissinger warned that a purely West European deterrent would 'in the last resort lead to a kind of neutralism'.[37] There is another – far more plausible – danger. It could precipitate even more discord than the MLF. The European revisionists may well be right to argue that there will never be a European defence community without a European deterrent, but they are wrong to believe Europe could deploy its own deterrent without destroying the all party consensus for nuclear weapons which already exists in France, and which is so often cited in the United States as one of the few elements of certainty in an otherwise confused and uncertain political scene in Europe.

As long ago as 1958 Ben Moore suggested that an independent European nuclear force would actually encourage the Europeans to spend more on conventional forces if only because graduated deterrence would be more realistic once Europe itself could take the ultimate decision to escalate.[38]

Europe has lived with the threat of nuclear war for 40 years because in the last analysis it has never really believed that the US deterrent would actually be used. And the French have managed to win a consensus for their own deterrent largely on the understanding (nowhere explicitly stated) that it would not be activated either. If the Peace Movement in France has little, if any, support could this be because the will to defend itself is weaker than in its neighbours? Could neutralism be weak in France, asks Dominique Moisi, because it has chosen to declare itself potentially neutral like Switzerland, because since leaving NATO's integrated command in 1966 France has been to all intents and purposes a neutral country?[39]

In a recent outspoken article in *Le Monde* Michel Pinton, the Secretary-General of Giscard's party the UDP blew the whistle on the *force de frappe* almost as decisively as Dr Henry Kissinger did for the American guarantee in his notorious Brussels speech four years earlier. In his article Michel Pinton contended that future French forward positions and even tactical nuclear weapons would be overwhelmed in a few minutes or hours of a Soviet invasion, leaving France with its strategic deterrent aimed exclusively at Soviet cities. 'In this situation the French people would naturally prefer to negotiate or surrender as in 1871 or 1940 rather than annihilate millions of Russians, inviting the same fate in return.' This has been known for years – it was only President Mitterrand's rather unwise suggestions of further Franco-German cooperation which has recently re-opened the whole question. There is certainly no evidence of the will to use nuclear weapons even at the risk of national suicide on which the Socialist CERES group has laid so much stress.[40]

Although President Mitterrand spoke rather generally of extending the French deterrent to Germany during his visit to Bonn in November 1982, the Germans are unlikely to be very reassured. Confidence may have declined in the American guarantee, but they can derive none at all from a French one. They cannot have forgotten that Monsieur Mitterrand himself served in every Fourth Republic Administration which tried to block German re-armament in the early 1950s and for a long time remained bitterly critical of the Franco-German Treaty of 1963. Today he seems to have accepted the logic of de Gaulle's strategic thinking – the offer to Germany of a nuclear guarantee exclusive to Europe; but the retention of a weapon that Germany itself is debarred from possessing, an ultimate guarantee against that same power whose economic dominance was always of such concern to de Gaulle.

France's offer of a German key in French nuclear policy – in keeping with its Military Planning Act of 1976 which insisted that the concept of sanctuarisation could only be conceived in a European context – might be more credible if the French were less evidently concerned about Germany as they undoubtedly are about the Soviet Union.

The broadening of Franco-German strategic consultation announced in October 1982 must also be questioned. What credibility has that commitment when France is actually limiting its capacity to collaborate effectively with the Federal Republic by cutting defence expenditure on conventional forces; when French forces in Germany were cut in 1982 by 10 per cent following a much larger cut of 25 per cent a year earlier. The money spent on constructing a seventh atomic submarine and buying the Hades missile for the early 1990s does not mean that France can forgo maintaining large conventional forces since it is only at the conventional level that Franco-German cooperation can really have much meaning. For the time being French thinking does not appear to have changed very much since 1972, when the Defence Minister, Michel Debré insisted that 'the decision to employ nuclear weapons can only be made by a single nation'.[41] There is no evidence that a French government now or in the future would disagree with General Pierre Gallois 'it is hardly credible that (a nuclear power) would expose its entire property to destruction merely to ensure the protection of another state'.[42]

CONCLUSION

The initiatives for which Europe has been responsible illustrate that it is inadequate and, even misleading, to suggest that there has been no progress on European defence cooperation. Whatever one's views of its nature and scope, it is still impossible to calculate and rash to predict what further progress will be made. Much will depend on the attitudes of three countries: the United States, France and the Federal Republic of Germany.

With regard to the United States, the Europeans will have to ask themselves whether their cooperation is intended to anticipate what many now expect: a reduction in the American conventional commitment to Europe, or to forestall it. There seems no reason, however, to assume that it will provoke it. There is no evidence that the Americans would feel threatened by the further development of the WEU any more than they have felt threatened by the development of the Eurogroup. Henry Kissinger advocated re-activating the WEU as long ago as 1966 when he appeared before the Senate Committee on Foreign Relations. To the extent that Europe was made to face up to its problems in a European context, he felt that it would be driven inevitably to working more closely with the United States.[43] Even when he was in office he was convinced that a European defence community would be less divisive than European economic unity. At the last session of the DPC in December 1973 the American Defense Secretary, James Schlesinger, threw his full support behind the Jobert initiative even though Jobert and Kissinger had clashed earlier in the year over the management of Atlantic relations.

In the 1970s one of the main breaks on the development of European cooperation was the very real concern of the smaller states that it would provide the United States with an excuse to reduce its military establishment in Europe. That concern has been expressed as frequently in the WEU as it has been in the Eurogroup which set out in 1969 with the express purpose of neutralising criticism in Congress that the Europeans were not pulling their weight.

But if the smaller members have remained unsympathetic to defence planning outside the framework of NATO in the past, their attitude may be about to change. It is the smaller states, notably the Netherlands and Belgium, who have clashed with the United States over the issue of theatre nuclear modernisation. In the BENELUX countries as well, bipartisanship has begun to break down more rapidly than in Britain or Germany. It is now very much in their interests to find a European defence policy which may complement that of NATO just as it has always been in the perceived interests of France.

At the end of the day, however, everything presupposes that the French will be prepared to throw their full weight behind it. Nothing in their most recent attitude suggests they intend doing so. And it is precisely on this point that the WEU Assembly has asked for greater clarification of the French position.

Whether one looks at Jobert's initiative in 1973, or President Mitterrand's most recent proposals, there seems to be no substantial basis on which the WEU might build. Lemoine's speech in 1981 was but the latest in a long succession of French inspired flirtations with a European defence community which were all based on the understanding that Europe would be able to spend more on defence if it acted independently of the United States while still remaining within the Atlantic Alliance. Europe today, however, would not be prepared to increase defence expenditure above and beyond the 3 per cent figure agreed in 1977 unless the Soviet Union were seen to be more threatening than it is perceived, at present, or Europe were to feel more alienated from the United States. It is, in fact, its reluctance to admit that *détente* has failed, or indeed, to admit that the Soviet Union is quite the threat that Reagan imagines that largely explains its frustration with America. In 1975, after all, Giscard d'Estaing repudiated Jobert's WEU initiative precisely on the understanding that it might provoke the Soviet Union and thus set back *détente*.[44]

It can always be argued, of course, that the advocates of defence cooperation found themselves in 1973 arguing from too slender a basis of experience. Their hope that it would help to make Europe, at least, in part independent of the United States and therefore, free to manoeuvre between the superpowers was true, if at all, only on the basis of certain assumptions and not on the basis of proofs made available by experience. In the mid-1970s European defence cooperation was seen to be a threat to *détente*; the United States was not. Today the relationship with the United States has become infinitely more complex at a time when its government is seen to be the real threat to *détente*. But it still remains as true as ever that greater European cooperation might send the wrong signals to Moscow. Even if it reassured the Americans, it would remain a very ambiguous symbol of European unity. The last transatlantic crisis in 1973 brought the Europeans together and produced a fairly coherent attitude to *détente* in the form of the Atlantic Declaration. The present crisis, despite encouraging France to look again at the WEU, has produced neither a coherent attitude to *détente* nor a consistent attitude to defence cooperation.

In the absence of both, the French government has been forced to confront an especially fine problem of political judgment. It seems likely that under the present socialist administration even more than its predecessor there will continue to be disagreement about how far defence cooperation can be taken without endangering what is left of *détente* on the one hand, and the relationship with the United States on the other. Its ambiguous support for the WEU must raise doubts about its real support for European defence cooperation, as too must its continued absence from the Eurogroup. The supporters of both institutions may well have based their hopes that they might play a more significant role in European security on assumptions and principles which run counter to several dominant elements in French thinking.

It is even doubtful whether much closer cooperation in the conventional field would be particularly welcome to the Federal Republic. In the 1950s Karl Deutsch and Lewis Edinger warned that West Germany could be trusted as an Atlantic partner provided it did not have to make a choice between partnership with the United States and relations with the GDR. The question that needs to be asked in the 1980s is whether the Federal Republic could ever be trusted as a partner in a European Defence Community if it should ever be forced to make a choice between Western Europe and relations with East Germany. We should recall that at the height of the movement towards European unity – at the Hague summit in 1969, Willy Brandt spoke out against a specifically European security organisation:

> We are surely agreed that our Community shall not be a new bloc, but a model system suitable as an element in the construction of a well balanced all European peace system.[45]

That concern probably still prevails even though the SPD has passed from the government scene.

Whether the creation of a European defence community would re-open the German question is less important in the short term than the fact that any movement towards it would probably highlight the divisions within France which have already been made apparent by discussion of closer Franco-German cooperation. It seems most unlikely that the withdrawal of the Seventh

Army would help both countries to realise the hopes for extending the Franco-German Treaty of 1963 which originally foundered on America's insistence that ratification of any further treaty would have to be tied to a statement of support for NATO. Even if the Germans believed it would not erode their understanding with the GDR and the Soviet Union, future French governments would have to decide whether there would be much public support for such a community in France, and whether it could survive for long without a nuclear umbrella which the French public might be extremely reluctant to provide.

In short it is not what one writer has called 'poverty of imagination' in conceiving alternatives to the Alliance which explains the lack of progress towards greater European cooperation[46] but an all too vivid imagination of what the future might hold if some of the alternatives so often talked about were ever to be revived. Simply because the case for greater European cooperation is more convincing than ever does not, alas, make it any more realistic. In this sense the main problem facing the Atlantic Alliance is not a 'progressive divorce' between the United States and Europe but the fact that the European Community, with every year that passes, is beginning to look like a marriage of convenience.

5 Alliance Management: Defence Costs and Equipment

Almost from the inception of the Alliance the United States and its allies have clashed over a number of issues of Alliance management. One of the most important has already been discussed: the modernisation of NATO's theatre nuclear forces. The most important issues outstanding are three in number: the proper level of defence spending; the standardisation of weapons; and finally differences of outlook about operations inside and outside the NATO theatre.

The debate over burden sharing is largely a political fiction – although it is politically significant for all that. The debate over standardisation is much more interesting for it reveals quite clearly the limits of European cooperation. Despite its best intentions Europe is no nearer agreement on how best to proceed than it was ten years ago. The same holds true for 'out of area operations'. A European contribution would be limited. There is little the Europeans themselves can do – acting together – beyond the European theatre. Here too the limits of European cooperation have been reached. Only a disposition to deplore a reliance on the United States which is palpably real would suggest that Western Europe could distance itself from American policy. Beyond Europe as well as at home the American commitment is still important.

BURDEN SHARING

The current emphasis by the United States on the need to strengthen its military capabilities has led to a persistent pressure on its allies to fall into line. In one sense the pressure is normal. As the largest and most powerful member of the Alliance the United States has traditionally exerted leadership within NATO in terms of assessing the requirements for collective defence. Its espousal of the 3 per cent annual real increase in defence spending and the Long Term Defence Programme were as much political as military, intended to demonstrate to a sceptical Congress that NATO was a functioning Alliance in which each member made an equitable contribution; as well as to persuade and motivate its own allies to actually contribute more.

In one respect both objectives have been reached. The LTDP has established a well coordinated package of measures which have gone a long way to eliminating major equipment deficiencies; while all but a few members were able at some time to meet the 3 per cent objective. But as with all political decisions of this nature there have been costs as well as gains. Both initiatives have remained permanent benchmarks against which allied performances have tended to be measured. In the case of the LTDP progress has not advanced much beyond the original endorsement and lies in the area of promise rather than substance. General Rogers told the House Appropriations Committee a few years ago (1980), 'the momentum of the past is slackening and commitments are becoming more and more promissory notes'.

With merit one could argue – and the Europeans have – that the weakening of NATO's conventional forces over the past ten years and beyond has been due to American cost cutting. Throughout the years 1971–78 France and West Germany, together with the Netherlands, increased their real defence expenditure by nearly 3 per cent. Since the adoption of the Long Term Defence Programme, these three powers together with Britain have been doing reasonably well overall, not as well as the United States would like, but well enough especially if one keeps in mind that the Europeans throughout the 1970s increased their defence expenditure in real terms whereas the United States did not. Between 1969–79 the United States decreased its contribution to NATO when measured by defence dollars as a percentage of GNP devoted to the Alliance and by the total of US dollars devoted to NATO as a percentage of total NATO defence spending. As a result the combined British, French and German defence budgets, which in 1970 totalled about one quarter of the United States', had by 1980 risen to about 40 per cent of America's.

Ten years after the Vietnam War the United States is still paying for that bottomless commitment. At the height of the war in Indo-China, the United States diverted $300bn (in 1982 dollars) to a secondary theatre of conflict. Vietnam was a tragedy not only for the United States but also for NATO, for it came at a time when the Soviet Union increased its own defence expenditure by nearly 5 per cent a year. As it happens the estimated difference between Soviet and American spending on defence between 1970–79 was roughly equivalent to the overall cost of the war in South-East Asia. Thus the United States not Europe must bear the main blame for the predicament in which the Alliance now finds itself. During the same period while US reserve troops strengths were falling from 3m to about 1.6m, non US–NATO reserves were increasing from 4 to 6 million. The 1970s in fact saw a dramatic reduction in US military power. 'Under Kissinger and Ford', Ronald Reagan proclaimed during his bid for the Republican nomination in 1976, 'this nation has become Number Two in a world where it is dangerous – if not fatal – to be second best. All I can see is what other nations the world over see: the collapse of American will and the retreat of American power.'[1]

Translated into simple statistics the picture was indeed a worrying one. During the period that Richard Nixon and Gerald Ford were in the White House, the United States deployed only two new strategic weapon systems – the Minuteman III and Poseidon, while the Soviet Union brought into service eight new ICBMs, two new SLBMs and the Backfire bomber. In the same period US ground forces were cut by 270 000 men – almost exactly the figure by which Soviet forces grew. The Soviet Navy, whose growth had gone almost unnoticed in the 1960s, approached parity in practically every form of surface warship except the aircraft carrier.

Not all this was the fault of the Administration. Congressional reaction to the war in Vietnam ensured that the defence budget would continue to be cut. Between 1950–69, Congressional cuts in the defence budget requests had averaged only $1.7bn annually, compared with $9.2bn for non-defence items. In the 1970s, the balance was radically reversed with defence requests incurring average annual cuts of $6bn while the non-defence budget was increased by an average of $4.7bn. As a percentage of total government expenditure, defence spending decreased by 16 per cent in seven years (1970–77), reaching its lowest rate since World

War II. 'In the anti-military orgy spawned by Vietnam', Dr Kissinger recalled 'to have challenged the overwhelming Congressional sentiment for "domestic priorities" (would have been) almost certainly an exercise in futility.'[2]

Even the new weapons systems which were planned in this period for deployment in the 1980s: the B-1 bomber, the Trident and Cruise missiles were made possible only at the expense of conventional forces which accounted for the bulk of 'controllable' defence spending. Between 1969–74, USAF squadrons were cut from 169 to 110; army and marine divisions from 23 to 16; naval ships (including submarines) from 976 to 495. As John Gaddis notes:

> Simple numerical indices can be misleading, and it is no doubt true that qualitative improvements compensated in part for these sharp quantitative cutbacks. It is also true that some such reductions would have occurred in any event in the wake of Vietnam and with the transition from the 'two and a half' to the 'one and a half' war standard. Still the scope and extent of these cuts was striking.[3]

It is American cuts in defence expenditure much more than European which accounted for the decline of NATO military spending between 1967–76 from $171bn to $147bn. This was a period when the defence expenditure of the Warsaw Pact rose from $92bn to $139bn (at 1975 prices).[4]

When one looks again at the balance sheet, the question of burden sharing looks far less divisive. One reason for the American suspicion that Europe is not pulling its weight is that there has been no parallel on this side of the Atlantic to the dramatic turn-about in the defence debate that has taken place in America. In 1972, the hawkish position of the Senate faced with Senator Mansfield's resolution was to advocate only marginal defence cuts; by 1979, the dovish position was to limit increases in defence spending by 3 per cent. Two years later only four senators out of 100 voted against a $200bn defence budget proposed by the new Administration. Obviously nothing like this has taken place in Europe; but then again there has been no necessity, for European defence spending has remained fairly constant since 1970 both in times of crisis and *détente*.

The calculation of how much each NATO partner should

contribute is highly complex as Caspar Weinberger's burden sharing report to Congress intimated in 1982. Competing needs vary from country to country. National commitments cannot be measured in terms of defence outlays and resource commitments alone.[5] The report stressed that many of the indicators which are often used (such as Gross Domestic Product per capita, or defence share in GDP) for measuring allied defence efforts can be misleading if considered in isolation. Applying more comprehensive measures of national performance, such as taking account of the lower cost of conscripted personnel, Europe does rather well.

TABLE 1: *Defence Burdens in NATO*

Country	Defence Expenditure as a Percentage of GNP (%)			
	1950	1960	1970	1980
Belgium	2.8	3.9	3.3	3.3
Canada	2.9	4.9	2.8	1.8
Denmark	1.8	3.1	2.8	2.4
France	8.3	7.4	4.6	4.1
Federal Republic	n.a.	4.6	3.7	3.3
Greece	6.6	5.4	5.6	5.6
Italy	4.2	3.7	3.0	2.4
Luxembourg	1.5	1.2	0.9	1.2
Netherlands	5.4	4.5	3.8	3.1
Norway	2.6	3.7	4.1	2.9
Portugal	4.1	4.5	7.9	3.6
Turkey	6.9	5.7	4.7	4.3
United Kingdom	7.3	7.3	5.6	5.1
United States	5.5	9.9	8.7	5.6
NATO Europe	5.8	5.7	4.2	3.7
Total NATO	5.4	8.2	6.7	4.4

SOURCE: *NATO Information Service, Brussels*

The three most important indicators commonly used are per capita GDP, the growth in real defence expenditure and defence expenditure per capita. On all three counts burden sharing appears far more equitable than often supposed.

Per capita GDP is a widely accepted measure of economic development. This indicator is normally used with the premise that the Alliance is better served if its poorer members use their resources on basic domestic programmes while the richer partners carry a larger share of the collective defence burden. In every alliance (and the Warsaw Pact is no exception) the larger members inevitably bear a disproportionately larger share of the common burden while the smaller members spend a great deal less than they would otherwise have to on their own.

Statistics show that during the 1970s US GDP per capita declined dramatically. Many European countries are now richer than the United States, but that does not mean they are necessarily free-riding. Fluctuating exchange rates and different inflation indicators often distort the picture. To eliminate such distortions the best method is the Purchasing Power Parity (PPP) system, a method used in Caspar Weinberger's report. Based on the PPP, a comparison shows that US GDP per capita still remains well above even the highest European figure. The much heard reproach that the Europeans are richer but spend less on defence is thus at best, questionable.

Real growth rates in defence spending are also misleading because it is only in the last few years that the United States has achieved growth rates higher than its European allies. Over the period 1970–81, US defence expenditure declined by an average annual rate of −1 per cent while the economy in terms of GDP grew by 2.9 per cent. The respective figures for Belgium are 4.2 per cent (defence) and 2.8 per cent (GDP). In the Federal Republic of Germany, real defence expenditure grew slightly faster than the economy. For Europe as a whole the growth figures are 1.7 per cent and 2.5 per cent (GDP), a fact which bears out the claim that Europe took on more of the common burden during the 1970s. It is only recently that this trend has been reversed.

Finally, defence expenditure per capita is an even more uncertain guide. In 1981 the US figure was $658, more than double the European average of $305. But then all the industrial European countries (with the exception of Luxembourg) are considerably above that average which is low because of NATO's three least advanced economic powers – Turkey, Greece and Portugal. The UK is highest with $486 followed by West Germany ($461), Norway ($418) and Belgium ($407). It should be noted that since 1973 all NATO European countries with the exception of Portugal have increased their per capita defence spending in real terms.[6]

The situation in NATO, in fact, is not quite as serious as often portrayed. Substantial improvements in force deployments have been made since 1977. The Seventh Army has been increased by two brigades; the United Kingdom and Germany have purchased several hundred new tanks; the F-16 has been introduced by five air forces; the Tornado multi-role combat plane by three others. Italy has begun to augment its naval strength in the Mediterranean by building six new guided missile frigates and a helicopter carrier. Even Norway has added a brigade to its active forces and has for the first time agreed to the pre-positioning of supplies for non-Norwegian reinforcements. The Long Term Modernisation Programme was the product of several years of planning; it was not the programme of an alliance that is unable to deal with the problems that confront it. Both the 3 per cent annual real increase agreed in 1977 and the decision to deploy a new generation of fighters, theatre nuclear forces and battle tanks are obviously products of serious military thinking – they represent a thoughtful response to NATO's deficiencies, many of which are serious, and a willingness to confront rather than shy away from the challenges that the Warsaw Pact now presents.

What the modernisation programme has done is to restore some credibility in conventional defence; it has done nothing, however, to restore the imbalance of forces which on SACEUR's own admission is now 2:1 in the Warsaw Pact's favour. It is difficult to believe that the 3 per cent annual increase or General Rogers' 4 per cent programme, or the massive 7 per cent increase in the US defence budget would ever be sufficient to narrow the gap, even if all three commitments were to be honoured.

NATO in that respect would be better advised to get more value for its money, rather than spend more. Almost half of NATO's total outlays are spent on personnel compared with only 25 per cent for the Warsaw Pact. The American All Volunteer Force (AVF) accounts for a massive percentage of the defence budget. The US's refusal to face the question of reintroducing conscription leads one to the suspicion that the United States would rather face an Atlantic crisis over burden sharing than confront a domestic crisis over registration for the draft.

The Warsaw Pact has substantially more fire power than NATO even though the Alliance spends considerably more. Some of the answer for this lies in the Pact's low military manpower costs but a large part of the combat imbalance lies in the Pact's

TABLE 2: *NATO Expenditures on Equipment*

Country	Equipment Expenditure as a Percentage of Total Defence Expenditure (%)			Total Defence Expend (US $m)
	Average 1970–74	1976–77	1980–81	1980–81
Belgium	10.6	11.0	14.4	4000
Canada	7.3	8.0	15.4	4400
Denmark	16.8	19.4	18.3	1600
Federal Republic	11.9	13.2	14.8	26700
Italy	15.4	13.1	17.5	8700
Luxembourg	1.6	3.4	1.8	n.a.
Netherlands	12.8	15.5	18.0	5200
Norway	13.5	11.4	19.3	1700
Portugal	7.5	1.9	6.1	800
Turkey	4.0	28.5	4.7	2100
United Kingdom	17.1	20.6	25.2	26300
USA	21.1	17.4	20.3	140500

SOURCE: *NATO Press Service*

greater degree of force integration. In spite of having more than twice the national product of the Warsaw Pact countries NATO possesses a collection of forces that are quantitatively inferior, qualitatively uneven and have only a limited ability to rearm, reinforce, support or even communicate with one another. One solution out of many would be to press for a much greater degree of standardisation.

NATO STANDARDISATION

Efforts to ensure cooperation between partners in the Atlantic Alliance have a long history and have taken many forms. In theory a strong interest in promoting such cooperation should exist for it would be possible to strengthen security at less cost. This could be achieved by avoiding loss, wastage, duplication and too great a variety of equipment both at the research and development level and at that of production and use.

Yet 30 years after the birth of the Alliance, it has to be noted that however long they have gone on, however diversified the initiatives may have been, however justified the grand design, the results are still meagre. And this is still so today despite rapid growth in the costs of armaments, the economic and financial crisis which oblige governments to devote dwindling resources to defence; the further reduction of the amounts available by inflation and, finally, knowledge that the conventional forces of the Warsaw Pact are superior in many respects and above all quantitatively, to those of the Atlantic Alliance.

Budgetary constraints have justified cooperation for major programmes such as the MRCA, Roland and Jaguar. The growing complexity of arms systems (and by correlation their cost) is beginning to upset all the conventional data of defence budgets and to slow down many programmes. This phenomenon is even evident in the United States which would have been unimaginable ten or even five years ago. The benefits of economies of scale resulting from long production runs, coupled with cost-sharing at the research stage, even if costs are all the greater in joint programmes, should alone be enough to explain the recent proliferation of multinational programmes.

Technological constraints are mainly a consequence of budgetary constraints. Most are due to the fact that few countries have sufficient means to pursue research in every branch of science and technology and hence it is only reasonable to pool their knowledge. Conversely the technological factor especially in the aerospace industry has been a deterrent to cooperation with the United States. Competition from the United States has been a spur for European cooperation. It should be remembered that the British Harrier jump-jet aircraft is one of the few planes that the USAF has ever purchased from a foreign buyer.

Finally, for some time political considerations have led to more extensive cooperation with a view to maintaining the competitiveness of the European defence industry in the present world crisis which has not spared the United States any more than Europe. The political determination to cooperate, sporadic at first and cautious in the late 1950s, has become much more significant since 1975.

European cooperation is hardly surprising when one considers that the research and development effort in the United States compared with that of all America's European allies together is in

TABLE 3: *Western European Participation in Cooperative Structures*

	NATO	WEU	Euro-group	IEPG	EC
Belgium	Y	Y	Y	Y	Y
Denmark	Y		Y	Y	
France	Y(a)	Y		Y	Y
Federal Republic	Y	Y	Y	Y	Y
Greece	Y(a)		Y	Y	Y(a)
Iceland	Y(a)				
Italy	Y	Y	Y	Y	Y
Luxembourg	Y	Y	Y	Y	Y
Netherlands	Y	Y	Y	Y	Y
Norway	Y		Y	Y	
Portugal	Y			Y	Y(b)
Spain	Y(a)				Y(b)
Turkey	Y		Y		
United Kingdom	Y	Y	Y	Y	Y

a) These countries have either major doubts about their future membership, or place major limits on their participation.
b) Prospective members.

the ratio of about 3:1 to the USA's advantage, and that its sale of arms to Europe is in the ratio of 10:1. The very fact that the European nations have attempted to establish cooperative programmes constitutes, in itself, a significant contribution to European cohesion.

That cooperation has taken place in three different forums: the Conference of National Armaments Directors (CNAD); the Independent European Programme Group (IEPG) and the Standing Armaments Committee of the Western European Union (WEU). Each will be discussed separately.

Conference of National Armaments Directors (CNAD)

The CNAD was originally set up to improve the mechanisms of cooperation in research, development and production of military equipment. At that time cooperation was accepted as a worthy goal in itself, with very little analysis to indicate what forms of cooperation might be worthwhile.

Since then the CNAD has concentrated on encouraging joint development projects among several nations with production shared among them, or production under licence of equipment developed elsewhere. The latter approach has helped to avoid the duplication of development effort and to achieve some production economies, although it has not, of course, helped to exercise the development capabilities of the licensee. The savings which have been achieved through such cooperation have been quite significant, although much more modest than the exaggerated claims made by the more extreme advocates of standardisation.

The second major area in which equipment cooperation has paid off is in increased military effectiveness. NATO's arsenals have been described as 'military museums' and considerable anecdotal evidence can be adduced to show the inefficiency resulting from the diversity of equipment. The problem can be overcome by ensuring interoperability, particularly where the acquisition of common equipment has for one reason or another proved impractical.

The work of the CNAD has not been spectacular but project steering committees have monitored a whole series of cooperative ventures including the Jaguar tactical aircraft, the Seasparrow surface missile system, the FH 70 155mm towed howitzer, the MK 20 rapid-fire gun, the Tornado multi-role combat aircraft, the F-16 combat fighter, cooperative support of the 76/62 Oto-Melara compact gun and the NATO Seacat system. In all these activities the Conference's principal role has been to exchange information and to write a large number of standardisation agreements which have dealt primarily with the interoperability of equipment.

Its most recent initiatives have been the establishment of two additional committees: the NATO Armaments Planning Review (NAPR) and the Periodic Armaments Planning System (PAPS). The first is primarily a scheme to discover opportunities for cooperation in the equipment replacement schedules prepared by the Independent European Programme Group (IEPG). These are collectively examined by the international staff with a view to determining whether they offer scope for cooperation. Follow up procedures have been established to ensure that they are considered by individual members and do not become victims of neglect.

The Periodic Armaments Planning System is much more

elaborate. Its purpose beyond the NAPR is two-fold: to include new types of equipment which would not appear in replacement schedules and to start the cooperative process early enough so that national programmes do not progress to the point where emotional commitments to particular solutions militate against cooperation. Its point of departure is usually a 'mission need' – a qualitative deficiency in military capability, or sometimes an opportunity offered by the appearance of new technology. Such mission needs are usually put forward either by the military authorities or individual nations.

Independent European Programme Group (IEPG)

The IEPG was set up in 1975 to tabulate on an annual basis the major equipment replacement intentions of all its 12 members. To permit comparison of the various national contributions the IEPG has devised a standardised format, a schedule divided into a number of general equipment areas such as guided weapons – air; and mine systems – land; within which there is a considerable number of sub-headings. In all some 160 weapon system areas were covered in the schedule put together in 1979. The information sought from each member in each equipment area is extensive. The task or mission of the equipment is described and the equipment presently in service recorded. For the intended replacement or new equipment the planned or expected in-service date is given, and where possible, the type of the replacement equipment and the quantities which the planners envisage.

National contributions are sent each spring to the Panel I Secretariat which is supplied informally by members of the Ministry of Defence in the United Kingdom who then assemble the consolidated schedule. This fairly laborious procedure is completed every year by mid-September when the Panel meets formally to consider what opportunities if any have been revealed. If cooperation seems possible in a particular area a recommendation is made to the IEPG National Armaments Directors that a group should be set up to examine the possibilities in detail under the aegis of IEPG Panel 2.

The form of any Panel 2 Group varies according to particular circumstances. It may take the form of an exchange of information on operational requirements for procurement options ten to 15 years in the future. It may be concerned with a small number of countries who wish to purchase a particular system and have agreed to cooperate in that purchase, or it may even take the form of procurement experts setting up a fully collaborative project involving joint research, development and production of entirely new weapon systems.

After the schedule has been examined it is passed to the NATO Armaments Planning Review Coordinator. There the information is tabulated together with similar information from the United States and Canada to form a fuller schedule covering all the CNAD members. This may seem like a duplication of effort but the IEPG puts together its own schedule first in order to be able to examine any possibilities for specifically European cooperation.

The main limitation to the IEPG procedure is that the scheduling exercise concerns itself only with proposals for the replacement of existing equipment. By its very nature it cannot readily take account of new mission needs arising from new tactical doctrines, nor of new technologies that may totally change the shape of procurement requirements. Taking account of these sorts of factors is a much more complex process.

Nevertheless, in the comparatively short time of the IEPG's existence a number of significant European projects have been identified. The most important perhaps, concerns a new tactical combat aircraft, a new family of European military helicopters and third-generation European anti-tank guided weapons. Some of the other cooperative projects identified by Panel 1's procedures are on a much smaller scale. One group for instance, has been working towards joint procurement and production of common ammunition for a 105mm tank gun. Although this scheme has not carried the same *kudos* as the European tactical combat aircraft, it represents a considerable step towards standardising ammunition and towards the equitable sharing of production work. Inevitably the rate at which new opportunities for cooperation have been opened up has slowed down considerably since the initial work of the first two years. After all, the European tactical aircraft and helicopter programmes represent a very considerable proportion of Europe's procurement expenditure over the next 15 to 20 years. New opportunities, however, will in all probability continue to be identified.[7]

Western European Union (WEU)

The last of the three forums in which standardisation is often discussed is the WEU's Standing Committee on Armaments. The WEU came into being in 1954, the Standing Armaments Committee (SAC) a year later (in accordance with Article 8 of the modified Brussels Treaty). Like most of the other committees it is composed of the representatives of the seven member countries who tend either to be permanent delegates or senior officials. Its main objective is to promote the standardisation of weapons systems. Frequent meetings take place between the armaments directors of member countries or their NATO representatives in SAC, its subcommittees or separate working groups have helped foster a number of multilateral production schemes.

Despite a fitful attempt to deal with standardisation in the mid-1970s and despite NATO's Long Term Modernisation Programme the subject has never been in the forefront of public attention except in France. French support for the Committee and its work has remained fairly constant since 1972 when Michel Debré, President Pompidou's Minister of Defence, tried to drum up support for a WEU initiative. True to its Gaullist principles, France was anxious that Europe should not agree to standardisation exclusively within the context of NATO. When Michel Jobert addressed the Assembly in November 1973 he called for 'a privileged framework for European cooperation' specifically to meet the threat of American competition.

Yet despite French support, the Armaments Committee has made little progress. The report which the Council authorised in May 1975 under the direction of the Belgian Foreign Minister van Eslande has still not been completed. SAC appears no more convincing than any other of the WEU committees and just as ineffective as most. The enormous gap between profession and practice reinforces the impression that it is somewhat remote from the actualities it has been asked to address.

Indeed, renewed French interest in its operation has left the situation somewhat obscure. It is true, that Georges Lemoine suggested in 1981 that the Council might allow the Armaments Committee to carry out studies in parallel with the Independent European Programme Group (IEPG) without requiring it to seek its consent. 'With, as it were, an information and research department available to it the Assembly would be in a position to initiate more ambitious studies. It could rely on an independent, specifically European agency whose work could not be suspected of being biased.'[8]

It is, nevertheless, puzzling that the French should want the Assembly to tackle the problem instead of the Council as authorised under Article 8. On past performance would they really be prepared to allow the Assembly to be independent of the Council? No other Assembly committee can undertake studies without its express consent. SAC has already met with serious difficulties in obtaining information for the van Eslande Report despite the fact that it is not intended for publication. Could it at one and the same time produce studies of the European armaments industry based on information supplied by the Council and provide the Assembly with access to the documentation received? And would the Council be able to waive its right of supervision without creating an unwelcome precedent for the future?

If Georges Lemoine's muddled proposals are any guide it seems highly unlikely that the French are politically or analytically prepared to allow SAC any real initiative in this matter. However unpromising the prospects, of course, the WEU is still committed to developing a vehicle for weapons standardisation. It would be perhaps, unduly pessimistic to deny that it is capable of succeeding, but unrealistic to overlook the fact that the Assembly, itself, is still in two minds about its own role.

On 21 June 1979, the Assembly passed a resolution, annexed subsequently to the van Waterschoot Report, which called for a comprehensive policy on European arms procurement. While acknowledging, however, that 'the modified Brussels Treaty is the only juridical basis for the organisation of defence and armaments in Europe',[9] it recognised that, at present, the WEU could not perform the role itself. The van Waterschoot Report, in fact, spoke of institutions other than the WEU which might fulfil the same purpose. Only the previous year the Assembly had recommended 'restructuring the European armaments industry under the aegis of the European Community relying on its responsibility in the fields of industrial and customs policy and research'.[10]

The van Waterschoot Report raised yet again those central questions of political cooperation in the Community that have been discussed repeatedly, though with varying emphasis, since the Hague summit of 1969. Although the Community has so far failed to extend the scope of its responsibility, the Commissioner for Industrial Policy, Etienne Davignon, reminded the European Parliament only three months after the Report's publication that it was within its competence to discuss defence questions relating to the '... healthy economic development of the Community and the strength of its domestic market'.[11] Etienne Davignon followed this up in January 1981 by presenting the European Parliament with a report on military and civilian cooperation in areas of high technology. Its author, David Greenwood, recommended that the Community establish a European bureau of defence analysis and an inter-government Task Force for public procurement. Davignon appended an explanatory note in which he proposed it would be more sensible to set up an organisation that could act as a communications link between the Community and the WEU.[12] Because of its semi-official endorsement and the arguments of its leading proponents the WEU now has a large following among politicians who, in all other respects, might have remained largely indifferent to its deliberations.

Until the publication of the van Eslande Report, of course, it is difficult to assess the likely role that the WEU might be able to play. But its main role is likely to be that of a coordinating body with a specialised secretariat in which armaments questions could be handled at the highest political level. The actual steps towards standardisation would probably be better handled by the IEPG which has taken over most of the activities of EURONAD, a committee of Eurogroup National Armaments Directors, originally set up within the Eurogroup in 1971 which still sponsors a few cooperative projects, notably the Maverick and improved Sidewinder missile. One recent proposal envisaged that SAC could be made responsible for collecting and collating all useful information about cooperative programmes; analysing the reasons for their success or failure; drawing up a list of priorities in the light of its assessment of future markets; and assisting governments to train future programme managers.[13]

The most detailed proposals to date were submitted by David Greenwood at a WEU Symposium in 1979 which provided a forum in a minor key for his submission to the European Commission. In his paper, Greenwood maintained that neither the present IEPG/NATO schedules nor the IEPG/SAC inquiries provide enough information on the demand and supply side of the European military equipment market. The first fail to provide crucial financial data of the kind found in the procurement programmes submitted by the Germans every year for NATO's defence planning questionnaire; the second amount to little more than an incomplete gazetteer of Europe's defence manufacturing industry. Neither provide the information which would enable 'matching' development and production capacity to be identified with reasonable precision. In Greenwood's opinion the work already undertaken by the IEPG and NATO on the demand side, and by the IEPG and SAC on the side of supply, went only half way to meeting that requirement.

Greenwood wanted to see the work continued in the case of the IEPG/NATO equipment schedules and completed in the case of the IEPG/SAC studies of the armaments industry. But in the light of the agreement reached by the European defence ministers in November 1975 to set up an independent European defence procurement secretariat, he suggested that a case could be made out for setting up a defence analysis office with close links with the IEPG, SAC and, in some circumstances, the European Commission. He also believed there was no intrinsic reason why such an office should not be put under the exclusive responsibility of the WEU.[14]

At the moment, neither Greenwood's proposal nor Davignon's appended suggestion to his report to the Commission have attracted general support. Nevertheless, the European Parliament's reluctance to discuss defence matters leaves SAC as one of the two institutions in which procurement decisions could be discussed prior to their adoption. Greenwood's report of 1979 is important precisely because it illustrates the potential of the Armaments Committee and the importance still attached to the WEU by, among others, the European Commission. Neither should be dismissed out of hand. Neither, however, can provide much hope for the possibilities of further European cooperation.

Moreover, however desirable standardisation may be in principle, in practice its gains are often questionable. On the military side there are advantages to interoperability but differences of language and tactical doctrine would set narrow bounds to the scope for 'coalition combat' even if equipment were fully interoperable. And since NATO's concept of operations for the defence of north-west Europe is based on ground formations (with air support) fighting in 'layer cake' dispositions on the central front the scope for flexible use of forces is strictly limited.

What may be even more significant is the fact that the

achievement of standardisation in major equipment categories presupposes harmonisation of doctrine – and in key areas such as armoured warfare and tactical air operations that would probably require enforced conformity to the lowest common denominator, tactics, to the likely detriment of combat performance.[15]

It must also be noted that nations quite rightly approach standardisation determined to weigh its gains, whether construed in terms of enhanced effectiveness or reduced expense, against expected costs either in degradation of their national competence, or in exposure to the problems of troublesome economic adjustment. Indeed, it would be unrealistic to expect them to do otherwise. This is no less true of the United States than it is of Europe. The true intentions of the United States with regard to military cooperation were revealed by an American Assistant Secretary for Defense in May 1975:

> We also have seen the recent development of the concept of 'common markets of technology' – attempts to aggregate economies . . . I believe we must approach this complex issue of the export of our technology with caution . . . Our technology is one of the few key assets we have left with which to barter on a world wide basis . . . competition for technological 'leadership' is fierce and getting fiercer. We are clearly being challenged and those same factors which have characterised our traditional leadership are not permanent . . . These comments apply to our 'friends' and potential foes alike. In the case of our NATO allies we should recognise that our military friends are also our industrial competitors.[16]

National interests will always predominate. The vitality of the armaments industries – illustrated by their exports and the role these exports play in a country's balance of payments, are very different. From these two standpoints, it is the French arms industry – the most varied and the largest exporter – that has the most significance for an independent defence policy; not only for the number of men employed (270 000) but also for the advancement of high-intensity research and develoment industries such as electronics, the second in the Western world, which has grown by more than 21 per cent per year since 1970 and devotes a quarter of its annual receipts to research and development.

In the light of such statistics, it seems doubtful whether any country could voluntarily restrict the development of its military-industrial complex which most see as a necessary condition for technical advancement, economic welfare and ultimately, social stability.

Of course, a distinction has to be made between two categories: firstly, countries that have a technological and industrial capability which enables them to develop complete weapon systems either on their own or in cooperation with other countries, a group which includes West Germany, the United Kingdom and France; and secondly, countries with a technological and industrial base which makes it possible to take part in the production of weapon systems or to produce sub-systems by itself, a group which applies to Italy and the BENELUX countries.

Moreover, it would be wrong to imagine that standardisation only discriminates against the countries of group one. The Netherlands does not have a particularly happy experience of the Leopard 2 tank which it decided to purchase in 1979 to replace its obsolescent Centurions and AMX-13 tanks. As the *Bundeswehr* had four army corps and the Netherlands army only one, it was not surprising that the German requirement was four times greater, (1800 and 450 respectively).

The programme costs for the Netherlands were well over $1bn. For some of the reasons mentioned before, in particular the balance of payments and employment, compensation orders were found to be necessary. Partially this was achieved by so-called single source production of parts for the whole series of 2250 tanks and partially by producing parts for its own 450 tanks only. The compensation however, resulted in a price increase of well over 10 per cent mainly because the production for parts for only 450 tanks was much more costly. One thing that became clear quite early was that only single source production, as opposed to the production in license of small series, was really cost effective.[17]

In short, there does not appear to be any real constituency in Europe for fully-integrated arrangements based on settling identical military requirements, or instituting highly centralised management of the arms production capacities of the Brussels Treaty signatories, or indeed of all NATO's European members. Since most countries, however, do appear to be disposed to cooperating on a case by case basis it seems reasonable to assume that greater standardisation is attainable within the institutions which already exist, whether they be the IEPG or the Western European Union.

6   Out of Area Operations

In the past, NATO has known no more divisive subject than the use of its forces outside the area to which they were assigned in 1949. From its inception, the Alliance has been designed solely to defend the North Atlantic area, not interests outside it. The suggestion that its defence perimeter should be extended to encompass the defence of energy interests in the Middle East has always been met with the objection that this would involve a strategic role for which NATO is not designed and which most of its members would resist for domestic political reasons.

The question has always been of concern to NATO because whether its members operate within the North Atlantic area or not, whenever forces have been used east of Suez they have had to be withdrawn from the front line. This was as true for the Falklands War as it was for the Indonesian Confrontation (1963–66) in which 50 per cent of the surface units of the Royal Navy saw service at any one time.

In May 1980, the Alliance took a potentially historic step when it agreed to the first phase of a plan enabling the United States to divert forces currently assigned to NATO to deal with emergencies in the Persian Gulf. By implication the Alliance for the first time in its history defined a security interest which lay outside its traditional defence perimeter.

This was reinforced nine months later by the decision of the incoming Reagan Administration to switch the command of the Rapid Deployment Force (RDF) from Readiness Command at MacDill Air Force base to European Command (EURCOM) in Heidelberg. Instead of making it an entirely new command in the Middle East, the United States transferred it to the control of the Supreme Allied Commander, Europe (SACEUR). By making clear that the RDF would rely on NATO bases and airfields in a crisis and on the diversion of supplies and even troops from the

European theatre in time of war, the Americans have effectively extended NATO's Southern Flank from Turkey to the Gulf of Aden. However, this has since been somewhat modified by the growth of the RDF into United States Central Command responsible to the Joint Chiefs of Staff, even if its forces are still drawn from those with a NATO role.

Many European governments have also become reconciled to the fact that the postwar framework of Western security will have to be changed significantly if they are ever to satisfy the changing expectations that the United States has of its allies. The United States which so often in the past criticised European intervention outside the north Atlantic area increasingly looks to its European allies for support. Reviewing allied relations in 1979, the former SACEUR Alexander Haig reminded the House Armed Services Committee that:

> At a time when several issues confronting the Alliance are not contained within its arbitrary boundaries, this traditional attitude creates an inflexibility and artificial constraint on Alliance action that will seriously impede its effectiveness. The entire globe is now NATO's concern.[1]

In principle, the Americans would welcome an allied contribution to the RDF, or failing that a contribution in the Indian Ocean. In his last State of the Union address (1980), President Carter declared that the United States could not be expected to shoulder the entire burden alone. The Reagan Administration has given the theme a new sense of urgency. It has shown signs of wanting to mend its bridges within the Alliance in order to secure full allied agreement for moves outside the Treaty area which in its judgment are allied interests as well. In a speech in London in October 1981, Caspar Weinberger the American Defence Secretary, insisted that Europe and America must work together in the Gulf. 'Given the absolutely vital nature of the goal, the means of attaining it can be broad and varied. But we can only secure the goal through unity of purpose and action.'[2]

It is a perception not shared by Europe. In his own State of the Union message to the *Bundestag* in January 1980, Helmut Schmidt warned against 'unconsidered talk about a geographical extension of NATO obligations' which would not help the developing countries of the world to help themselves.[3] Later that year,

NATO's defence ministers cautioned the United States against any move which might reduce its commitment to Europe to the advantage of a theatre of operations which was not under immediate threat.

Unfortunately, although the incipient crises which confront the Atlantic Alliance may be a testament to the success of its original objective – the defence of Western Europe – this is of small comfort to American planners who are trying to frame a new consensus around new objectives. Such a consensus is likely to prove elusive as long as each ally insists on resolving its own uncertainties before listening to the certainties of others; or as long as the United States expects to build consent around a policy that can only be discharged by American forces. While the United States and its allies frequently consult on matters vital to each other, they still prefer to keep open military options on matters vital to themselves.

Quite recently many Europeans have begun to wake up to the fact that a consensus on the protection of vital interests outside the Treaty area must be forged, and forged quickly. If the Europeans wish to keep their options open they may have to think very seriously about a European contribution to the collective defence. If they feel they do not have the resources to act alone they might act together. But it is time to recognise that unless they are prepared to act outside the bounds of Europe the United States may become increasingly impatient of consulting allies who are either incapable or unwilling to defend their interests themselves.

EUROPEAN CONTRIBUTION TO THE RDF

Unfortunately, the range of options open to the Europeans outside Europe has increasingly narrowed since the 1950s. Britain and France are no longer world powers, while West Germany still feels constrained from translating its economic influence in the developing world into a military presence. All three countries remain sceptical of proposals to extend the scope of the Alliance. The proposal might divide the Alliance rather than unite it, and give rise to concern among the developing countries that a NATO theatre of operations would in no time at all become a Western sphere of influence.

The distinction between NATO and purely American missions

might also be entirely obfuscated were the Americans sometimes to act on their own account, sometimes on NATO's. Despite all the arguments to the contrary, the Alliance has so far found conclusive arguments against NATO itself playing a role south of the Tropic of Cancer: why should it find these arguments any less forceful because America itself has offered to undertake the task?

Nevertheless, there is agreement that the interests of the United States and Europe in the Gulf are in all essentials similar. Indeed, all the European nations except the UK are even more dependent on Gulf oil than is the United States. In a recent Defence White Paper, the British government laid great stress on a collective response to a common threat. 'The West must make it clear that it is capable of protecting essential interests by military means should the need arise.'[4] Only a few years ago, Britain, like many other European countries, anxious to keep out of politically sensitive areas and to keep defence spending to a minimum, was reluctant to see vital energy supplies become part of the East–West equation. In 1979, however, it took the lead in persuading the Alliance to undertake a major study of its dependence on non-renewable resources from the developing world.

In 1979, the new Conservative government decided to improve the effectiveness of British forces to deploy outside Europe by providing extra transport aircraft, additional logistic support for the fleet and lengthened fuselages for the RAF's C-130 Hercules transport aircraft. The British continued to express interest in contributing forces to the RDF as late as February 1981. At a conference in Munich Geoffrey Pattie, then Minister for Air, added his support to the contention that NATO should help America defend not only oil in the Gulf, but also cobalt, chrome and other resources in Southern Africa. He went on to reveal that his government was considering whether or not to increase contingents of all three services in the area in consultation with the United States.[5]

But by then it had already become apparent that Britain simply did not have the resources to translate even these modest options into policy objectives, let alone significantly improve the strategic mobility of its forces, with all that this would have meant in terms of the restoration of amphibious capabilities, the development of staging and basing facilities, as well as changes in procurement priorities including the RAF's aircraft replacement programme.

Moreover, even if the resources had been found, the inescapable fact remained that the forces the United Kingdom would have deployed east of Suez would have been drawn from those already assigned to NATO, and which were already earmarked for European service in contingency planning. It would have had to call on the Puma and Jaguar squadrons, part of the Nimrod force and the Sea Harriers simply to provide the necessary air cover for an 8000 strong composite brigade group. The Royal Navy, in addition, would have been forced to draw on units assigned to the eastern Atlantic in order to provide afloat support for Royal Marine commandos and amphibious forces. Quite simply Britain was not equipped to engage in offensive or defensive operations outside Europe; it had neither the forces nor the transport to airlift a field force as it could have done in the 1960s.

But it must also be asked whether its contribution would have made any difference anyway. The cost of reintroducing a parachute battalion would have been $50m compared with the cost of the RDF estimated at the last count at more than $25bn over five years.

Contributions by other forces – even the French – would be modest. France could provide sealift for a motorised division of the army's marine infantry, or airlift a two brigade parachute division. It has already re-opened the C-160 Transall production line and is providing new aircraft with in-flight refuelling. But even when added to the existing airlift fleet they will still not be able to carry heavy artillery or tanks. French operations in Africa have merely highlighted the cost of intervention. The wars in the Western Sahara and Chad have seen the deployment of Jaguar fighter bombers, Breguet Atlantic maritime reconnaissance planes and Transall transports, in the case of the Jaguars 10 per cent, in that of the Transalls 25 per cent of the entire fleet. For reasons of cost even the French have begun to think in terms of a Western approach to problems which used to be seen as exclusively French in dimension.

Nor is the political outlet very promising. Both the extent and scope of any future contribution will almost certainly be influenced by the availability of enlisted men. Conscript forces as a rule are not sent overseas. The Foreign Legion, not the regular army, saw service in Zaire in 1978 and Chad in 1980. And with 10 000 men already deployed in Africa defending commitments which are fast appearing open-ended, the availability of any further forces must be considered somewhat doubtful.

If much of the focus of attention has been directed at Britain and France this is easily explained by the fact that none of America's remaining allies would probably be able to make a contribution. The Belgians have a few para-commando units which could be airlifted quite quickly in a crisis, as was made demonstrably clear during the Shaba 2 exercise in 1978. But they were soon airlifted back to Belgium to spare their government any further embarrassment at home. There is even less likelihood of German units being deployed outside Europe. Legal experts differ as to whether the Federal Constitution actually forbids their use overseas; indeed, there is a school of thought that maintains that Article 87(a) does not necessarily preclude such use where the reasons are exclusively defensive. But for the moment, confronted as it is with popular agitation against nuclear deterrence, no German government will wish to test public opinion on what, by any reckoning, would be a deeply divisive issue.

If Europe is going to provide any assistance it would probably have to be confined to logistic support. Such assistance could have a significant bearing on the RDF's budget, force structure, equipment programme and communications. Although the US Navy, for example, has negotiated right of access to a string of facilities from Berbera and Mombasa in East Africa to Oman in the Gulf, the number of personnel deployed there has been deliberately limited. Once troops and ships are deployed in the area in time of crisis, however, perhaps over a period of several months, on-shore support will become a critical factor in determining the success or failure of the mission. During the Proud Phantom exercise in Egypt in July 1980 accommodation had to be found for over 300 men who were needed to maintain a single squadron of F-4 Phantom fighter bombers in continuous operation. The deployment of the 15 700 strong 82nd Airborne Division would require the presence of 11 000 more service personnel.[6]

For deployments in Europe this is obviously not a problem since the support forces, for the most part, are already based in countries allied to the United States. But there is no guarantee that Kenya or Somalia would honour the agreements they have entered into if the presence of a large number of American personnel excited popular apprehension. In Oman, American servicemen have to wear civilian dress to spare their hosts embarrassment. The arrival of Americans in any large numbers might provoke nationalist discontent in a civilian population that has not always been sympathetic to the presence of foreign bases. The very presence of the kind of sprawling logistic empire off-shore that characterised American operations in Vietnam might incite precisely the anti-Western feeling to which the RDF is designed to respond.

The RDF may well have its quota of problems, but there is no reason why logistics should be one of them. America's allies in Europe could use their long standing links with East Africa and the Arab world to reconcile local communities to an American presence ashore, if that presence were seen to be part of a collective Western effort, and not merely another manifestation of American 'imperialism'.

They could also provide more concrete help in the shape of naval reconnaissance. European capabilities in this field are not extensive, but compared with what little they could contribute in the way of armed forces their impact would be considerably greater. Britain with her Nimrods and the Netherlands, France and Italy with their Atlantics and P-2 Neptunes are quite able to undertake reconnaissance missions either of their own accord or in collaboration with American forces. Although joint flights would be difficult to mount since the Nimrods and the P-2s are not interoperable, dual stocking arrangements in the theatre of RDF operations, particularly with respect to the P-3C Orions which are already coming into service with the Netherlands Navy and the P-3Cs operated by the United States, would go some way to removing this difficulty.[7]

EUROPEAN NAVAL TASK FORCE IN THE INDIAN OCEAN

The debate about a European contribution to the RDF is often conducted in a strategic void. Even at the present level of expenditure the strategy requires concentrating forces in the Gulf and neglecting the defence of shipping in the Indian Ocean. The United States seems more concerned with deterring the interdiction of oil at source than protecting shipping in mid-ocean.

In an attempt to keep defence spending within limits both the Carter and Reagan Administrations have framed the question in terms of one mission rather than the other, and subsequently ended up with a military force which is addressed to one threat only. Is Task Force 70, the USN force deployed in the Indian Ocean, with its single carrier, adequate for the defence of the sealanes? It is not that the debate about the RDF has raised a choice between the two roles – the choice has yet to be made. America's present strategy is perfectly sound if deterrence holds, but quite inadequate if it fails. The battle that matters may be fought with limited naval forces in the Indian Ocean leaving the Americans with the choice of reinforcing the Indian Ocean or remaining in readiness for a struggle in the Gulf that may never take place.

Since European shipping will be most at risk, the Europeans have a much greater incentive to contribute forces to a naval task force than they do to the RDF. Acting on their own it is clear that they do not have enough escort vessels to offer much in the way of protection for their own shipping. Their naval forces have been determined in recent years by different needs. Denmark has no ocean going warships; Norway has very few. The Netherlands occasionally deploys some in the Caribbean, more frequently in the eastern Atlantic but very infrequently in the Indian Ocean. The last joint exercises with the Royal Navy in that region were held in 1972. At the moment no country except France or Britain could mount naval operations east of Suez which would impress anyone, least of all the Soviet Union.[8]

Naval operations carried out in the past have revealed very serious deficiencies in home waters, a fact which weighed heavily with the Military Committee of the North Atlantic Assembly in 1980:

> When discussing re-establishing an allied naval presence in the Indian Ocean on a permanent basis, it should be remembered that naval assets in NATO's current areas of responsibility are already said to be below SACLANT's requirements and national replacement programmes do not provide for greater numbers. While the allies will have to cover any gaps left by American redeployments . . . it is unrealistic to expect a permanent contribution to the Indian Ocean without creating a shortfall elsewhere.[9]

Such observations offer a cautionary reminder about how

thinly stretched allied naval capabilities already are in SACLANT's current area of responsibilities without redeploying units beyond the Tropic of Cancer.

Since the conflict in the south Atlantic (1982) Britain has once again been party to a public debate on operations east of Suez, a debate which most defence writers had written off after the Defence Review of 1968 and the Heath government's brief and ill-conceived attempt to revise, if not reverse the decision two years later. It is remarkable that even in the mid-1980s Britain has still to discharge commitments to former colonial territories. The Falklands garrison now has 4000 men, with an aircraft carrier and nuclear submarine in reserve. The need to maintain the garrison has ironically involved the winding up of lesser commitments, that until recently successive British governments considered equally important. Under heavy pressure to find extra savings beyond the £230m already required by the Treasury, it is not surprising that the Defence Secretary has proposed withdrawing the garrison in Belize (1800 servicemen in all).

A perusal of the 1983 Statement of the Defence Estimates would lead the reader to suppose that a decision had already been made. Belize does not feature in the index; it does not feature in the descriptive text of the UK defence activities beyond the NATO area; it does not even feature in the statistical breakdown of the geographical deployment of UK service personnel overseas. It is only the list of the elements of the Belize garrison on the map of British military installations worldwide that reminds the reader that the Belize garrison exists at all. One day, sooner probably than later, the same may be the case with Fortress Falklands as well. This is certainly likely to be the case with a Labour government whose political credibility will not be invested in its retention.

Both parties will doubtless one day agree on the folly of maintaining 4000 men in a garrison which has no conceivable strategic significance for Britain. Nor, for that matter, can the country afford a Rapid Deployment Force, the minimal cost of which, one study suggests, would be as high as $385m, or $760m if allowance is made for its annual overheads. The sacrifices which would have to be made to maintain such a commitment would be extraordinary; $760m per annum is what it presently costs to maintain the RAF's front line force.

The different missions of the European navies and the need for

TABLE 4: *Costs of UK RDF (some options)*

Annual Direct Operating Cost, 1981 prices	£m
Option 1: Naval contribution only	
i) Aircraft carrier; cost per ships including 2 squadrons of a/c helicopters	25
ii) Destroyers, frigates; cost per ship	12
iii) Mine counter-measures vessels; cost per ship	3
iv) Possible force: 1 carrier + 5 destroyers frigates and 2 MCMVs	91
Option 2: Army contribution only	
Cost per 1000 men (BAOR standard)	23.7
Option 3: RAF contribution only	
i) Air defence; cost of 1 air defence and 1 GW squadron	34
ii) Strike attack support; cost per squadron	34
iii) Transport; cost per squadron	19
Option 4: An independent balanced RDF force consisting of:—	
i) RN contribution as above	
ii) 5000 troops	
iii) RAF force of 1 air defence and 1 GW squadron + 3 strike squadrons and 2 transport squadrons	174
Total	385.5
with overheads	760.0

SOURCE: Keith Hartley 'Can the UK afford a Rapid Deployment Force' *RUSI Journal* March 1982 p. 20.

economy of force both suggest the need for a NATO operation or, at the very least, in view of the Alliance's stretched forces, a degree of NATO coordination. At the moment SACLANT has merely drawn up contingency plans for the use of NATO forces in the Indian Ocean having been asked to do so by the Defence Planning Committee as early as 1972. These plans were only finally completed in June 1981. The focus of attention since then has shifted to the south Atlantic where shipping appears to be under a much more immediate threat from the Soviet West Africa squadron.

As the Alliance has become increasingly aware of the global Soviet threat, contingency planning has become increasingly complex. Provisional plans drawn up in 1976 actually included a design for a NATO Task Force composed of a large commando ship, four frigates, a submarine and several support vessels.[10]

There are many who would argue that any assistance to the USN at this stage is far more important than arguing over the form it should take. Initially, an allied task force need involve no more than three nations who would contribute forces on an *ad hoc* basis to begin with. One option would be to expand the concept of the standing force using as a model the highly successful Standing Naval Force, Atlantic (STANAVFORLANT) which came into service in 1967. The contribution of a frigate should not be beyond the resources of eight or nine NATO members, given that the ships would be rotated. That, after all, is what they have provided for STANAVFORLANT – the first multi-national naval squadron to operate permanently in peacetime. Its primary tasks are providing a 'presence', multi-national training and implementing new NATO procedures. When at sea it performs the role of an anti-submarine unit which can be expanded into an escort flotilla when needed. The ships of the squadron are grouped around those of the general purpose and guided missile class, ranging from the 2500 ton Köln class to the *Leander* and *Van Speijk* frigates. SACLANT has sole responsibility for deciding where the squadron will cruise, up to two years in advance, after first sounding out the defence ministries of the participating nations.

If a similar force were to deploy in the Indian Ocean it would probably resemble STANAVFORLANT in every respect except one: since operations outside the Atlantic area do not fall within Article 3 of the NATO Treaty the commander of the squadron would be responsible only to the participating nations and not to SACLANT or the local naval command or even the NATO Council. The difference may be crucial in at least two respects: first, it would meet the reservations of many smaller members who have always been wary of extending the Alliance's area of operation. As recently as July 1981 Norway pulled out of the Ocean Venture 81 manoeuvres because it objected to the fact that they were being held concurrently with three other naval exercises which involved the participation of the United States and several Latin American navies as well.

Even more important, a non-NATO command might persuade France to join. It should always be remembered that while Britain deploys a surface task force in the Indian Ocean every year and the Netherlands deploys a frigate or destroyer group every second year, the French maintain a permanent Indian Ocean fleet, which at one time (1976) eclipsed both the American and Soviet navies in the number of ship-days in the region. At present the French Indian Ocean fleet consists of 15 ships, including four corvettes, a command ship, a supply tanker, several patrol vessels (which patrol the Straits of Hormuz, the Persian Gulf and the Mozambique Channel) and occasionally an aircraft carrier which can be converted into a helicopter assault ship if required. The fact that the European naval presence in the area is as large as it is, is due in no small measure to the French contribution.

In view of perennial French suspicions about America's leadership of the Alliance, it would be over optimistic to expect the French to participate in a fully fledged NATO Task Force. Even when the French joined the British and American patrols in the Arabian sea during the Iraqi–Iranian war to prevent any interference to tanker traffic moving out of the Persian Gulf and through the straits of Hormuz, they refused to coordinate operations or even consult their allies since they had no wish to appear to be planning the defence of vital interests common to all over the NATO council table.

Nevertheless, the defence community in France has increasingly stressed the need for allied cooperation outside Europe. It is quite well aware that France has too few ships and too many commitments in home waters to maintain more than a token force overseas. In the past few years the evidence of such cooperation has been accumulating. In August 1978 the commander of the American Middle East Task Force (MIDEASTFOR) paid a visit to the commander of the *Forces Armees de la Zone Sud-Ouest de l'Ocean Indien* (FAZSOL) to discuss the coordination of their respective operational plans. Shortly afterwards the French commander paid a return visit to Diego Garcia.

One way of overcoming the suspicions that remain might be to rotate the units of the standing force every other year, while allowing individual members to patrol stretches of the ocean in which they are already active. An obvious area of interest to the French would be the Mozambique Channel through which oil tankers pass every day on their way to the Cape. Indeed, if the respective units of the standing force each covered a smaller stretch of ocean they would be able to benefit from shorter deployment times and higher employment cycles. This would allow a much greater rationalisation of units which would otherwise be deployed as part of a national task force, or not deployed at all.

Participation in a standing force might also be useful for Britain. At the moment the RN sends a task force into the Indian Ocean once a year, normally four frigates and a similar number of support vessels grouped around a helicopter carrier. Although it has still more experience of overseas operations than the French navy, the RN will soon lose most of its *County* and *Rothesay* class destroyers. From 1985 it will be primarily an anti-submarine force made up of two or three V/STOL carriers, anti-submarine frigates and hunter killer submarines operating almost entirely in the eastern Atlantic and the North Sea. The cutback in escort vessels has rendered incredible, if not questionable, the 1980 commitment to deploy an eight to ten ship task force in the Indian Ocean. It has even brought into question whether Britain will soon be able to operate East of Suez at all.

The Navy's problems have been compounded by the government's refusal to provide depots and prepositioned supplies which could resupply a task force in an emergency. Successive British governments have been unable or unwilling to justify the expense, partly because use of them would be infrequent, partly because it would mean locking up valuable stores and spare parts which are already in short supply at home. For this reason the destroyer and frigate squadron in each task force in the Indian Ocean usually comprises ships that are not due for refit for eight or ten months.

In the absence of depots, the operational capacity of a British task force would be limited. Even the FOF 2 group which entered the Indian Ocean in 1978 (the most powerful to deploy there since 1971) would have been deprived of almost all its 'teeth' once its guided missile destroyer had launched its Exocet anti-ship missiles. There is much to be said for British participation in a standing force grouped around an American or French carrier (or even one of its own V/STOL carriers) especially if the force in question had access to stores and equipment prepositioned for use by the RDF either in the Gulf or Diego Garcia. HMS *Invincible*'s 1983–84 tour of the Far East exemplified the problems of effecting repairs.

EUROPEAN DEFENCE ORGANISATION

It remains to consider the appropriate organisational framework within which a European contribution could be made. Agreement among the Europeans that a threat exists and that they must do something themselves to meet it has so far stopped short of any constructive suggestions about how best to organise a European contribution and how to resolve the thorny but vital question of French participation. What institutional arrangements would enable France to participate in a naval standing force? Would it be possible to associate France fully in what would be to all intents and purposes a NATO operation – albeit a European one – without radically altering the Alliance's command structure and raising questions to which there are no obvious answers in terms of the public commitment that could be expected from France itself? Long before the United States began to criticise its European allies for paying insufficient attention to the security threats outside Europe, the WEU Council expressed an interest in out of area operational planning. In 1963 Britain called for a comprehensive review of allied interests beyond the Tropic of Cancer as well as the means the allies had at their disposal for protecting them in the future.[11] It is not surprising, therefore, that the Assembly has been able to discuss out of area operations in recent years without arousing the controversy which has arisen over similar discussions in the North Atlantic Assembly. These discussions have focused not only on the Persian Gulf, but more recently on the south Atlantic and southern Africa.

NATO commanders have made no secret of their concern that it would be foolish to allow a strict interpretation of the Charter to prevent its members from meeting the threat to the free transportation of raw materials and petroleum products from the Gulf to Western Europe.[12] Despite the geographical limits of the Alliance, which have held good since its inception, there has been an exchange of information about matters outside the NATO theatre for more than 15 years. From time to time the North Atlantic Assembly has called upon the NATO Council to authorise the Supreme Allied Command Atlantic (SACLANT) to undertake whatever measures are deemed necessary to protect the shipping lanes in the south Atlantic.[13] Its concern has increased with the years. In only one instance, however, has NATO risked adverse publicity by drawing up collective defence plans and communicating them to the Defence Planning Committee (DPC). SACLANT's study on the south Atlantic approved in 1978 and completed three years later is limited entirely to planning and involves no contact with out of area countries, South Africa included.[14]

Since 1979 the NATO defence ministers have recognised the need for more than an exchange of information, however valuable. The DPC communiqués of December 1980 and May 1981 recognised the need for common policies and collective planning. In the words of the second communiqué:

> ... nations should be prepared to participate fully in consultations within the Alliance to enable NATO governments to share, and as far as possible coordinate, their assessments of the threat and its implications and to identify common objectives ... common objectives identified in such consultations may require members of the Alliance to facilitate out of area deployments in support of the vital interests of all.[15]

While all 15 members in the past have subscribed to the DPC communiqués, with the exception of France, not all European powers are reconciled to out of area operations. Very few have the resources to contribute to them and few, if any, consider it desirable to extend the geographical scope of the Atlantic Charter. The implementation has been left, in the main, to their military staffs, or the NATO Secretariat and this, in turn, has occasioned several acrimonious debates in NATO Council meetings.

It has become commonplace to discuss the growing and deepening rift between the United States and Europe in the way both view the world. Setbacks in the Third World, even if orchestrated or engineered by the Soviet Union, tend to be seen by the Europeans as just that – setbacks, not major reverses. And, in this respect, it is true that most European powers do not see the need for extensive military operations outside Europe. Nevertheless, the fact that the Europeans often find themselves in disagreement is frequently overlooked. The problem has as much to do with European politics as the crisis in US–European relations.

In the summer of 1981, for example, both Denmark and Norway pulled out of the Ocean Venture exercises in the north Atlantic despite Anglo-Dutch exercises in the Caribbean. Both countries also raised serious objections to France's intervention in Chad at a NATO Council meeting in 1977. The following year even the British raised questions about the Shaba 2 operation in which French and Belgian paratroopers intervened to prop up Mobutu's faltering government in the face of a rebel attack. The Europeans failed to agree at the Washington summit that force should have been used. Indeed, the final communiqué had to be rewritten to meet the objections of those countries, Britain included, who had taken issue with the French stand.[16]

It is possible that misunderstandings such as these might be avoided in the future by more open discussion of military operations in an exclusively European forum. As the WEU's General Affairs Committee reported two years ago NATO itself is no longer adequate. The Atlantic Treaty obliges neither the United States nor its European allies to come to one another's aid in a conflict beyond the North Atlantic theatre; nor does it oblige them to consult with one another beforehand. As a result, more often than not, they have been dissuaded from intervening.[17]

It is one thing for the United States and Europe to disagree on whether force should be used, quite another for the Europeans to be unable to intervene for disagreement amongst themselves. The agreement of the European defence ministers in May 1982 to develop the Eurogroup as a forum for 'a substantial politico-strategic discussion' is one solution, a potentially important step which, if followed through imaginatively, could improve the European contribution to NATO without embarrassing the United States.[18] But since France is not a member, although it has become the most important out of area power after the United States, the initiative appears, for the moment, to have only limited scope.

The WEU in fact, offers the only forum in which out of area operations can be discussed by European governments as members of its Council, and by European political parties through debates in its Assembly. Its responsibility in this sphere is actually set out in Article 8 of the modified Brussels Treaty. As the Assembly noted some years ago:

> ... even if it seems impossible to define a policy which the European countries should follow ... they can, at least, exchange information on a continuing basis about their respective interests and aims and thus avoid their legitimate interests bringing them into conflict or involving them in differences over which there has been no prior agreement.[19]

The Assembly's conception of how the WEU could provide a service without arousing adverse political comment may be a little unreal but in a general way it addresses a very real problem with a licence quite outside the experience of the NATO Council. Since the members of the WEU Assembly must be members of the Assembly of the Council of Europe in Strasbourg and are appointed by their national Parliaments on the strength of their respective parties, they should reflect a broad range of political opinions both in government and out.

Another option would be to make use of the Eurogroup, set up in 1968 at the instigation of Britain, to provide the European defence ministers with an opportunity of informal discussion on matters of European military coordination. The Group comprises all NATO's European members except France and Iceland. Normally, the Eurogroup defence ministers meet twice a year immediately before the regular meetings of NATO's Defence Planning Committee. At all other times, the permanent representatives of the member states to NATO together with a small staff, look after day to day affairs. Until now the Eurogroup through its various subcommittees has concerned itself mainly with procurement, logistics, communications and training. In *Europackage* for example, published annually as an annexe to the Eurogroup's December communiqué, the Group annually details its planned force improvements and the development and service procurement of new weapons systems such as the Panavia Tornado.

The fact that the Eurogroup already operates within NATO and that all its members with the exception of Luxembourg contribute forces to its integrated military command must be considered a significant advantage. Since its work is mostly carried out through its subcommittees a special defence committee for the Indian Ocean with an independent secretariat could meet from time to time under the chairmanship of the defence minister of one of the participating countries to coordinate joint exercises between a European standing force and the USN. It could perhaps, also prepare joint operational plans for the standing force, draw up specifications of the units comprising it and ensure that there was greater cooperation in the field of logistics as an incentive to greater economy. It might even undertake some of the contingency planning presently undertaken by SACLANT.

Yet despite considerable progress on technical matters the Eurogroup has not lived up to its original promise. Many of the smaller countries have shown scant interest in its deliberations and it is possible that any decision to extend the scope of those discussions might lead to even greater disenchantment. At present the Eurogroup obtains staff support principally from among the member delegations to NATO and has made a virtue of its informality. Its members might well not welcome discussion of an issue which by its very nature is bound to invite criticism and require clarification of its aims.

Nor is it clear that France would be prepared to join the Eurogroup after so many years outside it. And without French participation there would be no call for a European initiative. The closest that France has come to joining the group so far is its attendance as an observer at meetings of EUROCOM, the subgroup concerned with battlefield communications equipment.

Moreover, it might be argued that the Eurogroup would be ill-advised to extend the scope of its activity at present. It is already concerned primarily with the key task of joint weapon procurement and standardisation, a function that will become even more demanding at a time of contracting economic bases and reduced defence budgets. There are many issues in the Alliance where the Eurogroup might be able to play a useful role including the whole spectrum of theatre nuclear force deployment. Any additional responsibilities might jeopardise many of the associated activities in which it has been inconspicuously successful – especially in securing French participation in the Independent European Programme Group (IEPG).

In the confusion that exists at the moment there may be a temptation to use the NATO Council to arrive at a better understanding of what the allies can do collectively or individually beyond the Tropic of Cancer without being seen to engage the Alliance itself in these discussions. Even in the minds of the Americans the whole question of European participation revolves around the issue of cooperation rather than coordination, a clear division of labour rather than division of responsibilities. Thus in a speech in Munich in November 1981 the American ambassador to NATO commented:

> Some have suggested that we need new consultative mechanisms, or that we need to extend the operational boundaries of

NATO. I disagree with both these propositions. Existing structures are fully adequate for consultation and coordination if they are used properly. And what is required to meet the challenge outside NATO is not an extension of the NATO Treaty area but an enhanced effort by individual Western nations . . .[20]

Clearly the Europeans can do much more than they have to help the United States meet the threat to international security that has arisen in recent years. Invoking the Eurogroup or attempting to extend the NATO Treaty would entail considerable political and legal difficulties which would make such an approach quite impracticable for the forseeable future. But as we have also seen, attempting to preserve the distinction between planning and command is becoming increasingly dubious. It is all very well to argue that as long as security matters remain only the subject of discussion and planning and are not treated at the point of execution and command, the French will not object to participating. But what is the point of drawing up contingency plans if the Alliance is increasingly reliant on French participation?

As NATO moves towards the 1990s, questions about its purpose have become more pressing than they were in 1949. Granted that a European contribution in the Indian Ocean may be needed well before the decade is out, NATO might look seriously at a proposal made by Alastair Buchan almost 20 years ago: to set up a watch committee of four or five powers responsible to the NATO Council, not only for contingency planning but also for the execution of those plans. In the second of an occasional series of papers published by the Atlantic Institute, Buchan argued that such a body might be able to look after Western interests in Africa and the Gulf. He proposed that it replace the annual meetings of policy planners from the Atlantic Policy Advisory Group and the weekly meetings between the political advisers to the NATO mission.[21]

History has moved on since Buchan first developed this idea in 1964 but in the intervening period the problem has become more acute. In devising a collective response to threats outside Europe it may no longer be sufficient to look to the summit meetings which first began at Guadeloupe in 1975, in the hope of formulating an *ad hoc* framework for concerted action. For the problem may ultimately involve the future of the Atlantic Alliance just as much as the West's access to the commodities of the developing world.

THE UNITED STATES AND THE EUROPEAN COMMITMENT

It is probable, of course, that there will be no solution to out of area problems; that Europe and the United States will continue to disagree about operations outside the European theatre; that the Europeans will be unable to agree among themselves whether to defend their overseas interests or not.

The United States has never been keen on the presence of the Seventh Army in Europe. In the same year as its deployment, President Eisenhower hoped to convert it into a small contingent armed with nuclear weapons, a programme strongly endorsed by his chief rival for the Republican nomination Senator Robert Taft. In his *Memoirs*, George Kennan deplored the fact that America's membership of NATO had vitiated from the very beginning the sound principle embodied in the Marshall Plan: 'that they set up their own organisation and that we appear as great and good friends, but not the participating members of what they had set up'.[22] As recently as the mid-1960s, Zbigniew Brzezinski was reluctant to admit that the Atlantic Alliance was central to American policy, arguing that it should be merely one component in the Soviet–American relationship.[23] For Brzezinski NATO was no more important (and no less) than the Alliance for Progress in Latin America – a sentiment echoed many years later by the redoubtable Mrs Kirkpatrick, the US Ambassador to the UN.

In all three cases, those concerned felt that the United States would never be able to defend its own interests unless the scale of its European responsibilities was drastically reduced. More recently Jeffrey Record has criticised the United States for spending so much on NATO's Long Term Modernisation Programme at the expense of preparations for contingencies outside Europe. It is precisely because the United States cannot defend Europe by itself, he argues, that the American commitment should not be regarded as open-ended. It must of necessity be conditional like all its commitments overseas.[24]

This revisionist case has been taken up paradoxically by their European counterparts. If many Americans contend that the Alliance should be urgently restructured to permit the United States to play a more active role in the Middle East and even further afield, many Europeans look forward to a more active European defence effort which may permit Europe in the first instance to disassociate itself from the attempt to reassert an American *imperium*, and in the second, if necessary to oppose it.

The American conception of Soviet actions in the developing world, most Europeans would agree, is often gratuitously naive. They do not see the threat to the stability of Central America to be a threat to Western security. Setbacks elsewhere in the Third World, even if orchestrated by the Soviet Union, tend to be seen as just that – setbacks, not major reverses. Most Europeans simply do not find it plausible to picture the situation in the Third World as leaving the United States with no reasonable alternative but military intervention, or military support for local powers.

But the Europeans are equally mystified why anyone in the United States should feel that this difference of opinion about Soviet intentions and capabilities has inhibited it from acting in the Third World in the manner it sees fit. NATO has never been a properly integrated Alliance because America's commitment to the organisation has always been more restricted than its commitment to the Alliance. But for the Korean war NATO would probably have emerged as a transatlantic mutual assistance treaty, not an integrated military alliance – at most an American–Canadian non-reciprocal guarantee to the Brussels Treaty.

The developments which stemmed from the Korean war influenced the development of NATO to a much greater extent than it is often recognised. Until 1950 both Europe and the United States showed a peculiar disinclination to build up their conventional forces in the face of the Soviet threat. When Paul Nitze visited London in January 1949, he found that none of the putative signatories to the NATO Pact considered it necessary to increase their defence programmes. Washington did not press its allies – George Kennan whom Nitze later succeeded found no opposition to his own contention that the recovery of Europe should come first.

Even the development of a Soviet atomic bomb did little to concentrate the minds of European politicians. Neither the explosion of an atomic bomb by the Soviet Union in August 1949, nor the conclusion reached six months later that the Russians might be capable of launching a nuclear attack by 1954 altered allied thinking. Europe's economic recovery remained the first priority. In 1950 NATO estimated that it would need five times its present forces to deter a Soviet attack but nothing was done about it. The creation of NATO did not result in rearmament; rearmament was largely the result of the Korean War. Between 1950–51 NATO's defence expenditure doubled; it increased by a further 40 per cent the following year.

The deployment of US and Canadian troops in Europe was also a result of the war in north–east Asia. In 1950 Canada sent a brigade group to Germany. The effect on the United States was even more decisive. Senator Vandenburg had earlier opposed anything but 'an efficient nucleus' of American forces in an emergency; now he voted for the deployment of the Seventh Army in Central Europe.

The rearmament of the North Atlantic countries was one consequence of Korea. Another was the enlargement of the Alliance itself. The United States insisted on the admission of Greece and Turkey; on the rearmament of Germany and the appointment of SACEUR. The Korean war led to what Charles Bohlen described in his memoirs as 'the militarisation of NATO'.

The very fact that NATO owed its military structure to the perceived threat of Soviet aggression outside Europe, however, ensured that the Alliance would be divided in its response to the Soviet threat. For the Korean war left the United States at the head of an Alliance which faced a global threat, but whose treaty and procedures were limited only to the European theatre. Outside Europe the United States engaged in unilateral declarations, and unilateral actions. The conduct of the Korean war itself had begun to raise questions about US behaviour to China.

The seriousness of this situation should not be exaggerated but nor should it be minimised. The Korean war (1950–53) was a turning point in the history of the Alliance, only a year old when it broke out. It was the transitional war between World War II and all the wars that followed – from Indo-China to Central America. It was the first time that the United States army began to crack – not so much because of any fear of the enemy as because of its disgust with its local client. It was the last time that the United

States was able to engage in battle with its major allies fighting alongside.

Less than two years after NATO had come into being the Europeans found themselves so ill at ease with American initiatives elsewhere that they began to look for ways of translating the organisation into something more, and/or replacing/supplementing it with something different. The first led to talks on greater consultation; the other to the ill-fated scheme for a European Defence Community which eventually collapsed in 1954. In the same year Dulles specifically refused to discuss America's out of area operations with her allies in the West, asserting that Article 4 of the Atlantic Charter which required its signatories to consult with one another imposed no obligation on Washington to consult on questions which fell well outside the geographical parameters of the NATO treaty.

American forces which might have served in Europe served instead throughout the post-war period in the second theatre of operations: Asia and the Pacific. The commitment of the Seventh Army and a substantial air component in the early 1950s contributed very little to the Lisbon goals of 1952 which called for a force of 96 divisions. Two years later NATO had to settle for 70 divisions despite having larger manpower reserves than the Soviet Union and its East European allies. Within months of the Lisbon conference, the United States committed itself to a doctrine of massive retaliation precisely to avoid having to station large conventional forces in Europe. The justification for this was that if the threat was met in Asia it would never be put to the test in Europe. Typical of such thinking was General MacArthur's statement to Congress at the height of the Korean War 'if we lose the war to Communism in Asia, the fall of Europe is inevitable; win it and Europe most probably will avoid war'.[25]

America's propensity for deceiving itself that its operations in Asia adequately made up for a remarkably limited contribution to Europe should not have occasioned much surprise. Even in World War II more American troops were employed in the Pacific than in Europe. Such was Britain's concern that at the end of 1944 General Ismay wrote, 'I am afraid that our American friends . . . have only paid lip service to the fundamental principle that Germany is Public Enemy No 1'.[26]

The Pacific first strategy was hardly surprising given the fact that the United States really believed that it would be able to keep the peace in Asia after the war had ended, by leaving the Europeans to take care of themselves. 'I do not want the US to have the post war burden of reconstituting France, Italy and the Balkans,' Roosevelt told the State Department in February 1944, 'This is not our national task at a distance of 3500 miles or more. It is definitely a British task in which the British are far more vitally interested than we are'.[27] It was because the British were clearly incapable of undertaking the task that the United States had to step in. But it was because America preferred to limit its responsibilities in Europe that it abandoned the Lisbon goals within months of their formulation, obscuring the necessity for the review Lord Ismay had hoped for in the early 1950s: 'a careful appraisal of the economic risks involved in undertaking increases against the military risks of not doing so'.[28]

Even as late as Vietnam, the Americans continued to see the struggle as central to the defence of Europe. It was left to George Ball to question the opinion that the battle for Saigon was really a battle for Berlin on the grounds that whatever credibility the United States might gain by the steadfastness of its commitment to an ally of limited importance, it would almost certainly lose by the erosion of Europe's confidence in its political judgment.[29]

But there is not one instance of operations in which United States forces were involved in which it was prevented from committing as much force as it felt necessary as a result of its European responsibilities. Indeed quite the reverse. As Henry Kissinger reminded President Thieu in 1972, the United States had chosen to mortgage its entire military future in defence of a country that was not even a member of the Free World. At the height of the Vietnam War, the United States diverted $300bn (in today's Fiscal Year 1982 dollars) to a secondary theatre of conflict at the expense of its NATO commitments. Vietnam was a tragedy not only for America but also for the Atlantic Alliance for it came at a time when the Soviet Union increased its defence expenditure by nearly 5 per cent a year. As has already been stated, the estimated difference between Soviet and American defence expenditure between 1970–79 was equivalent to the total cost of the war in South-East Asia.

It must be up to the United States, of course, to judge whether the defence of Europe is still in its national interest or whether the cost of a force such as the Rapid Deployment Force in the Middle East is not disproportionately high. But the revisionists have really no reason to claim that America has been denied a proper choice by its European allies. The claim has always been a dubious one. When the Supreme Allied Commander Europe (SACEUR) can publicly reveal that America's air and sealift forces will be committed not to the Seventh Army, but the RDF in the event of a simultaneous conflict in the Middle East and Europe, such a claim seems disingenuous in the extreme.

If we take the revisionist case a stage further its plausibility seems even more specious. There is now some support in the United States for a much looser NATO framework which would allow the Americans to enter into bilateral treaties with their main European allies, while allowing those powers in turn to enter into bilateral pacts with one another.[30] It might well be the case that such a scheme would help to define obligations more explicitly, including the circumstances in which one country would be obliged to provide support for the operations of the other outside the European theatre. But cooperation outside Europe would inevitably take up resources that might detract from the ability of both parties to defend their other allies. This is particularly true of an accord between the United States and Britain which might easily become an excuse to reduce expenditure on forces earmarked for operations on the continent, or for that matter naval operations in the eastern Atlantic. The recent conflict in the south Atlantic required the active deployment of 70 per cent of Royal Navy units. During the Indonesian Confrontation (1963–66) 50 per cent of the navy, then twice its present size, served in South-East Asia.

Such force redeployments especially over a long period are surely much better discussed in a NATO forum where members can discuss which of their defence commitments are important to themselves and which are essential to the Alliance. NATO obligations need not run counter to national interests, but the obligation to consult all allies on major defence cuts or the reallocation of resources, at least, compels each member to think again about its real, as opposed to imaginary, priorities.

Secondly, it is doubtful what the Europeans would gain from such bilateral treaties. The French have long been active in out of area operations and have invited criticism from their other NATO partners for their activities in Africa, specifically in Chad at the NATO Council summit of 1977, and Zaire the following year. At times they have collaborated extensively with the United

States, both in the Indian Ocean where the French and American fleet commanders work closely together, and in central Africa. For this Giscard was condemned by the socialist party. After Shaba II, the opposition claimed France had become the *'gendarme Otanien de l'Afrique'* and the 'spearhead of the Atlantic Alliance'.

Although US European Command (EUROCOM) was nominally in charge of the 1978 airlift its primary role was to keep its NATO allies informed. EUROCOM had no operational role. The airlift was mounted from the United States not Europe. And it was in the United States that troops were alerted for possible deployment in Zaire. NATO as an organisation was consulted only after the episode was largely over, even though its channels of communication were used throughout. The most significant feature of the operation, however, was that the association was an *ad hoc* one. Nothing would have been gained by a bilateral treaty. Indeed, the extent of the collaboration between the two countries is not often discussed precisely because the French believe that they have more to gain by emphasising their independent posture.

Even during the Falklands conflict, conducted in an area of the world – the south Atlantic – where the United States would very much welcome some form of NATO commitment,[31] it is difficult to see what it would have gained from a bilateral treaty with the United Kingdom. During the conflict America was able to provide the British with extensive intelligence, logistical and material support in keeping with the spirit, if not the letter of the Atlantic Charter. To have honoured the terms of a bilateral treaty would almost certainly have brought it into conflict with the OAS. As it was, most of America's Latin American allies recognised in private that the scope of its NATO obligations was quite different from that of the OAS. Washington may fault the extent of cooperation on out of area contingencies, but the fact that those commitments are open to interpretation makes the options agreeably uncertain and the assistance one partner renders to another a matter for discussion. Their obligations beyond Europe are more or less what the parties wish to make of them. Most would not wish it otherwise.

7 The Need for an Atlantic Community

If one glances at any book on the Atlantic Alliance written in the late 1950s prognostications strikingly similar to those volunteered by today's pundits and politicians will be found. Klaus Knorr was only one among many to ask in 1958 whether the Alliance could survive a profound crisis of confidence, whether it could still defend Europe against possible aggression and aggressive threats.[1] The questions raised at the end of the 1950s, in retrospect NATO's first and most successful decade, reveal that today's crisis of confidence is not without precedent. Crises within the Alliance have been part of its history. Indeed, hardly a year has passed in which its future has not been questioned. If anything, those who write about the Alliance in the 1980s for the most part try to argue that NATO is not foredoomed to failure; that the Soviet Union can still be contained.[2]

Yet there seems little doubt that the present difficulties provoked in part by Europe's lacklustre response to the invasion of Afghanistan and the public response in Europe to the deployment of Cruise missiles have brought into sharp focus the doubts that have preoccupied many Europeans about the credibility of the American nuclear guarantee and the steady and seemingly inexorable decline of American military power – doubts which many American politicians have merely heightened by continually questioning their own strength.

At the same time, there is a widespread feeling in the United States that competition rather than cooperation has become the keynote of a coalition based more on sentiment and the similarity of political institutions than any real identity of economic and strategic interests. Many in the United States, not all of them neo-isolationists, are beginning to ask whether the Alliance is more of a burden than an asset. To exaggerate the importance of such opinions would be to deny the commitment that successive administrations, not least the present one, have made to Europe; to ignore them, however, would be to exaggerate the respect in which Europe is still held.

The succession of recent misunderstandings, conflicts and crises which have beset relations between the United States and Europe has traditionally been seen as the consequence of a shift in the balance of power that first became evident in 1973. The emergence of a European voice in the world has had inevitable repercussions for American policy as well. During the three months of regular session of the General Assembly between September–December 1981 when Britain held the Presidency of the European Commission, the British delegation in the United Nations delivered well over 100 statements on a wide range of agenda items which expressed the views of the Community's nine other members. Obviously this has led to conflicts of interest with the United States. Yet Europe's failure to develop institutions which would permit it to play a role more in keeping with its economic status has prevented the Community from challenging America's leadership of the Alliance. Indeed, unlike the early 1960s when France challenged America's leadership and failed, or 1973 when President Nixon challenged the Europeans to decide whether to work with the United States or go their separate way,[3] the present crisis has not been prompted by Europe at all – but by profound misgivings on the part of European public opinion which the individual European governments have been unable to allay.

The sensitivity of European politicians to the danger that too great a degree of unity might alienate the United States has in one respect been resolved; European unity is now less real than at any time since 1973. Both in Germany and Britain belief in the Atlantic Alliance is more deeply ingrained in popular experience than is the case with their own European institutions. The real challenge to the unity of the Atlantic world has arisen from the collapse of the bipartisan consensus which has existed on all defence matters since 1949. This has made it increasingly difficult for governments which are in all other respects committed to the American connection to deliver what they have agreed. Yet the problem has been unnecessarily compounded by the present

Administration in the United States by challenging a consensus that has existed for the last 20 years on the most important problem of all: how to deal with the Soviet threat.

The current tendency in American thinking to regard its relationship with the Soviet Union in essentially combative and doctrinal terms and to make it the predominant issue in areas of regional instability provides a contrast with the more relaxed and pragmatic view of East–West relations prevalent in Europe. European governments are not convinced that the ability to display military power in regions of endemic instability constitutes the most effective method of ensuring Western security. To that extent there is a growing and deepening rift in the way that the two partners view the world.

In further contrast to the United States, European public opinion has also continued to maintain high confidence in the principle of arms control negotiations. Most European governments still place a high premium on negotiations as an essential component of Alliance security. European support for SALT 2 was virtually unanimous and agreement on the modernisation of theatre nuclear forces would have been impossible without an American commitment to enter into negotiations about the limitation of intermediate range systems.

These transatlantic divergences in mood and attitude have been present for many years, but they have been highlighted in the last few. They have produced in particular certain trends which, unless corrected, could have serious repercussions. Unless the two problems are resolved there will be little communication between the two sides, and a very real danger that the Alliance will become so divided that its members may be incapable of taking concerted action.

If Europe manages to restore a public consensus on defence – Alliance management will be that much easier. But it also needs to be said that the Europeans too need to become more mature in their public attitudes; to come to terms with the fact that European unity has made but little progress and has produced consistent views on no more than a few, mainly economic matters. The need for the American connection is as great as ever, and it will only be maintained by taking into account American interests outside the strict parameters of NATO. Europe too often forgets that it is the United States which has made most of the concessions in recent years: for example, entering into disarmament negotiations with the Russians earlier than it had planned to, and keeping in operation one of the few remaining channels of *détente* by going through the motions of negotiation at the European Security Conference in Madrid in spite of the continuing repression in Poland.

If it is important for the United States to recognise the need for European governments to respond to public opinion particularly concerning the need for arms control and the general desire to preserve the balance of power in Europe at lower, rather than higher, levels of force, it is equally important for the Europeans to recognise and understand the special role of the United States as a superpower with interests and responsibilities beyond NATO boundaries.

* * *

The past explains a great deal about European attitudes to defence within the Atlantic world, and even more about the recurrent bouts of Mansfieldism on the other side of the Atlantic Ocean. It would be a great mistake to imagine, for example, that European unity would have been possible without an American guarantee to Europe, or outside that Atlantic Community which André Malraux predicted would come into being in the early 1950s. European unity, in fact, would have little meaning outside the Atlantic world.

But if Germany can draw very little reassurance from the Gaullism of France and neo-Gaullism of Britain, its own allies can draw little confidence from the SPD's attitude to nuclear weapons. Like most other European social democratic parties the SPD now faces very real problems in maintaining any consensus on matters of defence. Like the Labour parties in the Netherlands and Norway who took their countries into NATO in 1949 the British Labour Movement seems set to embrace policies which can be reconciled only with difficulty with its Alliance obligations.

This question of political management is possibly the most serious challenge NATO now faces. It is worth pointing out that since 1945, Labour Party conferences have considered 72 resolutions on defence and thrown out a third of them. In the same period the Conservative Party has considered only 30 and carried every one. The problem is not so much that the Labour Party has always found it difficult to agree on defence issues but that the 100 MPs who abstained in 1949, on the decision to take Britain into

NATO would today find much greater support. The profound isolationism of the British Labour Party finds emotional gravity in unilateralism; and draws inspiration from the belief that protesting French farmers are more likely to reach Dover before Russian troops.

Most social democratic parties like to insist that when they are not concerned with the immediate defence of the nation their principal concern is the survival of NATO. But their attitude to the Alliance can hardly be described as one of respect for an organisation with its own sense of purpose and conception of security. Their commitment to NATO will almost certainly become more qualified and less open-ended. This may be more true of the rank and file membership than their political leaders but the fact that the two most recent leaders of the British Labour Party have been convinced unilateralists, and that Helmut Schmidt's successor voted against the deployment of Cruise missiles adds very little credibility to their description of themselves as Atlanticist parties. This is a conclusion that has been reached before, but it is one against which the Labour Party and the SPD protest too much.

This study has also shown that doubts about NATO's nuclear posture will persist well into the 1990s. The task of balancing the competing requirements of nuclear and conventional defence and deciding on an order of priorities for future resource allocation will be a very complex matter. It is very possible that NATO's assessment of trends in international relations and more certainly the need to keep abreast of military developments in the East, will provide a very strong incentive for prolonging the present pattern of deterrence. There may nevertheless be penalties in neglecting public disquiet about nuclear weapons. Although NATO's individual governments are not likely in the foreseeable future to forfeit public support, there may be an increasing rejection of a nuclear defence and a concomitant mood of apathy which might act as a negative force in its future development.

The effects of increasing anti-Americanism cannot be ignored. In an extreme case there could be a dangerous loss of legitimacy for an alliance which still depends for much of its cohesion on the American nuclear guarantee. As there appear to be no immediately obvious solutions to these problems, Western leaders will most probably want to investigate the implications of adopting a no first use strategy, or greater reliance on conventional defence, expensive though such solutions may obviously be. There is, in the final analysis, no real prospect of defence on the cheap.

This study has been, in large part, critical of many recent studies which have talked somewhat glibly of reforming NATO, especially those that have looked forward to the creation of a European Defence Community. Unfortunately, the past which saw such remarkable progress towards European unity is now beginning to act as a hurdle to further cooperation, in the one area in which progress has never matched its achievements elsewhere: that of defence. Indeed, the defeat of the plan for a European Defence Community 30 years ago was one of the few setbacks to European unity in the 1950s.

The foundations on which NATO was built in the late 1940s – the preservation of German sovereignty but the division of the German nation, the international harvesting of the West German economy to continental economic cooperation, and the security guarantee given to France by Britain in the Brussels Treaty, and the United States in the Atlantic Charter – might all have come about long before the Soviet threat at any time between 1919 and 1923, the year which saw Aristide Briand's ill-fated scheme for a European union.

We now know that an American security guarantee to France might have met with considerable Republican Party support had President Wilson chosen to present a convincing case for it.[4] When Aristide Briand revived the idea of a French security treaty in 1927, however, Secretary of State Kellogg transformed it into an anodyne multilateral pact against war. If the United States had not withdrawn support for France, and Britain had not reneged on its commitment in 1916 to maintain allied currency and commercial controls after the war, both powers might have underwritten a Franco–German economic community instead of forcing the French to rely on German reparations.

In short, a European defence community has always been predicted on the link with the United States as a filter of European rivalries. Even when France occupied the Rhineland to secure German payments it wanted an international occupation to maintain a semblance of the Atlantic community which had come into existence briefly during the war: including allied ownership of the Rhenish railways, an allied customs regime, in effect Anglo-American financial support for the franc and the integration of the Franco-German economies. As the young Konrad

Adenauer, one of the eventual architects of such a scheme in the 1950s wrote when Mayor of Cologne in 1923, a separate West German state presupposed both a united Western Europe and an Atlantic community. Although the French eventually left the Rhineland, they still tried to exact the only military guarantee they ever received from the United States: an allied army of observation including an American contingent which remained on until 1935.

In this context the revisionist claim that European unity can only progress outside the Atlantic community begins to look historically suspect. Even within it, the movement towards unity appears to have run out of steam. The political confidence that will allow the European powers to resolve their outstanding differences may well not exist. For the forseeable future, it seems that Europe will continue to remain what it is at the moment: a theatre for national rivalries. Unity is still a long way off. Only a refusal to take heed of the historical record would seduce the unwary into believing that it will be realised very soon.

A close understanding of the historical record also explains why many Americans are as reluctant to continue their guarantee as they were to extend one in 1949: why many would prefer the Atlantic community to be a much looser affair. America's deepest instincts differ very little from those expressed before the outbreak of the last war which dragged her into a conflict with Germany against her own better judgement. As late as February 1939, Franklin Roosevelt wrote:

> What the British need today is a good stiff grog inducing not only a desire to save civilisation *but the continued belief they could do it*. In such an event they will have a lot more support from their American cousins . . .

It is this lack of belief in themselves which seems so widespread among the Europeans which explains America's occasional frustration with its allies. As one American spokesman recently observed, 'those who march in opposition to measures designed to strengthen NATO do so, in large measure, not because they think defence no longer necessary, but because they think it no longer possible.'[6] Revisionist prescriptions are hardly likely to reassure American opinion: indeed, by reopening the deep fissures which lie along the undersurface of Europe's international institutions they will in all probability make it even more difficult to communicate either to the United States or the Soviet Union a continued willingness to defend itself or be defended.

It is time, not to rewrite the Atlantic Charter as the revisionists demand, but to reaffirm its principles. It is time to adhere to the Charter both in spirit as well as the letter, for it is the spirit which has suffered most from the collapse of a European consensus on defence issues. It is time to recognise that the present crisis is serious, and that its resolution will require governments on both sides of the Atlantic to tackle their own political problems so that they can better communicate their legitimate concerns to each other.

The greatest danger of Atlantic revisionism lies in the realm of self-fulfilling prophecy. It is the doubt that NATO has a future which poses the gravest challenge of all. In such circumstances it may be useful to remind ourselves of Paul Valery's admonition 'We fear the future not without reason. We hope vaguely, we dread precisely. Our fears are infinitely more precise than our hopes.' It was that same Valery, of course, who recognising the decline of Europe in 1938 wrote that the Old World was ready to be governed by an American commission. After the war Europe obtained an American guarantee instead. If NATO should collapse the only prospect for Western Europe may be that of being governed by a Soviet commission.

Part II

Perceptions of the Atlantic Alliance

8 NATO: The Next Decade

GENERAL BERNARD W. ROGERS

Supreme Allied Commander Europe

The issues we are seeking to explore are among the most critical affecting the citizens of our nations. I am grateful, therefore, to have this opportunity to discuss with you the direction the Alliance is taking now and should take in the next decade. This informed audience need not be told that NATO is in the midst of critical times. Many statesmen and scholars are calling it a crisis. Certainly, there is cause for concern, especially given a number of worrisome trends that threaten Alliance security and the foundation on which that security is built. The signals are too serious and the tensions too high for us simply to muddle through another of NATO's many challenging periods. To move ahead we need a strengthened consensus on the fundamentals of NATO security objectives and on the more divisive questions of what must be done to achieve those objectives.

In moving towards such a strengthened NATO consensus we must face up to the basic reality, the fundamental challenge to the Alliance: convincing the peoples of our nations, especially in Western Europe, that there is a threat to their freedom and security. To meet that menace we must elicit from our peoples the willingness to make sacrifices in other areas in order to enhance their collective security. Undermining public support for such sacrifices in most NATO nations is the understandable desire to preserve the level of prosperity and social gains our peoples enjoy. Governments, meanwhile, must wrestle with the unhappy state of the economy in today's world. Further complicating and emotionalising the situation is the growing public alarm over the size and destructiveness of burgeoning military arsenals, especially nuclear weapons. What prevails is public uneasiness and uncertainty which provide fertile ground, either for our NATO message or for what seem to be more tempting ideas which appear to some to promise continued peace without greater individual sacrifice.

Those seeking a path out of this uncertainty rightfully look to NATO and the leaders of NATO nations. Unfortunately, what they find is a mixed consensus and considerable support for some disturbing proposals striking at the very foundation of NATO security. They also find an Alliance frequently torn, as now with the Soviet pipeline, by issues over the manner of dealing with our major potential adversary.

These disturbing conditions do not mean that the Alliance is in crisis. But NATO does face a critical choice of either allowing its unity and resolve to be further eroded at a time when cohesion is vital, or seizing the opportunity for solidifying a consensus on which to sustain its future security. We must ensure that the latter is the direction in which our Alliance heads. Towards that end I wish to set forth what I consider the main elements of that consensus, explore the causes of its erosion and suggest a general direction that we should follow.

There is no real debate over NATO's basic goal, the maintenance of peace. But what we seek is not only peace, but peace with our freedom intact, a distinction often missed – or dismissed – by some popular movements today. Disagreements emerge over the means to achieve our goal, or, more specifically, the means to achieve the three supporting security objectives that most Alliance leaders would agree contribute to peace with freedom. Those objectives are:

To maintain security through deterrence.
To seek a less hostile world with lowered tensions.
To seek reduced and balanced force levels.

The objective of maintaining security through deterrence requires defence capabilities sufficient to dissuade a potential aggressor. Consensus on this objective often founders over how much military capability is required. To deal with this latter question, we must assess where we stand today and what is required to achieve this security objective.

NATO's current security posture should be assessed against its ability to implement its deterrent strategy of Flexible Response. That strategy is based not only on adequate forces being available but also on the uncertainty in the mind of a potential aggressor as to our response to his aggression. There are three responses envisaged in our strategy which our triad of forces is intended to support:

> Direct defence, to defeat an attack or place the burden of escalation on the enemy.
> Deliberate escalation on NATO's part; or
> General nuclear response, the ultimate guarantor of our deterrent.

The Alliance confidently can continue to build its consensus on this strategy of Flexible Response, which is still appropriate, if given an adequate capability for each leg of the triad of forces it requires: strategic nuclear, theatre nuclear and conventional. Assessing our ability to implement our strategy, we find NATO has been surpassed by the Warsaw Pact in all three categories of forces supporting Flexible Response. Fortunately, at the strategic nuclear level, the United States and Great Britain are taking actions to ensure the continued deterrent value of those forces. At the theatre nuclear level, NATO's two-track decision of December 1979 to modernise our long-range theatre nuclear forces while negotiating their elimination is aimed at restoring the balance and filling a gap in our deterrent spectrum.

However, it is in the conventional area that we find consensus most elusive. NATO's lack of consistent resolve in providing a credible conventional capability has led to our having mortgaged our defence to the nuclear response because our nations have not been willing to pay the price of an adequate conventional defence. Although Allied Command Europe (ACE) gets stronger every year because of commitments that are met, the gap between the force capabilities of NATO and the Warsaw Pact gets wider each year, decreasing the credibility of our deterrent. Instead of possessing genuine flexibility of response, NATO's military posture will require us – if attacked conventionally – to resort fairly quickly to the second response, 'deliberate escalation', if we are to defend successfully. Basing our deterrent on that response, especially given the theatre nuclear imbalance against us, puts a strain on the credibility of our deterrent.

There are many reasons for NATO in general and for most of the member nations in particular having failed in their commitments to conventional security. One dominant reason is that many citizens and leaders in NATO apparently do not believe that the threat justifies additional sacrifice. To these sceptics we should make several points regarding threat capabilities and intentions.

Considering threat capabilities, NATO now faces imbalances of more than 2:1 in virtually all areas of comparison. Soviet military spending consumes about 14 per cent of its GDP, well over twice the percentage of Gross Domestic Product which the United States devotes to defence. There are sceptics who acknowledge the NATO/Warsaw Pact imbalances, but who believe that many Pact problems and numerous NATO strengths overshadow the numerical disparities. To be sure, numbers do not say it all and there are compensating factors. But today's imbalances, including present and imminent Pact qualitative advances in equipment, have grown so serious and the trends so adverse, that we no longer can rationalise away the ever-widening gap.

Considering threat intentions, it is preposterous in my judgment to dismiss the threat posed by Pact capabilities by claiming that its growth of military power is directed solely at defence, reflecting no more than traditional Soviet insecurity. The size, type and location of Pact forces go far beyond the requirements for defence. The offensive nature of numerous Pact manoeuvres demonstrates both the capability and readiness for aggression. The invasion of Afghanistan confirmed it.

Warsaw Pact military capability and readiness for aggression need not necessarily manifest themselves by a massive military attack against NATO 'out of the blue'. NATO's strength still makes the risks and costs of such an attack high enough for the Pact not to favour that course. More likely, and to my thinking, the most disturbing menace is that Pact military power eventually may permit the Soviet Union to achieve its long-term goal of domination of Western Europe without having to fire a shot. Thus, maintaining sufficient and credible military power in NATO is important not solely in terms of its ability to deter military attack but also because such strength can enable the NATO allies to resist the threat of political and economic intimidation as well.

Assuming that we carry through on the critical actions being taken to improve the nuclear legs of our triad, the key to increasing Alliance security is the strengthening of NATO's conventional capabilities. Such strengthening will enhance our deterrence and raise the nuclear threshold, which are especially important if one believes that a potential aggressor might question the credibility of NATO's intention to escalate to nuclear weapons.

The military situation as I assess it, though unfavourable, is not yet unmanageable or beyond restoration if we resolve to act before it is too late. As a defensive Alliance we need not match the Warsaw Pact one for one in any area of comparison. But we do need a conventional capability adequate enough to provide a reasonable prospect of success utilising NATO's preferred response, the first: to 'defeat an attack or place the burden of escalation on the attacker'. Such a capability demands, among other things, the exploitation of our technological superiority to develop the electronic warfare capacity to disrupt the highly centralised control and direction of Warsaw Pact operational military units; and to implement our recently agreed ACE doctrine of holding the lead Warsaw Pact divisions long enough to destroy with conventional means the follow-on forces before they can reach the line of contact. Then the aggressor – should it attack conventionally and its attack be frustrated – would be forced either to withdraw or make the agonising decision to be the first to escalate to nuclear weapons. Faced with that unpleasant and credible prospect, I do not believe Soviet leaders would attack. They are no more anxious than we to cross the nuclear threshold because of the mutual uncertainty about further escalation fairly quickly to the strategic nuclear exchange.

A conventional capability sufficient to deter both aggression and intimidation can be achieved by the end of this decade if the Force Goals 1983–88, agreed by nations, are fulfilled on the time scale set out. Meeting these agreed commitments to force improvements will require an average annual real increase in defence spending of about 4 per cent per year, Alliance-wide, for the next six years. This would represent a sacrifice in the first year, 1983, for every man, woman and child in our West European nations of about £7. This cost is affordable and reasonable if we are serious about maintaining peace with freedom; after all, the total Gross Domestic Product of NATO nations is more than three times the estimated GDP of the Warsaw Pact. The annual performance of each nation should be judged by how well it meets its force goals for that year.

A final point is that security through deterrence also requires protection of our collective vital interests outside NATO boundaries. The United States has accepted the responsibility to protect those interests on a global basis. Our nations must concert their efforts, as allies, to assist the US in discharging that responsibility, while, as an Alliance, we seek the means to retain the ability to meet commitments within our boundaries. These, then, are the requisite elements of a consensus on how to achieve the objective of security through deterrence.

Our second and a somewhat longer-term security objective is the quest for a less hostile world with lowered tensions. Although clearly central to the political consensus of the Alliance, this objective has been plagued by real and perceived differences about how to achieve it. Most differences revolve around the manner of dealing with the Soviet Union, differences which are not surprising in an Alliance of sovereign nations. Still, a greater consensus on this objective is important to our goal of peace with freedom.

Certainly the foundation of this objective should be the desire for more constructive relations with the Soviet Union. A continuing dialogue between West and East is essential. However, the objective should not become cooperation at any price, regardless of Soviet actions and behaviour. Nor should we allow the need for better relations to impact unfavourably upon our other interests, such as promoting trade with the East but ignoring the effect that the transfer of high technology can have on the military balance between NATO and the Warsaw Pact. Finally, disagreements over issues such as the pipeline, trade and sanctions must not be allowed to erode the basic NATO consensus on collective security or to stifle initiatives directed towards other crucial Alliance concerns.

A third and longer-term security objective – to me the most essential and one to which the other two objectives contribute – is the successful negotiation of equitable and verifiable arms reduction accords and control measures for all categories of forces and arms. Only such accords can lead to reduced and balanced levels of forces; only such control measures can inject some predictability into the military situation and thereby make it more stable and more manageable.

To be successful in negotiating arms reductions and controls we must ensure that the Soviets have incentives to negotiate seriously. This, in turn, requires that the USSR views our Alliance as one of political unity and cohesion, and as militarily strong and resolute. The political imperative demands that we maintain our resolve to implement both tracks of our vital decision of December 1979 regarding the modernisation of and negotiation about long-range theatre nuclear forces. We must also overcome the transatlantic tensions, which I believe can be reconciled if we are patient enough to listen to each other and wise enough to take account of the problems and interests which are peculiar to individual nations. The military imperative requires that we be perceived as capable of implementing our strategy of Flexible Response.

To achieve this objective of balanced arms reduction and controls – to me the only course for the future we seek – there are no magic strategies, no credible short cuts, no reliable hope in unilateral restraint. Indeed, any of the increasingly fashionable diversions from what is required undermines our chances of successful achievement. On the other hand, successful arms negotiations are possible, if we are patient, unified, strong, resolute and consistent of purpose.

If we are to strengthen the consensus on Alliance objectives and their achievement, we must also address directly the attitudes and beliefs of our vocal minority about the military situation. We find some of our peoples are lulled into a sense of complacency because of NATO's success in keeping the peace. They disregard the fact that the balance for each leg of our triad of forces has shifted from NATO to the Warsaw Pact over the past 30 years. Too many of our fellow citizens exhibit a false sense of security and engage in wishful thinking that Soviet problems will cause that nation to reduce the amount of resources devoted to its military budget; they disregard all projections which show the continued unabated growth of Soviet military power along the rising glide path of military expenditures which the USSR has followed since the mid-1960s. We find others attracted to freezes or moratoria on nuclear weapons, disregarding that they would freeze a sizeable imbalance against us, thus eliminating all incentive for serious Soviet negotiation of arms reductions. Others are drawn to pacifism, neutralism or unilateral disarmament, disregarding that history confirms that such movements might maintain the peace but would surely lead to the loss of our freedom of action as we know it.

We must also disabuse those who believe that the two superpowers should be placed on the same moral plane. That is wrong. Nor can we tolerate a double standard, one for the Soviet Union, another for the US. NATO leaders and citizens must direct their criticism to the continuing Soviet military growth and its deployment of missiles, rather than to proposed NATO actions designed as a response to what the Soviets have done and continue to do. We must continue to remind our peoples that they are the object of a massive Soviet propaganda and disinformation campaign, which is unobstructed by internal constraints and unconcerned by inconsistencies between words and deeds. Our citizens are the targets of a well-financed, centrally directed Soviet campaign which fosters policies, activities and movements which seem attractive to some of our people, but which are designed to undermine NATO resolve and split the US from the Alliance. The Soviets find particularly lucrative the publics who would like to believe that their security can be achieved through restraint rather than by sacrifice.

We must also demonstrate to our peoples that the international interests of the Alliance and the national interests of each of its member nations are interwoven. For example, it is crucial that Americans remain convinced that US vital interests are inextricably linked with those of Western Europe, making the continued forward deployment in Europe of US forces an essential part of US defence arrangements. It would be disastrous to withdraw those forces and foolish to reduce them.

A strengthened consensus on the objectives I have discussed – security through deterrence, lowered tensions, and reduced and balanced force levels – and on their achievement, is crucial because: these objectives are mutually reinforcing; an eroding consensus on issues as fundamental as our objectives would prevent NATO from steering on to a path promising both short-term benefits and eventually a fundamental re-ordering of expenditures away from larger and more expensive arsenals; deep disagreements on objectives can mean that the misguided pursuit of one objective undermines another, for example, trade with the Soviet Union without care for technology transfer undermines military balance; failure to show the resolve to maintain military balance undermines success at arms negotiations.

The urgency of a strengthened NATO consensus is compounded by the convergence and cumulative impact of the worrisome trends I have touched on, that is firstly, the ever-increasing Soviet threat; secondly, the continually widening gap between relative force capabilities; thirdly, the attitudes, beliefs and impact of the vocal minority; fourthly, the growing impatience with traditional arms control efforts and the appeal of seemingly quicker remedies; and fifthly, the pressures to reduce the financial burdens of security rather than those of other programmes.

I mentioned earlier that being a defensive Alliance, the military situation is not yet unmanageable or beyond restoration. However, the important question we must keep before us is: how long can we permit those trends to converge before the military situation does truly become unmanageable and we feel political and economic pressure, coercion and blackmail from the East which we are unable to resist. Should this occur, the Soviet Union will have indeed accomplished its long-term objective cited earlier. Peace will have been maintained, but our freedom of action will have been forfeited.

The approach I have outlined can guide us down a path that will preserve our freedom and move us toward greater stability and eventually, if we persevere in our search for arms reductions, to reduced financial burdens upon our peoples.

As you and I know, it will not be until the voice of the people is heard by their parliaments, telling them that they – the people – are prepared to sacrifice for their own security, that we can expect the requisite priority to go to security arrangements in the national allocation of resources. Our task of influencing the people will not be easy. We must raise our voices in every available forum and medium if we are to get public support of our objectives. And somehow we must be able to explain the inescapable paradoxes: that we must arm today in order to disarm tomorrow; that we must sacrifice more today for security so that, being successful in negotiating arms reductions, we will need to sacrifice less tomorrow without risk to our security.

In our efforts, our greatest obstacle may well be complacency and an unpersuaded younger generation. The former US Under-Secretary of State George Ball has used an interesting parable to illustrate this possibility. He tells of:

> A village in a valley that had for decades been periodically devastated by floods until one day the villagers gathered resources and built a dam that for more than 30 years kept the village safe and dry. Then a new generation, disdaining the wisdom of their fathers, looked at the dam with abhorrence. It blotted out the sunset, they complained, and threatened the ecology. Who needed it? Since there had been no floods for over 30 years, it was obvious that the dam was no longer required. So they held a rock festival, blew up the dam, and sank beneath the advancing waters.

We must not let that happen to our Alliance. Numbers are in our favour, but zeal, enthusiasm and vigour are not. Public opinion is not anti-NATO, but the number of those willing to stand up for the Alliance in public is smaller than the minority of our vocal critics. We must ensure that our political leaders know that pro-NATO forces also must be reckoned with. And we must challenge those who, through ignorance, fear or faulty logic, would destroy the structure which has held back the flood waters of aggression, safeguarded the peace and preserved our freedom for over three decades.

(*Address given to the RUSI on 29 September 1982*)

9 The United Kingdom's Strategic Interests and Priorities

THE RT HON MICHAEL HESELTINE MP

Secretary of State for Defence

I have been asked to talk about the UK's strategic interests and priorities. I am glad to have the opportunity to do this so soon after the British people have given such a clear and decisive verdict on where they think that our national interests and priorities lie. I would like to draw a few lessons from the 1983 general election which I believe to be relevant, not only for Britain's place in the Alliance but also for the future of NATO as a whole. I should also like to say a few words about my own personal priorities as Secretary of State for Defence over the coming months.

One of the most notable things about the election was the importance which was accorded to defence as an issue throughout the campaign. In an analysis of the vote carried by Gallup for the BBC, 38 per cent of those questioned said that defence had been one of the two most important issues influencing their vote. Defence was second only to unemployment (72 per cent) and well ahead of prices (20 per cent), hospitals (11 per cent), pensions (8 per cent) and the EEC (5 per cent). The change since 1979 is striking. Then only 2 per cent felt that defence was one of the major issues.

The reasons for this are clear. The heightening of East/West tension over recent years and, in particular, increasing concern about nuclear issues, has brought defence to the forefront of public debate. This is, of course, natural and healthy in a democratic system. But it is also central to my theme. Britain's strategic interests and priorities depend on world realities which are, to a large extent, outside our control. Our national strategic interests are inextricably linked with those of our partners in the Western Alliance. Our economic interests are closely bound up with those of the EEC and the world economy as a whole. British elections do not change these realities in any fundamental way.

But, at the end of the day, our national strategic interests and priorities depend ultimately upon the perceptions of the British people. And it is here that a message of great comfort for the Alliance can be drawn. British politicians do not have the luxury – and I personally would certainly not wish to have it – of dictating to our people where their interests lie. For the first time since the war, the British people were presented with a radical choice on defence. They were offered a policy of abandoning Britain's strategic nuclear deterrent, stopping Cruise missile deployments without conditions, removing American bases from this country and cutting our defence expenditure to the proportion of GDP spent by our major European allies. Such a policy, if it could have been put into effect, would have represented a complete reversal of the consensus which has been maintained by all British governments since the war. On the other side there was the choice of continuing support of the NATO strategy of strong conventional forces, coupled with a nuclear capability, including that provided by the British independent nuclear deterrent. The people's choice was clear and decisive – not only in their general rejection of the radical alternative but also in terms of particular issues.

Taking the issues by turn, and returning to the Gallup analysis, over half of the people questioned – 55 per cent – felt that Britain should rely on both nuclear weapons and strong conventional non-nuclear forces for our defence. None of the alternatives – no or few weapons of any kind, strong conventional but no nuclear weapons or nuclear weapons only – received more than 20 per cent support. In other words there was a strong endorsement for current national and NATO policies of balanced nuclear and conventional forces. Again 73 per cent of those polled thought it was a bad idea that Britain should give up nuclear weapons for defence whatever other countries decide. On the issue of Cruise missiles which had generated great heat and emotion before and during the campaign, over half – 56 per cent – thought it was a good, or fairly good, idea that Cruise missiles should be sited in Britain as part of the West's defence.

These figures are significant. But we do not have to rely on polls alone. The evidence was clear, both on the hustings and in the decisive votes cast at the ballot box. The British people rejected the radical alternative and opted for the policies which have successfully kept the peace in Western Europe for nearly 40 years.

The question now is what does this mean for our future defence policies in Britain? First, it means that the British people recognise that there is a threat to our national strategic interests from the Soviet Union and her Warsaw Pact allies. The realities of that threat are very familiar to all of you. Second, I believe the people have massively supported British membership of the North Atlantic Alliance and the policies which NATO has adopted to contain the Soviet threat. In rejecting a non-nuclear policy and massive cuts in both our conventional and nuclear forces, they have agreed that NATO needs balanced forces to deter across the spectrum of the threat.

In turn this means that we shall continue with the four main contributions which Britain now makes to NATO. First there is the defence of the UK base. This is a vital task which has been neglected in the past. It is not, of course, simply a matter of protecting our own homeland. The UK is also an important base from which many tens of thousands of reinforcements, Americans as well as British, would reach the Continent. Thousands of reinforcement and resupply sorties would pass through our airspace and millions of tons of transatlantic shipping would pass through British waters. We shall continue with our plans to enhance and upgrade the defence of the UK home base. The TA expansion will continue and the Home Service force concept will be implemented. Major improvements to the air defence of the UK, including extra fighter aircraft, will be made.

On the Central Front of Europe we will continue to provide the powerful land and air forces which provide the tangible evidence of Britain's commitment to European defence. Our forces will be upgraded with new equipment such as Challenger and Tornado. At sea, in the Eastern Atlantic and Channel, our strong maritime forces will continue to be modernised with the acquisition of new weapons systems, new ships and more nuclear-powered hunter/

killer submarines. Finally we shall continue to provide an independent UK strategic nuclear force, currently Polaris to be replaced in the 1990s with Trident.

The main focus of our defence policy will continue to be on NATO to which 90 per cent of our defence effort is currently devoted. The Falklands campaign showed that we must be prepared for the unforeseen and that we must be ready to defend our vital interests outside the NATO area. We have already announced – in the Falklands White Paper – a number of improvements in ability of our forces to operate outside Europe, such as the purchase of a fleet of Tristar strategic tankers and the upgrading of our out-of-area formation, 5 Infantry Brigade. But the main emphasis of our out-of-area policy will continue to be on promoting peace and stability by deployments and exercises, by seconding personnel, by training and other assistance. These are economical and cost-effective ways of protecting our interests in a world in which we can no longer aspire to the role of international policemen.

So I do not see any fundamental shifts in our national strategic priorities over the next five years. But defence policy and international affairs are dynamic not static. We must be prepared to adapt to unforeseen developments. We must be prepared to take the initiative to preserve the peace and to reduce the level of tension in the world. And we must be prepared to be constantly vigilant in trying to ensure that the vast resources which we devote to defence are managed in the best and most effective way.

I should like to conclude by mentioning two areas to which I shall be devoting my attention over the coming months.

The first is arms control. Again I derive a message from our election – and from that in Germany. It is clear that our people want peace and a reduction in the massive nuclear and conventional arsenals which exist in the world today. But it is equally clear that they recognise that you cannot negotiate with the calculating hard-headed realists in the Kremlin from a position of weakness. The British and German elections, together with the stand of the French and the cohesion showed by the Western allies at Williamsburg have given the lie to Russian attempts to divide the West. They have tried to persuade our people that there is a nuclear and conventional balance of forces which is being destabilised by a massive Western arms build-up. This claim has been decisively rejected and Western solidarity and cohesion are greatly strengthened as a result.

We now have a great opportunity to push forward with the series of radical proposals for arms control and disarmament which the Alliance has put forward. Up to now our initiatives have been rejected. The zero option was rejected. The withdrawal of 1000 NATO warheads from Europe was ignored. In the START talks the Americans have proposed a reduction in the number of strategic warheads on each side by a third. The Russians have stalled. There is a stalemate at the MBFR talks.

But now, in the face of a cohesive and united West, I believe that there is better chance than for many years that real, fair, balanced and verifiable measures of arms control can be achieved. There have been successes in the past – the Test Ban Treaty, the ABM Treaty, and, to some extent, the SALT process. And there are signs of hope now. The first sign of movement has come in the INF negotiations. After initially refusing to negotiate at all they have put forward some proposals, albeit heavily balanced in their favour. There are some signs that they might be willing to discuss a ban on chemical weapons now that the US has announced plans to modernise its ageing stocks. We must build upon these small glimmers of hope over the coming months and years.

The second area to which I shall be devoting my attention is the management of defence. I do not need to emphasise how closely defence policy is interlinked with the question of resources. The Ministry of Defence employs well over half a million Servicemen and civilians. My budget this year is £16 billion. Yet, despite the vast sums, our resources are never sufficient to allow us to do all that we would like. My task as Secretary of State is to ensure that every penny that the taxpayer provides is spent in the most efficient and cost effective way. We must get value for money in terms of the maximum frontline hardware and defence capability and the absolute minimum of overheads and support.

Many of you will have heard of MINIS which is now being introduced in the Ministry of Defence. MINIS is not intended to be a criticism of existing MOD management. The Ministry has been a pioneer in the introduction of management and budgetary accounting systems in Government. Rather, the objective of MINIS is to expand upon and link in with existing systems to ensure that the objectives and priorities of defence policy are translated into effective programmes of action throughout the defence organisation. Managers at every level, both military and civilian, must be aware of the functions they should perform and the value of the resources with which they are charged. MINIS will provide detailed information about the MOD's activities, costs and performance. It will be the tool through which Ministers and senior managers can assess the efficiency of the organisation and decide where changes are necessary. It is not just a theoretical system for the top bureaucrats. It is intended to give managers at all levels, across the range of defence activities, a feel for the costs and performance of the resources they control. The benefits, in terms of reduced MOD overheads and more to spend on defence hardware, will be as obvious to you as they are to me.

I shall also be pursuing value for money in our massive equipment procurement – nearly £8 billion this year. Efficiency is also vital to the health of our defence industrial base. Our defence industries must be lean and fit if they are to live in the market with fierce international competition. In my judgment we need a sustained drive to introduce much more competition into the provision of equipment, its repair and other areas of defence effort. I have my own ideas about how to achieve this and I shall be working on them over the coming months. But the presumption I shall take will be on competition and dual sourcing unless overwhelming arguments point another way.

(*Address given to the RUSI on 24 June 1983*)

10 The Way Ahead: Britain's Roles

AIR MARSHAL SIR PETER TERRY, KCB, AFC, RAF

Deputy Supreme Allied Commander Europe

In this address, I shall concentrate on air aspects and attempt some conclusions about the structure of the RAF in NATO. One can, of course, only arrive at such conclusions logically by starting with a strategic perception, making assumptions about priorities and resources, taking account of what our allies are thinking and doing and, not the least, recognising that when talking about possible new priorities for the Services, none of us is starting with a blank sheet of paper as far as equipment is concerned. Change – fundamental change – takes a long time to implement. The time constraint today means that I will have to assume a lot and leave out a lot.

We would not, of course, be talking about 'Britain and the Alliance' and the roles and priorities of the Services if there was not the feeling abroad that it was time once again to pull up the defence roots to see if the plant is still living and bearing the sort of fruit we want. I must admit that I am not much of a man for 'fundamental reviews' – I have taken part in too many and been too often disappointed by the results. I am a gradualist by inclination and I also happen to think that the UK has pretty good machinery for identifying and handling the need for change and NATO's machinery is also much better than it used to be. However, it is always useful to examine the pressures for change even if the outcome confirms the *status quo*.

It is sometimes argued that the RAF specifically does not need to take a position on strategic priorities because, whether the emphasis is on a maritime or land based strategy, there will always be a major role for the RAF to play. This view does less than justice to the importance of the debate. At the end of the day, adequate affordable defence is about priorities and options, because we can never be as strong everywhere as we would wish. In this debate, the middle of the road is no place for the Air Force to be: quite apart from 'ducking' the issues, it leaves you vulnerable to traffic coming in both directions. So I shall start by nailing my strategic colours to the mast.

The first point I want to make is that I am not at all convinced that, for all the talk about problems within the Alliance, there is yet, a significant strategic dimension to them. I would not for one moment deny that there are important issues with which the Alliance has to deal – the growing threat, recently flagging or at best patchy Alliance defence efforts, lack of progress in arms control, the nuclear debate (currently Cruise and Pershing II, but I suspect with much more to come) out of area operations and, not least, the re-emergence of an assertive America on the world stage and in the councils of NATO. To be sure there are military, resource, presentational and political dimensions to all these problems, but that is a far cry from believing, let alone proving, that individually or in aggregate today's problems cast doubt on Alliance strategy or call for fundamental restructuring in Alliance defence arrangements. Having said that, unless these problems are solved, they could in time develop a strategic dimension that could shatter the structure of the Alliance as we know it today. Already the seeds are there – an unwillingness in some countries to face up to the cost implications of meeting the threat, justified concern at the slow progress of arms control, divergent attitudes on nuclear issues, and unnecessary misunderstandings on burden sharing and other matters across the Atlantic. It is not necessary nor helpful to the thrust of today's debate to take the point further. I have said enough to indicate that while we have problems and some are potentially serious problems, in essence I believe they reflect, on the one hand, a lack of consensus about how best to proceed in certain areas and, on the other, the perennial problem of resource constraints. And by the way of the world, you are not going to make progress on the latter without first solving the former. No, our problems are not problems of strategy. I would go further and simply assert that with today's constraints I cannot conceive of an acceptable alternative strategy that would offer a way out of today's resource problems by providing equivalent security at less cost. We have to succeed with today's strategy or face a substantially different future in which NATO, as the guarantor of our security, becomes progressively more fragmented and less valuable.

Within a strategic framework that is dictated by the threat, the existence of nuclear weapons and the security requirements of the Alliance there is, of course, a continual process of change, of evolution of defence forces. The relative wealth of nations changes over time and forces have to adapt. Changes in the threat or in technology prompt changes in force structures and weapons. In front of this audience I have no need to spell out Britain's current contribution to NATO. It is enough to say that it is, as it has always been, a balanced contribution and includes a nuclear element. And on the latter point, I believe most strongly that it remains in Britain's and NATO's ultimate interest for the UK to continue with an independent strategic nuclear deterrent which, to be credible, must be underpinned with shorter range nuclear options and balanced conventional forces. If we get the equation right, even if the Russians turned up in Calais having conquered Europe without triggering a NATO nuclear response, it would be a brave Russian who risked a Polaris or Trident response to any attempt to subjugate us by force. My conclusions, thus far, are that our strategy is the only one open to us, we have to join with our allies to recreate the consensus which alone can ensure it will continue to be viable and, for the UK, balanced forces including nuclear weapons are the best guarantee of our ultimate national security and survival.

What then is the place of the RAF in such a force structure and what are the trends that may alter the relative effectiveness of Air Forces in future? I do not feel that I need to argue the air defence case and particularly the air defence of the UK which has high priority for NATO, given the importance of the UK base, and even higher priority when considered from an exclusively national point of view. What the RAF is doing today in this area, is totally relevant to both NATO and national needs; we could certainly not do less and retain any confidence in our national defences. Where we can do more – such as providing more fighters – it would obviously be worthwhile. By the end of this decade, UK air defences should be in better shape than for many years and I doubt that anyone will seriously disagree with the need for that.

In the maritime area, we have made major progress in recent years in demonstrating how land based air can effectively contribute to the maritime battle – on, beneath and above the surface of the sea. Here the RAF has largely set the pace in NATO. In all areas of maritime air warfare the RAF is as capable as the best and better than most; and improvements still to come will maintain that position. If the other European members of NATO put proportionally as much effort into maritime air warfare, the maritime scene would be transformed, particularly in the Mediterranean. That they do not, is partly a matter of money and partly a matter of even more pressing priorities for direct defence on land.

On the flanks of NATO, the RAF provides offensive and transport support for UK reinforcing forces and for the UK element of the Allied Command Europe (ACE) mobile force. It is an expensive business due to the special skills and equipment that are needed for the conditions found on the flanks – especially in north Norway or east Turkey – and because of the long distances involved. The arguments for continuing such support lie principally at the political level – to demonstrate solidarity and to support nations whose only hope for successful direct defence lies in early reinforcement. But the skills and equipment developed through accepting this commitment are also essential if we are to have the flexibility nationally to intervene in operations outside Europe – as the Falkland Islands campaign so convincingly showed.

On the continent of Europe, the RAF is fully integrated into the Five Nation Second Allied Tactical Air Force of which it is also about one fifth by numbers. The RAF, as is sometimes thought, is not exclusively in Germany to support 1st British Corps, although obviously by its location immediately to the rear of the Corps, by its equipment such as Harriers and Chinook, which are important to Corps plans, and by long association, it is likely to be the preferred force to support the Corps. The RAF's specific current commitments in Germany are: a contribution to Central Region integrated air defence, met by Phantoms maintained in peacetime in Germany for air policing under the Bonn convention; helicopter and offensive air support of land forces which, in the case of the helicopters and Harriers, is likely to be provided to 1st British

Corps as a matter of priority; and with Buccaneer and Jaguars – soon to be Tornadoes – to provide offensive counter air and interdiction of the battlefield.

As you would expect, it is in the Central Region of ACE – the most densely packed and sophisticated battlefield of all – where the major challenges lie for the RAF. Helicopter and Harrier support for 1st British Corps is a well established, well practised, highly effective and an essential operation of war. I do not foresee any change in the future requirement except to do it progressively better through the normal process of aircraft and weapon modernisation and through improvements in command and control. Whether and how the RAF might get into the anti-tank helicopter business is still, as far as I know, a matter of debate within the MOD. The arguments will obviously turn on cost and effectiveness. I can only say that I would like to see the RAF take on the task, if we can afford to do it properly.

In air defence, on the continent, the RAF may well be affected by the major review of Europe's air defences now under way. The availability of new weapons systems such as the Patriot SAM, new generation fighters – F-15, 16 and 18 – and the introduction of the NATO Airborne Early Warning Force, raises fundamental questions of airspace structure and control in defence. This review may well confirm what airmen have long known, that modern air defence fighters are highly capable aircraft offering substantial improvements over their predecessors and, if they can be given the airspace in which to develop their full potential alongside modern SAM systems, then we have within our grasp the correction of one of the major weaknesses of NATO – air defence in the forward regions of ACE. Whatever the outcome of the review, adequate numbers of air defence aircraft will be essential for any workable concept of air defence in continental Europe. For the RAF the answer must lie in the eventual acquisition of an aircraft capable of both air defence in the continental environment (good radar, all weather and agile) and ground attack (good range, payload and penetrability) – in short, the proposed advanced combat aircraft now being developed with Government support as the Jaguar replacement. This aircraft – with a swing capability between air defence and ground attack – would, with similar types such as the F-16, give us a much better chance to meet and defeat an enemy air assault in the early stages of a battle, create with all the other air defences at least a tolerable air situation and then contribute to the offensive battle as priorities switched from defence to offence.

While it goes without saying that unless we win the air defence battle there can be no successful defence of continental Europe, it is also true that unless conventional offensive capabilities are improved in land and air forces there can be no chance of successful sustained defence on land. The only way that we can ultimately offset Soviet numerical superiority is being able to kill more of them than they can kill of us. There are two ways of killing the enemy – by attrition in contact at the Forward Edge of the Battle Area (FEBA) and through attrition of reserves and follow-on forces by attacks at longer ranges behind the FEBA. This latter is not a task for air forces alone and the ability to do it at all depends on introducing improvements in intelligence gathering, evaluation and dissemination which are now possible on better target acquisition systems and on the development of the more effective conventional weapons that new technology has the potential to provide.

There remains a great deal of work to be done to establish the feasibility, costs and trade-offs involved in extending the effectiveness of weapons systems into the enemy's rear areas, and we cannot expect to pay for it by cutting investment in direct defence at the FEBA; but technology is inexorably pushing land/air warfare in this general direction and we have to go down the path to see where it leads or, for sure, the enemy will be there ahead of us. In the Tornado, the RAF has a ready-made platform for this concept and the general thrust of our target acquisition and weapons development is in the right direction. It seems to me to be entirely logical and likely that if alternative and more cost effective means can be found to attack fixed targets such as airfields, other than by manned aircraft, then air forces will increasingly be used with increasing effect to attack mobile and deep interdiction targets to the obvious benefit of sustained defence on land and the level of the nuclear threshold.

Finally, in this brief review of current commitments, I must say a word about intervention forces. Not so long ago it was virtually impossible in the UK to justify additional capability against the possibility of fighting outside the NATO area. The Falklands have shown us both the dangers of having too little flexibility and the remarkable flexibility that can be achieved with comparatively minor modification to forces that already exist. One can press the Falklands point too far, but I am sure that a reasonably sized transport force (from wherever it may be drawn) inflight refuelling for most if not all aircraft and a decent tanker force are the main ingredients of sensible and affordable flexibility for air forces. But now, of course, comes the crunch. Whether or not the future emerges as I foresee it, there are always likely to be more potential commitments than cash and the opportunities for cheapening the cost of forces by specialisation and improved standardisation seem to me to offer only the promise of uncertain and long term gains, even if it is accepted that a measure of specialisation is sensible for a country such as Britain where the maintenance of balanced forces seems to be so strongly in our national interest.

For Britain, I see the rest of the 1980s as a triple challenge: a challenge to provide the resources to fulfil current defence plans; to do our best to cheapen the cost of existing forces and to apply the money saved to improving the sustainability of existing conventional forces; and to take every opportunity to exert British leadership and common sense within the Alliance to re-establish the consensus that is necessary to underpin everything else. For the Alliance, it is a time to stand firm and display solidarity. Only by so doing will we have a chance to accomplish that other goal – mutual and balanced force reductions and thereby in the longer run regain some sort of control over escalating defence expenditure.

(*Address given to the RUSI on 24 June 1983*)

11 The Maritime Extension: The Restoration of US Naval Strength

HON JOHN LEHMAN

US Secretary of the Navy

My purpose is to review with you the state of America's defence recovery – with particular emphasis on naval forces – and then discuss the key role technology plays in that recovery. Though there is good news to report, much remains to be done. Part of the reason for the good news is that we are getting a balance – at long last – in our approach to the development of military technology. As you know well, the West relies upon advancing technology to compensate for numerical weakness. In recent years, however, the cost of technology has threatened to price an adequate defence out of our budgetary reach.

My point is simply that, as we grapple with this problem, we must be wary of falling into the two extremes; first, that the more advanced the technology, the better it must be – the constrictive spiral of 'gold-plating' – secondly, that the simpler or cheaper the technology, the more cost effective it is automatically presumed to be. Lastly, I will stress that the loss of our technological advantage would bring about a strategic change of the greatest magnitude. We must not transfer to the Soviet Union unknowingly the very technological edge that helps to ensure our continued peace and security.

Let me begin with the good news. In 1981, President Reagan boldly proposed a major programme to re-order national priorities, to rebuild American military strength, and to stabilise the nuclear balance through negotiations. The President's recovery programme was founded on three objectives. First, a realistic approach based on an accurate assessment of Soviet strength and a renewed commitment to our defence alliances in Europe, in the Americas, and in Asia. Second, a well-ordered programme of defence investment based on increased current budgets not wishful promises for future years. Third, a fundamental reorganisation of defence management to break away from well-established cycles of inefficiency, waste and uncontrolled cost growth. Guided by these objectives Secretary of Defense, Caspar Weinberger, developed a balanced programme across the spectrum of strategic, theatre and conventional forces.

The military programme put before Congress at that time is now well established and on course. In fact, as Congress considers the fourth Reagan defence budget, few are fully aware of how much has already been accomplished. After nearly a decade of steady decline in budgetary resources, force structure, readiness, modernisation and personnel manning, the trends have now been sharply reversed. We can see dramatic improvement across the board, especially in those critical areas of readiness that give our forces not only fighting capability but staying power as well. A key element of America's return to strength is reacquiring clear maritime superiority in partnership with allied maritime forces.

As President Reagan said in December 1982 at the recommissioning of the battleship, *New Jersey*:

> Freedom to use the seas is our nation's lifeblood. For that reason, our Navy is designed to keep the sealanes open world-wide; a far greater task than closing those sealanes at strategic choke points, maritime superiority for us is a necessity. We must be able in time of emergency to venture in harm's way, controlling air, surface and sub-surface areas to assure access to all the oceans of the world. Failure to do so will leave the credibility of our conventional defense forces in doubt. We are ... building a 600-ship fleet ...

In stressing the importance of maritime superiority, the President was not advancing a new concept. Maritime superiority has been fundamental to NATO strategy since 1949. It remains fundamental to any strategy of coalition warfare. But for Europe, it has additional importance. NATO requires not only the unconditional control of the Atlantic lines of supply, but also control of the Northern and Southern Flanks. Soviet control of these flanks would seriously threaten, if not destroy, our capacity to defend the Central Front for any length of time. The successful achievement of NATO objectives on both flanks has, in itself, an added effect on the Central Front – for the Soviets would be forced to divert forces to their own areas adjacent to NATO's flanks, ultimately denying Moscow the advantage of concentrating all its energies against Central Europe. Thus, maritime superiority is by no means an alternative to a coalition defence of Europe, nor does it impede a strong, improved, and modernised conventional land defence of NATO. Instead, maritime superiority complements those objectives. It is, in fact, a prerequisite for the success of any defence of the Central Front. We have made great progress. The approval of the FY-1983 Navy budget last December, with its two nuclear aircraft carriers and balanced shipbuilding programme, puts the 600-ship Navy essentially in hand. We now have 518 ships – up from 479 when the Administration came into office – with 100 more currently under contract.

Any discussion of our successes, however – both as a nation and as a member of the Alliance – must be viewed in relative terms. We must measure ourselves realistically, with the integrated forces of both allies and sister services, and against the current and projected threat. Certainly one of the key elements in any such measure would be our success in maintaining a broadly-based technological lead. Unfortunately, it is in this very area – technology – that there are grounds for serious concern.

Estimated Soviet outlays for military research and development have been steadily increasing for years. These outlays now nearly double those of the United States. The Soviets have mounted a steady and persistent force expansion, which combines the historic Soviet emphasis on producing large quantities of military equipment with more recent efforts to field technically sophisticated systems. Their success in this endeavour has placed a major challenge at our doorstep.

We cannot be as certain as we once were that the quality and superiority of US and allied technology would offset the quantity of Soviet weapons; taken together, the growth of Soviet weapons in quantity and quality, have diminished the relative technological advantage of allied weapons systems. The Soviets have invested heavily in technologically-advanced platforms, sensors and weapons. The Soviet Navy, once a coastal defence force, now leads the US in numbers of surface combatants and submarines. Yet they continue to strive for further advances in sophisticated systems. The principal surface warships the Soviets are building today are among the most seaworthy and heavily armed in the world, having far greater endurance, fire power and electronics capabilities than their ships of the past.

The Soviet Navy has long led the world in the production of Cruise missiles for naval warfare. Some 70 cruisers, carriers and destroyers, about 70 submarines, 150 smaller coastal combatants and 300 land-based aircraft have an anti-ship Cruise missile capability. Their operations are increasingly integrated through long-range reconnaissance aircraft and satellite surveillance systems, using advanced communications for coordination of simultaneous strikes against surface naval targets over wide ocean regions. These capabilities have been clearly demonstrated during world-wide exercises.

To match such an enormous development programme in numbers, the US and its NATO allies would require sums far beyond today's fiscal realities, but if matching numbers is not the total answer – even when we consider the superb quality of allied personnel and equipment – then there is only one other factor which can affect the balance – technology – long a key Western strength. It has, in fact, become axiomatic that only with superior technology can we in the West remain militarily competitive.

To cope with the 'high-threat' environment today found everywhere at sea, the US Navy has rapidly transformed over the last decade from manual, analogue and loosely-coupled systems, to a fast-reaction, digital, automated and highly-integrated combat force. The four-dimensional capability of our aircraft carrier battle groups must satisfy the demand that we be able to take our forces into a very hostile environment – and prevail.

A recent US Defense Science Board Study discussed the operational readiness of high technology military systems, I found the conclusions interesting:

Notwithstanding current numerical advantages, the study said, the Soviets continue to aggressively pursue high technology applications across a broad spectrum of military applications. Given the ratio between allied and threat forces, the Alliance must continue to seek qualitative superiority through technology. Modern systems designed to meet the demands of diverse and complex missions have requirements which can only be met through the exploitation of high technology.

One of the study's principal recommendations was that we continue to exploit high technology as a continuing edge in combat capability. We must be sure that this recommendation is carried out.

The permanent inability of the allies to match the Soviet bloc in trained manpower numbers all but precludes the armchair strategists' dreams of greater numbers of simple platforms. Technology – not simplicity and numbers – will give the edge to the West. At the same time, effective use of technology will itself help compensate for lesser allied personnel numbers. As an example of increased effectiveness at lower manpower costs, the new, highly-sophisticated Aegis cruiser has a crew of only 350, compared to the far less capable cruisers of 20 years ago, which required crews of almost 1300; but Aegis is many, many times more capable. We simply must have that kind of efficiency.

Advanced technology is sometimes characterised as 'gold plating' and 'frills'. Often, however, the versatility of high technology brings about reductions in the number of units required at equivalent levels of effectiveness. The Navy's F/A-18 Hornet, for example, serves as both a strike and fighter aircraft. Accident rates for the F-18, the F-14, and similar high-technology aircraft are only about 5 per cent of what they were with the 'simple' jets of the 1950s. Their black boxes reduce maintenance hours – allowing more sorties per aircraft, and fewer personnel assigned to repair functions. All of this translates into cost savings.

Perhaps the most apt example concerning technological efficiency is the story of an Air Force bombing mission over Schweinfurt, Germany during World War II. 291 B17s participated. 60 B17s were shot down on the mission with over 600 men lost. Only 228 B17s got to the target and, due to haze and smoke, only about 10 per cent of the bombs dropped hit the target area. Today it is estimated that just eight of our new F/A-18 aircraft could fly the same mission profile and put almost all of their bombs on the target.

Availability for combat, however, is not solely dependent on system reliability. It is also dependent on the capability of the system to operate at night, in bad weather and in the hostile environment of electronic countermeasures. In most cases, simpler systems do not have these sophisticated capabilities and thus are not truly available for combat under these difficult conditions, conditions which, statistically, prevail 60 per cent of the time in northern Europe.

Some believe that current systems are not only too expensive but also difficult and costly to maintain, and less operationally available and combat ready. In most cases, the opposite is true. System performance, as a rule, has been increasing faster from generation to generation than either procurement or support costs. For systems of equivalent performance and cost, application of new technology actually increases reliability, because – although the cost per repair increases as technology advances – the frequency of repairs actually decreases to a greater degree.

The acid test of any system or theory, of course, is how it fares in actual combat. The importance of high technology in modern warfare was graphically illustrated during this past year's conflicts in the Middle East and the south Atlantic. In the air battles over Lebanon, Israeli forces achieved an 87–0 record, primarily with the sophisticated F-15 and F-16 fighters, while losing only two aircraft to surface-to-air missiles. The bulk of the kills were by radar-directed aircraft using missiles. In 1982, the Israeli success in destroying the same surface-to-air missile systems that were such a dangerous problem in 1973 can be directly attributed to application of high-technology systems. The use of the E-2C, reconnaissance drones, and anti-radiation missiles were all new factors that negated, along with superb training and tactics, this once formidable threat. Technology also played a prominent role in the Falkland Islands, as you all know well. Use of AIM-9L Sidewinder missiles accounted for 16 of 20 confirmed kills by the British Sea Harriers. The elimination of the Argentine surface Navy as a factor in the conflict by British nuclear attack submarines was a total success.

I recently observed a large Atlantic Fleet exercise that included over 70 ships of the US Navy, the Royal Navy and representation from other nations. This major training effort illustrated several technologically-advanced dimensions of modern naval warfare. The exercise included the practice deployment of fighter aircraft against incoming bombers hundreds of miles from our carrier battle groups, missiles destroying ships 50 miles away, and missiles being used to destroy incoming missiles. I was gratified to see that our tactics and equipment were up-to-date, and our naval professionals intent on mastering the complexities of today's warfare environment at sea. The Soviets, who watched the exercises closely, were probably not as pleased.

Our dependence on technological superiority raises another thorny problem – technology transfer from West to East – a serious situation, made still more so by recent trends in the military balance. As I have said – selected technology remains among our few decisive edges of military superiority in today's fragile balance. But this edge is being eroded by our own negligence.

The West has long depended on its ability to research, develop and effectively employ new concepts – of being in the forefront of applied scientific achievement. The Soviets, of course, are not blind to this. They know that much of our military and economic power lies in our steady flow of technological successes. Alarmingly, it is a stream that they have often tapped in the past – and continue to tap today – with extraordinary success.

All too often we develop, test and field new high-technology systems aboard our ships and aircraft – at enormous expense – only to learn that the Soviets have easily, cheaply, and rapidly, acquired this same technology for their own military use. In fact, it generally appears on the scene shortly after initial deployment in our own fleets. This demands, of course, that we again develop, test and field a new system superior to its compromised predecessor. Again and again we perform this costly 'technological leap-frog'. Any doubt about this trend may readily be dispelled by a chronological survey that traces the introduction of innovative military designs – such as hull types, aircraft and missile aerodynamics, and avionics and electronics break-throughs – into our allied forces, followed by a similar chronology of Soviet design introductions.

Soviet aircraft designers, for example, have long been interested in US military transports and wide-body jets, and managed to accelerate the development programmes for their

Il-76 Candid and Il-86 transports by obtaining our latest developments in this area. The Il-86 is based on the same jumbo construction processes as the Boeing 747, and the Il-76 closely resembles the C-141. The Il-76 also is used by the Soviets as the platform for their new AWACS, which is expected to be operational in the mid-1980s.

We must face the facts. The Soviet Union and its surrogates have long been embarked upon the most impressive, systematic, and calculated effort – using both legal and illegal means – to raid the free world's technological base. This effort has paid big dividends, in some instances shrinking our once eight-to-ten year technology lead to two or three years – or less.

Technology transfer is often thought of in terms of clandestine activities – and certainly much of it is exactly that – but the great bulk is legal and subtle – very hard to detect and deter. It is found in the open marketing literature of our defence industries, which often feature technical achievements derived from nuggets of militarily-critical technology provided by the government. It is found published in unclassified journals – and in scientific and student exchanges. But the most important and self-defeating of all areas of technology transfer is Soviet importation of sophisticated manufacturing technology, delivered by the foremost manufacturing firms in the free world's military-industrial complex. Much of this is done, as I said, openly and legally, often within the terms of trade agreements between the US, other Western nations, and the USSR.

The gains of the Soviets are sometimes astonishing. Not long ago, a radar project engineer for a high-technology US defence firm was recruited and paid a total of $110 000. In all, over 20 highly classified reports on future US advanced weapon systems or their components were passed over to Bloc intelligence agents. Among the classified reports, those of prime importance to the West included the F-15 look-down shoot-down radar system, the quiet radar system for the B-1 and Stealth bombers, an all-weather radar system for tanks, an experimental radar system for the US Navy, the Phoenix air-to-air missile, a shipborne surveillance radar, the Patriot surface-to-air missile, a towed-array submarine sonar system, a new air-to-air missile, the improved Hawk surface-to-air missile, and a NATO air-defence system. The information in these documents put in jeopardy existing weapons and advanced future weapons systems of the United States and its allies. Just think of the implications – cost, compromise, countermeasures.

This transfer of military and dual-use technology forces our combat professionals to face a much higher risk; in many cases they may have to contend with extremely capable weapons systems that we ourselves have developed; computer software and hardware, and microprocessing to name recent concrete examples. If it has application to military systems, its transfer spells danger to Alliance interests. In borrowing our ideas and equipment, the enormous savings to the Soviets in development costs allow them to expand production quantities of military equipments still further to threaten world peace – while our need to provide the next generation of technology that will again outpace the threat costs our taxpayers billions of dollars.

There is no reason to flinch in the face of the most brassy Soviet efforts to steal our technology. The gratifying precedent, years back, of Britain's expulsion of 105 Soviet officials has received solid reinforcement in the past few weeks with the expulsion, by the Socialist government of France, of 47 Soviet officials for and I quote, 'The systematic collection of scientific, technical and technological information, particularly in the military field'. There have also been other recent expulsions of Soviet officials in Western Europe – in Italy, Spain, the Federal Republic of Germany – here in Britain and, just days ago, in the US. These actions indicate that we are becoming more serious about this critically important issue. In fact, these actions – and the recent NATO study on the transfer topic – represent the first time in 30 years that NATO has addressed this issue directly and agreed by consensus on the damage caused thereby to the Alliance.

Western intelligence sources estimate that from one-third to one-half of all Soviet representatives in Western nations work directly for the KGB secret police or GRU military intelligence. When combined with the typically relaxed approach to information control within open democratic societies, this formidable intelligence capability can achieve alarming results. To a considerable extent, our ability to develop – and protect – our technology determines the future destinies of the Western nations. Far-sighted proposals from the allied scientific community, based on the feasible development and integration of current concepts and systems – bold attempts to make technology work at the pinnacle of our efforts for peace must be forcefully encouraged.

We must come to understand that anything dreamed by the mind of man will probably come to pass. The bold – not the naysayers – control their own futures, as history has taught us again and again. In 1940, US Naval Intelligence scoffed at the idea of the Germans developing anti-ship guided missiles; four years later they were being launched at us in the Mediterranean. Dr Vannevar Bush, the scientist who successfully convinced President Roosevelt to proceed with the atomic bomb in 1941, was a man of remarkable scope and vision yet he scoffed at the possibility of space travel. That he was wrong does not indict him – no one can reliably predict the future – but it does remind us of the compelling need to stretch ourselves in scientific exploration – to strive to maintain that vital technical edge – and to keep what we have developed secure for our own use.

In a speech to the RUSI in February 1947, that eminent British scientist and thinker, R. V. Jones, said:

> In the past war the nature of the weapons, the brilliance of our intelligence sources, and the mistakes of our enemies all weighed the balance in our favour. It may well not remain so in the future. But though the fortunes may vary, and methods change, the principles will remain the same.

In speaking about technology in his book, *Future Conflict and New Technology*, Professor Jones went on to comment that:

> Sudden changes of scale of other qualities besides numerical strength can produce dramatic effects . . . something to be anticipated whenever a major technical development is exploited. If victory sometimes goes to the side that can hold out the longest, it can also go to the side that reacts the quickest.

The dangers arising from science and technology were seen at the outset of the scientific revolution by Francis Bacon, who in his *Novum Organum* of 1620 – the year the *Mayflower* landed at Plymouth in America – correctly anticipated the charge that would be levelled against their pursuit and gave an answer that still stands:

> Lastly, let none be alarmed at the objection of the Arts and Sciences becoming depraved to malevolent or luxurious purpose and the like – for the same can be said of every worldly Good: Talent, Courage, Strength, Beauty, Riches, Light itself. Only let Mankind regain their rights over Nature assigned to them by the gift of God, and obtain that power whose exercise will be governed by Right Reason and true Religion.

The thought was put rather more succinctly by the American philosopher, Damon Runyon: 'The race is not always to the swift, nor the battle to the strong, but that's the way to bet'.

(*Address given to the RUSI on 26 April 1983*)

12 Security by Negotiation

PROFESSOR HEDLEY BULL

Montague Burton Professor of International Relations, Balliol College, University of Oxford

The negotiations about arms control and disarmament, that now occupy so prominent a place on the agenda of international politics, have as their chief purported objective the advancement of our security. There is, however, a great deal of scepticism today as to whether our security can in fact be advanced in this way. On the political right in Western countries – especially in the United States – there has occurred a resurgence of belief that our security rests chiefly on measures of defence to strengthen the West's position relative to that of the Soviet Union, that arms control negotiations are the impediments to this and that serious negotiations about them should be postponed until the West's defences are stronger. But on the political left also, the movement for unilateral disarmament expresses a lack of confidence in negotiated measures, a search for security independent of the reciprocation of measures we take by other parties.

There is, I believe, a good deal of ground for this scepticism. First, while the advancement of our security is the purported objective of these negotiations, it is not the only objective or always the main one. Arms control negotiations are always driven by political objectives – on the one hand, domestic political objectives such as that of satisfying public opinion and negotiating the problems of security are being explored; on the other hand, international political objectives, such as that of the maintenance of status or reputation or the infliction of propaganda defeats on adversaries.

The purpose of the negotiations on general and comprehensive disarmament in the 1950s and the early 1960s was to meet political objectives of this kind. The general and complete disarmament plans of those days were put forward so as to satisfy the illusions of the public that nuclear weapons and arms and armed forces could be got rid of, and also to demonstrate to other nations that one was making an effort to this end, and that the reason why no progress was made towards the goal lay in the policies of rival states and not in one's own policies. Nor has this changed today. The United States Government is surely negotiating with the Soviet Union in the Intermediate Nuclear Force (INF) talks less because it has faith that these will lead to negotiated solutions to the problem of European security than because a demonstration of willingness to negotiate is necessary to sustain European support of plans to deploy theatre nuclear forces. The United States is negotiating with the Soviet Union in the Strategic Arms Reduction (START) talks less because of belief in the possibility of negotiated alternatives to its new strategic weapons programme than because the negotiations are thought necessary to sustain domestic support for this programme, and to sustain America's international image as a nation devoted to the arts of peace.

I do not wish to suggest that concern for these political or public relations purposes of arms control negotiations is always wrong or misplaced. It is difficult to see that any government is in a position to ignore them. Arms control negotiations are a ritual aspect of modern defence policy, in which all governments in some measure are bound to engage. But their engagement is not necessarily a sign that they are pursuing security. Secondly, our experience with the SALT talks disappointed many of the hopes invested by theorists of arms control in the negotiation of formal arms control agreements. The hope was that agreements would be reached that would lead to a more stable balance of nuclear forces, and also to lower levels of nuclear forces, to actual reductions; and that even if these objectives were not reached, visible agreements between the superpowers would help to promote a process of *détente* or loosening of tension, as the Partial Nuclear Test Ban Treaty of 1963, and other measures in the 1960s, had done.

The SALT I agreements signed in Moscow by Presidents Nixon and Brezhnev in 1972 appeared to confirm these hopes. The treaty prohibiting, or virtually prohibiting, ABM systems, did appear to remove one potential destabilising threat to the stability of the nuclear balance. Nothing was done substantially to reduce the level of strategic arms. But the ABM treaty, together with the interim agreement on offensive strategic arms, did apparently demonstrate agreement on a methodology that might ultimately lead to reductions, as well as to further measures to promote stability. The idea of equality or parity in numbers of strategic nuclear launchers as the basis of negotiation, verification by national intelligence means rather than by third party or international inspection, cooperation between the parties in facilitating verification by national means or in not providing obstacles to it, joint management of the treaty system through a standing consultative committee. The 1972 agreements were also thought to have a great impetus to the process of *détente*, and were themselves put forward as part of a large package of American–Soviet agreements which aroused hopes that a comprehensive relaxation of tension between the superpowers was under way.

But after these early successes the SALT II talks, beginning soon after SALT I and leading to the agreement signed in 1979 between President Carter and Mr Brezhnev, led to disillusion. The SALT II treaty based on high ceilings of numbers of nuclear launchers and other high ceilings for (MIRVed) launchers failed to make any contribution to the central objective of a more stable strategic balance. By this time the threat to stability came not from the anti-ballistic missile but from the possibility of a disarming strike by strategic offensive forces. This possibility arose chiefly because of the development of multiple and individually guided warheads or re-entry vehicles and because of improvements in accuracy. But these were factors which the SALT II treaty failed to regulate or at least to regulate sufficiently. Nor did the SALT II treaty lead to substantial reduction of numbers. The ceilings proposed for the Soviet and American forces were immense. It was noticed that in the long years during which the SALT negotiations had been going on the American and Soviet strategic nuclear forces had grown vastly in size. It was pointed out the negotiations themselves were supplying new incentives to the increase of armaments, as new programmes of defence expenditure were agreed so as to compensate for limitations accepted under the agreement or so as to provide bargaining chips with which to strengthen one's position in the negotiations.

The SALT talks did not appear to be contributing even to the relaxation of tension between the superpowers. This was the period when American–Soviet relations were put under strain by Soviet interventions in the Third World and by a series of reverses and humiliations suffered by the United States. The strategic arms negotiations, by placing at the forefront of public debate such sensitive and divisive issues as that of whether or not the military relationship between the United States and the Soviet Union should be based on equality, and how this equality was to be expressed (issues, incidentally, which have inherently nothing to do with the stability of the American–Soviet balance or the security of the two parties). This seemed only to exacerbate the rising tension between the superpowers. It does, indeed, seem in retrospect that the promise held out by the success of SALT I was illusory. It rested on conditions which proved temporary. One of these conditions was a balance of strategic nuclear strength. The Soviet Union had built up nuclear forces enough to achieve parity with the United States in certain key industries of strength, but not yet enough to create a fear in America that its overall lead would be lost. Another temporary situation was that a limitation of numbers of strategic nuclear launchers was still significant. This was later invalidated by the fact that the centre of the arms competition shifted away from numbers of launchers and towards accuracy of missiles, numbers of warheads and survivability of launchers. A situation where verification of limitations by national intelligence means alone was possible came to be invalidated when verification became essential of limitations on numbers of warheads: this cannot be done by national intelligence means alone. Thirdly, even at best, negotiated solutions to the problems of our security cannot be sufficient in themselves. They may be an important supplement to unilateral measures of defence but they cannot be a substitute for them. The reaction against arms control that took place in the late Carter and early Reagan period was brought about in part by a feeling that arms control was being made a substitute for defence.

In the present clamour from elements of public opinion in Western Europe and the United States for negotiation we need to remind ourselves of the truth that underlay that perception. The United States government, I believe, is right to insist that while negotiated SALT or START agreements may help to make the US–Soviet balance more stable, the United States has first to ensure, by unilateral measures of defence policy, that there is a balance. If a negotiated freeze of strategic nuclear weapons deployments would in fact freeze Soviet superiority (just as President Johnson's similar proposed freeze in the 1960s would have frozen American superiority), then it is understandable that the Administration in Washington should adopt a guarded attitude. Western European opinion, in my view, places too much emphasis on the pursuit of an agreement with the Soviet Union that would make it unnecessary to deploy theatre nuclear forces. I believe that the deployment of US Cruise missiles and Pershing IIs will not in fact benefit our security and that we should seek to extricate ourselves from fostering this policy irrespective of Soviet responses.

Partly, I base this on the feeling that no land-based nuclear forces should be deployed in densely populated areas, and a feeling that in the long run we shall turn away from this course. But partly, also, I believe that the security of Western Europe at present is not assisted by the deployment of further nuclear forces that are subject to solely United States positive and negative control. The argument for Cruise and Pershing II is that these deployments will couple Western Europe more effectively to the United States. It appears to me, however, that in a period in which United States and Western European policies in the world are so divergent, Britain and its Western European partners should be seeking in some respects to loosen the arrangements to tie them to the United States, not to strengthen them. I believe that in Western Europe we do need a theatre-based nuclear counter poise to the SS-20 and other Soviet forces, both medium range and inter-continental range that threaten us.

But I believe that to provide such a counter poise we should look to nuclear forces that are controlled by European governments and serve the interests of European peoples. If we were to pursue this course of building up a European counter poise to the Soviet Union, we should certainly need to negotiate with the Russians. But we should not allow them to have a veto over the build-up of European nuclear forces to a level sufficient for adequate deterrence. We should certainly not accept the suggestion of President Andropov that there should be equality or parity between all the combined British and French nuclear forces, and simply one component of the huge Soviet nuclear arsenal, such as the SS-20 force.

The British government, I believe, has reason to view with particular scepticism the idea that arms control agreements can be made a substitute for unilateral measures of defence policy. The rationales given by British governments, both Labour and Conservative, for the nuclear force that they have sustained for so long, have been marked by the British national vice of hypocrisy. We are constantly being told that the purpose served by the British nuclear force is not any national one but that of contributing to NATO. And we are told one of the reasons for having it is so that Britain can contribute more effectively to arms control. These bogus rationales are today the source of a good deal of embarrassment. If it is indeed the case that the British deterrent contributes to NATO then President Andropov must be right in insisting that the British forces be counted along with the American ones in the INF negotiations. If the purpose of the British deterrent is to enable Britain to speak with a louder voice in favour of arms control, then this implies that Britain will be willing to enter negotiations ready to accept on her own armaments some of the reductions or limitations that she will be urging so persuasively on others.

The reality, of course, is that Britain's nuclear deterrent force serves chiefly national purposes that have little to do either with NATO or with arms control. It is, moreover, a minimum – the bare minimum – deterrent force, if not a less than minimum one. And Britain has little or no surplus to trade away in negotiations with other states. Britain's true position is, therefore, not that of a champion of arms control but rather like that of a country such as France or China which, because of the uncertain state of its own deterrent force, is basically hostile to nuclear arms negotiations. Whilst there are some arms agreements that help Britain's nuclear position – the ABM Treaty which eases the problem of penetrating Soviet defences or the Non-Proliferating Treaty that imposes handicaps only on non-nuclear weapons states while leaving early members of the club free to develop their own arms – the British deterrent is actually threatened by such possible agreements as a Comprehensive Nuclear Test Ban Treaty and INF agreement including all the forces threatening the Soviet Union, or even a START agreement that might lead to pressure on Britain to reduce her arms.

I have so far been giving you reasons why the scepticism about arms control so widespread today among the *cognoscenti* has some strong foundations. Let me now try to restore the balance by giving you some reasons why we should nevertheless remain faithful to the idea that security can be negotiated. First, the claims made originally on behalf of negotiated security by the founding fathers of arms control in the late 1950s and early 1960s never focused exclusively or even chiefly on formal arms control agreements. The basic idea of arms control was that it was cooperation in military policy between states that were antagonists but which nevertheless recognised certain common interests. These common interests were first in security and secondly in reducing the economic burden of arms competition, although it was clear that the latter was subordinate to the former. The outstanding common interest was that shared not only by the superpowers but by all peoples in the avoidance of nuclear war. The two chief proximate goals were to stabilise the United States–Soviet balance, preferably at a lower level, and to control or inhibit the spread of nuclear weapons.

Now, there were not one but three categories of steps by which these goals were to be pursued. One category was actions which, while they were unilateral or non-reciprocal, were taken to promote the common interests of both sides. The classic example of this was action to reduce the danger of war by accident or miscalculation, which although unilateral is in the interests of both sides. A longer catalogue of such steps would include various measures to avoid crises or control them if they occurred, measures such as steps to make retaliatory invulnerable, to reduce the premium on surprise attack and create an atmosphere in which decisions did not have to be taken hastily. A second category was that of so called tacit or informal agreements. The outstanding tacit agreement that underlies our security in the nuclear age is that among the nuclear weapon powers not to use their nuclear weapons, even in conflicts with lesser states. We may dispute whether or not this is an agreement, but it is at all events the pattern of the nuclear powers' behaviour, and is brought about in part by reciprocal action. The third category is that of formal arms control agreements. In the course of the 1960s, it was the negotiation of these formal arms control agreements that came to occupy the centre of public attention. It was always a surprise to me that these negotiations, first the Partial Nuclear Test Ban Treaty and other minor treaties in the 1960s, then of the more ambitious SALT agreements, came to be so central in international political negotiations as they did do. They came to take on a life of their own, sometimes remote from matters of actual security.

The attachment to parity or equality of numbers of weapons between the superpowers was itself a departure from the close consideration of security. The formal arms control agreements moreover came to be pursued for their own sake and so as to promote *détente*. The early theorists of arms control never saw these agreements as being concerned with the promotion of *détente*. When from 1963 onwards, these agreements were concluded they did have the effect of providing evidence of *détente*; but the idea of the arms control theorists was actually the contrary one, namely that the superpowers had common interests and could pursue them, even against the background of continuing political tension and of failure to resolve political disputes.

My present point is that if we look not simply at the record of formal agreements but at the prescriptions of the arms control theorists as a whole, we shall see that much of what they recommended has come to pass and has made the world more secure than it was before. The nuclear powers did move away from the view of their defence policies as concerned simply with the promotion of their own strength, and came to discipline their views with the consciousness of interests shared with the adversary. They did carry out many of the unilateral actions taken in the joint interest and enter into some of the informal or tacit understandings that were prescribed. As a result of this there did arise, in the 1960s and 1970s, an environment that was to this extent more secure. And even now in the more unsettled 1980s much of this survives. Secondly, the formal arms control agreements concluded in the period from 1963 to 1979, although they were not the main elements in our security at that time and were certainly not substitutes for unilateral measures taken by both sides, nevertheless made an important contribution. Certainly in that period the conclusion of a series of agreements and the evidence of an on going process of superpower negotiation did a great deal to bring about a restored belief in security after the anxieties that had been felt in the early period. In the Western World, public opinion became more relaxed about nuclear war and little was heard in those years from the movements for nuclear disarmament. As between the West and the East a new note of confidence and trust, at least in one another's sanity in relation to nuclear war, became noticeable. Even in the rest of the world, the superpowers were able to make credible, at least to some of the states some of the time, the idea that they were responsible custodians of nuclear weapons.

This sense of confidence and trust has now been destroyed by the policies the superpowers have pursued in the 1980s. It is possible to argue that the sense of relaxation about the dangers of nuclear war, brought about by formal arms controls in that period, was misplaced. My own view is that this is not so, that some of these agreements represented genuine advances. The ABM Treaty, for example, did not itself create the stable nuclear balance of the 1970s or even do a great deal to maintain it, but it did serve to advertise the agreement of the superpowers, even if only indirectly and tacitly, to a doctrine of stable mutual deterrence. The Non-Proliferation Treaty was not the only, or even the most powerful of the forces stemming nuclear proliferation, but it did do a lot to advertise the fact that nuclear proliferation was not inevitable and to rally some of the other forces making for control of it.

Finally let me add a few words about future policy. We shall continue to need negotiations in all of the three senses which I have mentioned: actions taken unilaterally in the common interest, tacit or informal negotiations and the pursuit of formal arms agreements. We should try to ensure when we are negotiating that security is actually the goal of the negotiations. Too much of our negotiating policy is mere pandering to public illusions about the possibility of nuclear disarmament. I believe that governments could be more honest with the public in recognising that we are bound to live permanently in a world of nuclear armaments rather than pretending that there can be some escape from them. The two chief goals of our security are still to stabilise the central nuclear balance and to control nuclear proliferation, though there will have to be increasing attention to the fact that we live in a world of five or more nuclear powers. In the START talks we should seek to resist the degeneration of negotiations about mutual security into negotiations about a balance or ratio of armaments in which the chief considerations are not about security but simply about national status or prestige. This is one of the chief lessons of the SALT period. I believe also that we should seek to place less emphasis on agreement about numbers and types of weapons and more on agreements about doctrines or philosophies of deterrence and stability. It may be too much to hope that the nuclear powers will come to share a common strategic ideology but they could develop much more common ground than they have done now. Whichever course we pursue, however, our security will still depend on negotiation, even if not on negotiation alone.

(*Address given to the RUSI on 18 May 1983*)

13 Changing Roles in the Alliance

JOHN WILKINSON MP AND COMMANDER MICHAEL CHICHESTER

If a text were the required preamble to our review of changing roles in NATO today, it would be the words of the late Alastair Buchan from his book, *The End of the Postwar Era*, published by Weidenfeld and Nicolson in 1974, in which he warned that 'NATO had come to display all the characteristics of ossification that affect any organisation – national or international, which is not regularly overhauled by strong leadership'.

The question of leadership lies at the heart of any discussion of the so-called Atlantic crisis. In the immediate post war period, when the support of the New World was invoked to redress a dangerously growing military imbalance in the Old, the leadership of the United States was unquestionably supreme in every sphere of relevance to the construction of an effective collective security system – political decisiveness, military power, technological capability, economic strength and the moral authority which derived not just from the largely American liberation of Western Europe in World War II but from its wholly American-assisted post war economic reconstruction also.

Today it is our potential adversaries of the Warsaw Pact who enjoy the advantages of a single, centralised, undisputed leadership exercised on their behalf by the Soviet Union. By contrast in NATO well over a generation after its inception, the United States' European protegés are Alliance partners who have more than come of age economically and politically and who although they choose for their mutual security and protection still to live under the same NATO roof as their American allies, have developed a very different view of their own interests and of the world strategic balance from that of the United States.

Collective security systems owe their inception to a shared perception of a common threat. In the earliest post war period such a threat to Western Europe was immediate and real. In March 1948, the defenestration in Prague of Czech Foreign Minister, Jan Mazaryk, was followed within a week by the signature of the Brussels Treaty by the BENELUX countries, France and the United Kingdom to assure that should any of the contracting parties be the object of armed aggression in Europe 'the other signatories would afford that country all the military and other aid and assistance in their power.'

However, the immediate threat lay not to the freedom of the five nations of what was to become the Western European Union but to the survival of the people of West Berlin who, within three months of the signature of the Brussels Treaty, found themselves under Soviet blockade. The shared experiences of the British and French Air Transport forces with General Lucius Clay's gallant American airmen on the Berlin airlift undoubtedly heightened the sense of Western Alliance and Atlantic partnership. Before the Berlin Blockade was lifted, the NATO Treaty was signed in Washington.

It is to be hoped that it will not be a calamity in Poland, or a *coup détat* in the strategically vital out of theatre area of the Arabian Gulf or an extension of the Iran-Iraqi war which will force upon today's collective leadership in NATO the fundamental reappraisal of the roles and responsibilities within the Alliance which is long overdue. The realities which confront NATO are profoundly disturbing: the prospects of an early agreed response to anticipate them seem alarmingly remote. After all the crucial two-tracked decision on NATO Intermediate Nuclear Force (INF) modernisation of 12 December 1979 was preceded by Soviet SS-20 deployments by a full two years. The Soviet invasion of Afghanistan was verbally condemned and provoked the wishful thought especially on the part of the French and Germans that *détente* in Europe would remain unaffected.

The imposition of martial law in Poland demonstrated, that in the chancelleries of Western Europe at any rate, the Sonnenfeldt

Doctrine still rules today. The dissociation of the European allies in NATO from the US Government's linkage of the issue of human rights in Poland with the Siberian gas pipeline, owes much of course to their perception of the paramountcy of their own domestic industrial, economic, social and political interests. However, it would be naive to pretend that West European support of the existing Eastern European order by upholding Soviet gas pipeline contracts and by rolling over the debts of Warsaw Pact countries is not influenced by an appreciation that a position of military inferiority precludes the European members of NATO from orchestrating a more assertive foreign policy which might destabilise and set in dangerous and unpredictable motion the Communist *glacis* in Eastern Europe.

However, an unprovocative foreign policy on the part of the Alliance is actually no guarantee against an over spill of Polish instability. The longing for freedom of the people in neighbouring Lithuania and Ukraine, for example, will not be diminished just because the West Europeans insist that come what may in Poland it is business as usual for them over the gas pipeline.

These contemporary European security preoccupations are, in essence, little different from those which exercised NATO planners in 1953, 1956, 1966, 1968 and 1971 crises in Eastern Europe, except that they have to be addressed in an era in which the balance of military power has shifted markedly in favour of the Warsaw Pact. In the words of General Rogers published in *Foreign Affairs*, Summer 1982, 'Instead of possessing the variety of capabilities which would truly translate into flexibility in response, NATO is left in a posture that in reality can only support a strategy more accurately labelled a delayed tripwire'.

Public opinion now appreciates that the dangerously low nuclear threshold which has ensued from NATO's inadequacy in conventional forces could mean, since NATO is a defensive alliance, catastrophe for Western Europe – as the debate over the proposed deployment of the enhanced radiation weapon showed. It is not just the Peace Movement which deplores the prospect of West Germany becoming a tactical nuclear battleground. So do NATO Defence Ministers, but they consistently fail to persuade their parliaments to vote the 4 per cent increase in annual defence spending in real terms which SACEUR now believes to be the average increase in yearly defence expenditure within NATO necessary to make credible a secure conventional defence of

Western Europe by 1988. Even the existing 3 per cent annual increase is consistently not met.

That is not all. Even if the latter day Maginot Line on the river Weser remains inviolate and deterrence holds in Western Europe, the West's interests, its economic welfare, and ultimately its security are equally affected by developments in the wider world. If seapower is the cement that holds together the North American and European components of NATO, the foundation of the whole structure of the Western economies and social order lies on the shifting sands of global access to markets and raw materials, worldwide trading and political relationships, far flung associations of economic and strategic interest.

This is the area of global grand strategy for which the Soviets have demonstrated a willingness to back the long range projection of Marxist political influence by military means specially adapted for the purpose. The Soviet Union manifestly does not limit its attempts to export Marxist Leninism to the arc of countries laying between the North Cape and the Caucasus. It does so and with much more success, worldwide, as evidenced by developments in recent years in all the continents except Australasia.

A strategy of the indirect approach is judged by the Soviet Politburo to be likely to bring better results than a direct attack upon Western Europe. By fostering subversion and surrogate expansionism in the Arabian Gulf area, the Horn and Southern Africa, Indo-China and Central America, and by building strategic bases in Afghanistan, the USSR is greatly increasing its power and political influence worldwide. Indeed the risks are less in this process than in a confrontation in Central Europe which apart from the dangers of a nuclear exchange would almost certainly precipitate the uprising against the Communist system of the captive nations which the Soviets so much fear.

If we accept that the primary threat to the nations of NATO lies in a Soviet grand strategy of the indirect approach on a worldwide basis and assume that the Western democracies with the exception of the USA continue to maintain existing projected defence expenditure of at best a full percentage point below the revised target set by SACEUR, then drastic steps will need to be taken by the NATO Alliance to make better use of its joint resources. Certainly the current economic recession and political uncertainties in Western Europe and the USA make any substantial increase in NATO defence expenditure unlikely. The immediate necessity, therefore, is for the Western Alliance to get better value from its existing budgetary allocations for defence.

There are three areas in which roles and responsibilities will have to change within the Alliance to use more effectively the joint resources of NATO which actually easily surpass those of the Warsaw Pact but which was wasted by duplication and bureaucratic inefficiency.

First, total defence should become an accepted concept for the whole of NATO and not just for its Scandinavian members. The mobilisation and effective deployment of a nation's full manpower, industrial and economic resources in time of emergency or war should be fundamental and must be pre-planned. This is the true lesson of the Falkland Islands war. Secondly, for historical and geographical reasons as well as on grounds of national interest, there are specific roles which can naturally be assigned to a particular NATO country or group of countries. Specialisation is fundamental to a collective security system in which resources are at a premium. Lastly, the West's economic and technological wealth should be pooled to create a genuinely Atlantic-wide market for defence equipment and armaments to ensure not merely standardisation on the basis of the equipment of the most economically and industrially dominant nation (which is how the Warsaw Pact operates), but on the best equipment in terms of both cost and performance regardless of the country of origin within NATO. We are advocating in essence a freer market for armaments within the whole Alliance. In some instances, a requirement will be met by a national supplier. In other cases it will be met by an offshore procurement. In others again, it will be fulfilled by a co-productive or collaborative programme on either an intra-European or US-European basis. New mechanisms for armaments cooperation are not required; certainly not new bureaucratic structures, rather instead a clear determination and will to succeed.

How should the Western Alliance tackle the problem of establishing a realistic and cost effective strategic and defence policy to deal with the world situation of the 1980s and beyond? The foregoing analysis of the political, strategic and economic realities facing the allies today points in our view to one inescapable conclusion; that this problem can only be solved by the calling of a strategic summit conference of the heads of state of all the NATO allies, including France, at which after study and discussion of a well prepared agenda agreement would be reached on four fundamental points. Firstly, the nature, the extent, and the objectives of the Soviet threat to Western interests and territories both within and beyond the NATO 'area', including an assessment on a global basis of the various strategic options now available to the Soviet Union in the development of its campaign to destroy the Western capitalist system and further the advances of international Communism. It is only by a global evaluation of the threat that the full extent of the United States commitment to deploy military power worldwide can be measured. Secondly, the scale, and type of conventional military forces required to provide a sufficient deterrent to this threat, and how and where such forces should be deployed, and what proportion of them must be kept permanently 'in place' in areas of threat in peacetime. Thirdly, how to provide these forces by organising and coordinating the whole spectrum of defence and military resources available to the allies, armed forces and reserves, civilian assets which can be utilised for military purposes in an emergency, notably merchant shipping and civil air transport, defence industries, research and development capabilities, bases and facilities; in short the allocation of 'total defence' assets so as to share the burdens of implementing a global defence policy. Fourthly, the political framework of such a comprehensive strategic plan, notably the role and responsibilities of NATO in a global defence context, and the possibility of establishing new collective security alliances beyond the NATO area, for example to underpin the northern defences of the Gulf oilfields, or to assist the USA in the Western Pacific area.

What would be the advantages of allied agreement on these matters? It would establish a division of strategic responsibilities between the USA in its role as the superpower of the West prepared to deploy military force unilaterally to counter the threat to vital Western interests outside the historic NATO area, and the European members of NATO who collectively, are equal in economic strength to the United States, but who as yet have not assumed a military role commensurate with their industrial and financial resources.

An examination of the threats facing the Alliance on a global as opposed to a theatre basis would allow the question of the defence of the NATO area as defined in the Treaty to be considered in the wider geographical context which is now required. It follows that a judgment on the relative importance of the various components and sources of the Soviet threat and on the allocation of resources to meet them would be necessary. Such a judgment is long overdue.

As regards the defence of the NATO area there would be the advantage of examining in its entirety what has become a three dimensional problem; the defence of territory along the Central Front and on the flanks, the defence of air space against long range bomber attacks and against the 324 Soviet SS-20 triple headed missiles which now threaten the whole land mass of intercontinental Western Europe as well as the United Kingdom, and the defence of the Atlantic reinforcement route and the sea approaches to Europe. Again this review of the overall threat to the NATO theatre could not be concluded without some plans on what proportions of NATO's, particularly European NATO's, limited defence resources should be allocated to countering each of the three components of the threat to the NATO area and which countries should contribute these proportions. We would have advanced a useful way along the path of military burden-sharing and possibly also of role specialisation. In our view this is the path that must be followed when the modernisation of the Alliance is undertaken.

When considering the numbers and types of military forces required for a Western global strategic plan the United States has already stated its intention to provide the bulk of the forces needed to meet Soviet threats to vital Western interests outside the NATO area, particularly in the Middle East, but it has also asked its European allies to help in this global task. There are mutterings in Washington about demands for US withdrawals from Europe if these requests for a bigger defence effort by the European allies are ignored.

Yet NATO Europe faces a dilemma here and Washington should at least recognise the fact. As we recently heard, SACEUR estimates that the NATO European countries need to increase their defence budgets by 4 per cent annually in real terms, up to 1988, merely to meet the force goals which he thinks are needed to produce a satisfactory counter to the expected level of Warsaw Pact forces in the European theatre. And the growing demands in Europe for greater spending on conventional forces so as to raise the nuclear threshold above its present dangerously low level will hardly encourage governments to spend some of their limited defence budgets on distant deployments.

In any case, in order to play any useful part in the defence of Western interests outside the NATO area, US or European forces must possess two essential qualities, flexibility and mobility; in other words the categories most suitable for this role are naval and air forces, land forces capable of rapid deployment by sea or air such as those which were sent to the Falklands, and long range air transport forces together with tankers for inflight refuelling facilities so that shore based aircraft can augment the maritime air effort. In NATO Europe today only Britain and France possess sufficient forces in these categories to be able to launch more than a token force out of area and French forces are not part of the NATO military structure.

This leaves Britain. In any modernisation of the NATO Alliance and of the military roles of its European members, we believe that British out of area capabilities should be increased and that such forces should be made available in emergency to assist the US in out of area deployments. In making this proposal we are mindful of the fact that our naval and air intervention forces are also suitable for vital tasks within the NATO area as well, in particular for the defence of the Eastern Atlantic and Channel and the reinforcement of the Northern Flank. This ability to fulfil important roles both within and beyond the NATO area makes them a particularly cost effective component of Britain's armed forces and one which should receive a greater proportion of the defence budget than is likely if the conclusions of the 1981 Defence Review remain unaffected by the post Falklands War Defence White Paper. Any plan for burden sharing and role specialisation amongst the Western allies must initially be aimed at making the best use of existing resources and organisations to meet the new situation. It must also accept the political realities within the Alliance and the limitations that they inevitably impose in the search for the ideal solution.

For this reason we consider that in the setting of a global grand strategy for the West, NATO should remain in its present form, responsible for the defence of the NATO area, but, it should recognise that threats to the vital interests of its members, particularly its European members, now exist outside the official limits of its area and that its members may consider it necessary to deploy forces to deal with these threats. This situation does not yet call for any formal extension of the NATO area nor for the establishment of new NATO command organisations but we recommend that in both the supreme headquarters of the Alliance the joint contingency planning teams which prepare plans for out of area deployments by NATO forces, should be strengthened.

In its superpower role, the US should accept that it is unrealistic to expect any more formal commitment from its European allies to help in its global tasks bearing in mind the need, which we have discussed, for any increases in continental European defence budgets to be devoted to the defence of the Central Front and the flanks. Conversely, NATO Europe must accept that the 4 per cent increases required during this decade will be seen by Washington as proof that Europe is doing its best and that US deployment to Europe in peacetime need not be increased.

We come now to another reality which soon must be squarely faced in preparing any new strategic plan for the Alliance. Britain will, before long, be unable to afford to continue to the full her traditional range of nuclear and conventional roles in NATO. The imbalance in the size and capabilities of armed forces which her heroic but outdated efforts to continue with, is bad for the Alliance and bad for Britain. Her share of the future military burdens of the Alliance must become more concentrated, and less diversified, less multi role and more specialised. How can this be achieved? First by renegotiation of the Brussels Treaty commitment by the UK to maintain four divisions and a tactical air force permanently in Western Europe in peacetime until 1992. The political situation which gave rise to this commitment has long since ceased to exist and in today's strategic situation, there are commitments of even greater importance to British security than this increasingly expensive static and inflexible contribution to the defence of one sector, albeit a vital one, in the NATO frontline. Secondly, the British government should explain to NATO more forcefully than it has done in the past that the assignment to the Alliance of the British strategic nuclear deterrent force represents a primary British contribution to Alliance military power and that whilst the modernisation of this force is under way there will eventually be limitations on the size of her conventional contribution to NATO war plans, unless the defence budget in future years grows more than is currently projected.

Let us now bring all these pieces together and describe the outlines of a plan for modernising the Alliance. The US will provide the bulk of the forces needed to counter Soviet strategic expansion and threats outside the NATO area. Provided her European allies do indeed increase their defence spending as SACEUR demands and so relieve the US of the need to increase its deployments to Europe, Washington should accept that for the next few years at least, with the possible exception of Britain and France, her European allies will be unable to maintain forces for intervention out of area in peacetime. But this should not preclude, as we have mentioned, NATO contingency planning to cover the possible out of area deployment in an emergency of SACEUR's Allied Mobile Force, or elements of it, or of NATO's naval and air forces.

The defence of the NATO area should be organised so as to share its burdens amongst the European allies in the most logical and cost effective manner and on the assumption that the level of the US contribution will remain static. The defence of the Central Front and of the flanks against an offensive by land and air forces will become the prime responsibility of those NATO members whose territories are situated within the confines of the European mainland and this task will be the first priority in their defence budgets.

The British role in NATO war plans will be redesigned to take account of her unique geostrategic position as an offshore island base of major importance to the Alliance in war, of her maritime capabilities and her responsibility for the defence of the ocean approaches to Europe (a responsibility which no other European NATO country can easily assume), and of her possession of air mobile and amphibious intervention forces which can be used throughout Western Europe or out of area if needed.

Britain's new look armed forces for the 1990s should therefore be built round four core elements. Firstly, maintenance of the most powerful naval and maritime air forces in Western Europe responsible for the defence of the East Atlantic and Channel and for Northern Flank reinforcement, and also able to operate out of area. Secondly, sufficient air forces to defend the UK base and its surrounding air space, support land forces in the European front, and provide adequate numbers of maritime patrol, AEW and strategic transport aircraft with enough of the latter to lift a brigade group and supporting units over long distances. Thirdly, an army in which the rapid deployment and intervention forces and their tactical air transport element and offensive air support form a greater and the armoured forces a smaller proportion of the whole than is the case today. Fourthly, adequate defence of the Home base and a strong Territorial Force and Reserves of all three Services.

Britain would of course maintain her commitment to reinforce the Northern Flank and also the Central Front in Europe in emergency or war and as token of this intention would maintain a land force of some two divisions in West Germany in peacetime and a Tactical Air Force based on the three clutch stations west of the Rhine. These forces would have minimum civilian support, they would preferably serve on unaccompanied tours, and be augmented by Royal Auxiliary Air Force Squadrons and Territorial Army Units in time of emergency or war which would also deploy in Germany regularly in peacetime thus providing valuable training opportunities which will be hard to provide in UK.

Here is a plan which faces the realities of today and which should therefore improve the prospects of the Alliance, but any realistic plan will require some major changes in the roles of the NATO European countries, particularly the British role. On the degree to which this inescapable fact is accepted will depend the future health and usefulness of the Atlantic Alliance but it will be reform and rationalisation by agreement and consent. We seek to present no *fait accompli* on our allies.

We must recognise that it is unlikely that the Alliance will find sufficient resources, particularly if the present economic recession continues, to provide the extra 4 per cent per annum in real terms which is needed for NATO to assure a secure defence on the basis of the current strategy with a high nuclear threshold. Even today, a measure of national specialisation exists within NATO. The British and French independent nuclear deterrents are one example, the French and British blue ocean navies are another, the British amphibious forces are a third example, the preponderance of the German Army on the NATO side on the Central Front is a further example.

Interdependence is already the principle upon which the collective security of the members of the NATO Alliance is founded. If we Europeans assign to our American allies, as we do, the supreme responsibility for providing the nuclear guarantee of our ultimate survival as free and democratic nations why should we cavil and complain about a further agreed specialisation of national roles and responsibilities at a conventional level?

Of course individual member countries will for reasons of strategic prudence and domestic politics wish to keep a sound degree of balance within their armed forces but it is undeniable that the logic of their existing capabilities and force dispositions leads already to certain clear conclusions. Only the French, Dutch and British navies are capable of major out of area deployments. Without a strong *Bundeswehr*, the Federal Republic of Germany would be indefensible. Unless the Royal Navy and Royal Air Force can assure control of the Channel, Eastern Atlantic and UK Air Defence region command areas, the whole reinforcement plan for Western Europe from North America in time of war would be imperilled.

As no one can realistically envisage the European members of NATO rebuilding the network of global bases they enjoyed in the 1950s and 1960s, out of area intervention will have to be executed by forces which they already assign to NATO. As far as the British Army is concerned tanks in Germany are not ideal for this purpose, whereas a ready constituted airborne brigade with appropriate air transport, inflight refuelling and offensive air support would be. It would also much enhance SACEUR's Allied Mobile Force.

Furthermore as the resources to ensure an effective conventional defence for Western Europe will continue to be limited, a strategy based on mobility, fire power and flexibility is essential. For a defensive alliance this must put a premium upon the importance of air forces which are the most appropriate medium for concentrating fire power rapidly at the decisive point.

Finally we must all within the NATO Alliance realise that only the complete mobilisation of the full potential of the resources of our civilian economies in emergency or war can make good the inadequacy of our combined budgetary provisions for defence in time of peace. Preplanned and well exercised total defence which will involve the wealth of talent and the rich diversity of skills in our highly advanced pluralist industrial societies would put the NATO nations at a great advantage against the centrally planned and bureaucratically directed socialist countries of the Warsaw Pact.

The Western Alliance needs a global perspective more than ever and a wide imagination. The convenience of familiarity must never be the justification for preserving an outdated and ossified strategy. The variety of the skills and expertise within the NATO Alliance is its greatest strength. New goals, new strategies, new force levels, new tactics and new contigency plans are required to adapt the Alliance to the realities of the Soviet global challenge. If they are brought to fruition the menace of Soviet influence worldwide in the 1980s and 1990s can be resisted by the NATO meeting as successfully as was the immediate post war Soviet threat to the heart of Western Europe on the Central Front.

(*Address given to the RUSI on 10 November 1982*)

14 NATO's Forward Defence: New Strategy

D. R. COTTER AND DR N. F. WIKNER

A provocative seminar held at the RUSI on 9 March 1983 gave rise to much discussion in the continuing debate about the way the NATO Alliance can meet the overwhelming superiority of the Warsaw Pact (WP) forces facing it along the borders of the Federal Republic of Germany (FRG). The speakers, D. R. Cotter, formerly Assistant for Atomic Energy to three US Secretaries of Defense, and Dr N. F. Wikner, former director of the SALT Task Force and Scientific–Technical Director for the US Defense Nuclear Agency, were well prepared for conducting the seminar, both having had long experience with the problems of nuclear weapons, employment, and defence. They provided a background to the growth of the Pact's present advantage, an explanation of Pact strategy and its necessary vulnerabilities, and a proposal now widely discussed in NATO for an 'integrated concept for the forward defence of Western Europe'.

This 'integrated concept' recognises the inherent limitations of traditional NATO defence plans (in the event of an attack NATO would have to destroy much of Germany to save it, a defence hardly likely to endear itself to the FRG). The speakers' proposal would put at risk all echelons of the WP forces, *on Pact territory*. Taken together with the remarks made at the RUSI by General Bernard Rogers, SACEUR, by General F. M. von Senger und Etterlin (both reproduced in this volume) and the debate about the US Army doctrine, ALB 2000, this seminar offered some possible solutions to the difficulties facing NATO's planners.

Forward Defence: New Strategy

Despite the confusion created by the unilateralists and despite the successful propaganda of the Soviet sabre-rattlers, the facts remain that the Alliance is outgunned in Europe. The imbalance is preponderant. Including all land-based missiles, for example, the existing Warsaw Pact advantage is five-to-one both in warheads and aggregate yields. And that ratio does not reveal the whole story. About 60 per cent of NATO's tactical nuclear weapons have a range of 15km or less; thus, most would have to be exploded in West Germany if NATO's forward defence were not able to stop a massive Soviet attack – a likely possibility with only 26 divisions to oppose the WP's 110 divisions facing NATO.

The Alliance has but 180 missiles (108 US Pershing I plus 72 under *Luftwaffe* control) in the medium-range category (700km), insufficient to put Soviet second and third echelon forces at risk or to threaten Soviet territory. In contrast the Pact – with forces now in-being – can blanket Europe and the United Kingdom with nuclear explosions covering 85 per cent of all NATO territory or destroy population centres three times over. Further, WP aircraft surpass NATO's in number and range; its ground attack aircraft outnumber the Alliance's by three or four to one. With those sorts of threats confronting them, NATO's planners have been faced with a nearly overwhelming challenge.

As early as 1974, NATO's Nuclear Modernisation Programme was prepared to answer the questions, 'How can NATO deter Soviet/WP aggression and raise the threshold at which nuclear weapons would be employed, especially when the WP has superiority in both theatre nuclear weapons and conventional forces?' The answers were, briefly, firstly, to improve NATO's conventional capabilities and secondly, to improve the NATO nuclear force's ability to survive a mass attack and still operate effectively. The programme – not yet carried out – aimed at increasing the percentage of intermediate and long-range strike systems and at significantly strengthening conventional forces. This most recent proposal is a continuation along the same lines but with greater emphasis on deeper strikes and on conventional non-nuclear munitions.

The proposed changes to NATO thinking have two aspects: strategic and logistic. They will require NATO forces to continue to defend forward but will now recognise the need to strike deep in Pact territory to prevent Pact reinforcement or exploitation of massed armour. This thinking is at once both new and timeless.

TABLE 5: *Comparison of existing NATO/Warsaw Pact Land-Based Surface-to-Surface Warheads in Europe (Aggregate Yield in Approximate Megatons)*

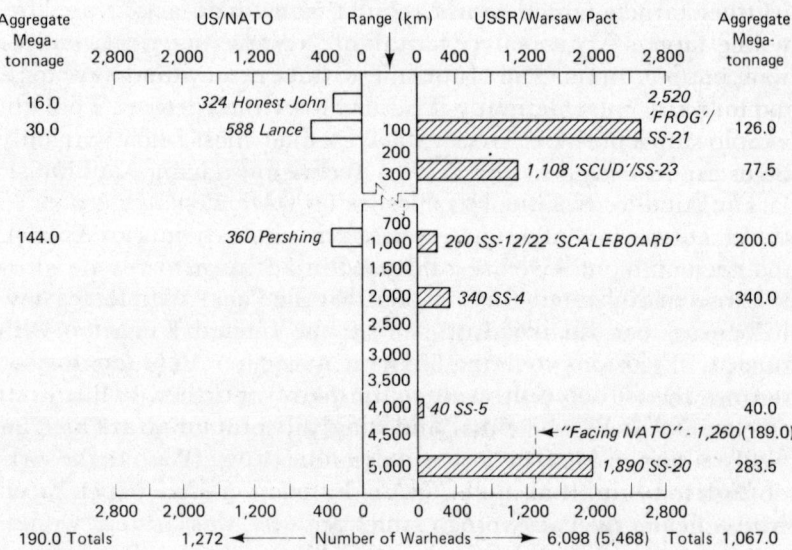

Existing Warsaw Pact advantage = 5 to 1 in warheads and megatonnage

Take the threat to the enemy, fight on his soil, disrupt his sanctuary. Two targets of this strategy are relatively simple to plan: the Main Operating Bases (MOB), which support Pact offensive air operations against NATO's rear areas, and the bridges and natural 'choke-points' in the Pact lines of communication – those bottlenecks in any attack through which their reserve echelon and follow-on forces must move. Both classes of targets are 'time-urgent'; the air bases and interdiction points must be struck within the first day if NATO is to survive. Doing so requires an all-weather and night capability in the designated weapon.

If those attacks, especially on the MOBs, are successful, the theory is surviving Pact aircraft must return to dispersed operating bases (DOB), less well-defended and relatively bare of hardened aircraft shelters, and, therefore, vulnerable to attack while on the ground. Similarly, second and third wave Pact aircraft would be forced to the by then overburdened DOBs, sitting targets for attack by aircraft or missiles.

Other targets which would require immediate action are the mobile targets – manoeuvre battalions, reserve troop concentrations, support units. The problem is to have accurate surveillance and targeting information systems to allow timely strikes. Though complex, the problem is solvable. Despite high mobility, Pact forces are restricted to well known avenues of advance and must pass inevitable choke-points, becoming stationary targets for a significant amount of time. Because these choke-points are known and predictable, they can be targeted in advance.

Those who present this proposal believe that the strategy of dedicating massive strikes to the second and third echelon WP forces will have two effects. First, it will deter Pact aggression because the threat of destruction of follow-on forces (while first echelon attackers, about 20 per cent of the total force, are held in check or turned back by forward defenders) would make the risk too high to begin. If, despite certain destruction of the second and third echelon, the Pact were to attack anyway, this strategy would prevent them from exploiting any breakthroughs, for there would be no operable forces to pour through the gaps the first wave had created. Second, this strategy would raise the nuclear threshold because it calls for employing conventional, non-nuclear weapons, but weapons with new capabilities, new destructive power, new technology. Such weapons, their proponents say, will give NATO 'conventional equivalence' to the Pact's overwhelming conventional force, but achieving that equivalence depends on carrying out the proposed upgrading (the spokesmen are careful not to call it an increase) of the Alliance's forces.

The success of the integrated strategy depends on three requirements being met: adequate surveillance and targeting information, survivable command structure and operations forces, and new weapons. The new weapons, all in-being if not in production, are essential, planners say, if the conventional deterrence is to work.

The ground forces require a Multiple Launch Rocket System (MLRS) with a range of about 30–50km to destroy enemy armour and troop concentrations in the forward area. To provide longer range cover, a Corps Support Weapon System (CSWS) with a range of about 300km would be employed to destroy second echelon and follow-on units. Deployed at the rate of one battalion per corps, these forces would have 72 missiles on launchers for quick response, in part replacing some of NATO's quick reaction aircraft. They would be armed with conventional search-and-destroy-armour (SADARM) or area denial submunitions.

NATO's air forces would require two sorts of new weaponry: a Standoff Attack Weapon (SAW) with a range of 18–35km and a Conventional Standoff Weapon (CSW) with a range of about 300km. Like those of the ground forces, airborne weapons will be 'smart' with a variety of submunitions for anti-armour, area denial, or airfield suppression missions. Such systems as West Germany's MW1 submunition dispenser used on the Tornado, the Hunting Engineering JP233 or Thomson-Brandt BAP-100 on various aircraft for runway breaking, are already in the pipeline to be operational this year.

Total costs for the new equipment and weaponry are estimated to be roughly $10bn to buy the hardware and to pay the personnel costs for 10 years. Planners argue that much of that cost could be paid by savings resulting from the increased efficiency of the new weapons. For example, they reckon that 2200 aircraft sorties are required to make a Pact division ineffective if 500lb free fall bombs are used, but only 300 sorties using the MW1 submunitions dispenser or 50–60 sorties using guided, sensor fuzed submunitions. That amount of money is also about what NATO is currently spending to modernise its Theatre Nuclear Force, including about $3bn for Pershing II and $4bn for the Ground Launched Cruise Missile (GLCM). One argument its proponents make for the new strategy is that if the West is to raise the nuclear threshold it ought to spend at least as much on updating the conventional force as it is on the nuclear force no one wants to use. In his speech to the RUSI, General Rogers suggested that the new strategy 'would not cost as much' as its critics suggest; he added that if NATO members increased their defence spending by as little as 4 per cent the Alliance could put this strategy in effect.

Should this strategy and its attendant conventional force upgrade be adopted, the implications affect both the military and political sides of NATO. The new weapons and the strategy to employ them would provide NATO with forward defence capabilities using non-nuclear weapons that approach the destructiveness of low yield nuclear (2–5 kiloton) weapons. That increased capability would thus provide a credible, conventional deterrent without resort to nuclear weapons, thus raising the threshold.

By reducing the need for large numbers of nuclear warheads, the West stands to benefit politically from the new strategy. If some of the munitions were put aboard helicopters, for example, the Alliance could well lower its defence profile, thereby reducing the ojections of many of the vociferous opponents to the current, high-visibility defence force.

Militarily, the integrated force strategy compounds the problems of WP planners by adding to the numbers and kinds of targets, by reducing NATO's dependence on airfields, by making more doubtful the success of a massive attack. In these ways, the conventional upgrade would be profoundly effective.

Whatever the benefits, however, one must ask questions about the strategy that calls for expending major portions of the defensive force on second and third echelon units. How are the 20 per cent of the WP forces that would be committed to an attack to be defeated? How can a commander commit an attack on the second or third echelon if frontline defenders are in desperate positions? Despite the effectiveness of the new standoff weapons or the MLRS, their kill rate substantially declines over distance; how much more efficient would the new weapons be if employed against forward echelons of an attacking force rather than on the second or third? Other than WP main operating bases which must be destroyed if NATO is to survive the first 24hr, would the new munitions and their targeting systems be more accurate, more deadly, at close ranges, employed to prevent a massive attack from developing any momentum? If second echelon choke-points are susceptible to planned targeting, are not first echelon attack points equally vulnerable? It is possible this strategy will result in the destruction of reserves and follow-on units but leave the main attack force relatively unscathed? Is this strategy merely another fashionable theory of defence or is it a way to meet the legitimate needs of the Alliance to provide a credible deterrent? Questions like these and many more must emerge in the next few months as the debate about the best use of finite resources is joined. Its proponents believe that upon the answers to these questions and the implementation of the integrated concept our survival depends.

TABLE 6: *High Value, Time-Sensitive Targets in Central Region*

Mobile Targets	Range (km)					
	0–30	30–100	100–200	200–300	300–800	Total
Manoeuvre Units	409	124	294	96	198	1,121
MR, Tk, and Arty Bns	423	8	30	6	96	563
Tactical Ballistic Missiles	256	120	84	12	84	556
('Frog', 'Scud', 'Scaleboard')						
Critical Logistic Support	–	9	6	2	3	20
Total Mobile Targets	1,088	261	414	116	381	2,260
Total Fixed and Mobile Targets – 2,685						

(*Report of an Address given to the RUSI on 9 March 1983*)

15 New Operational Dimensions

GENERAL DR F. M. VON SENGER UND ETTERLIN

Commander-in-Chief, Allied Forces Central Europe

It is tempting within the framework of the theme 'the Atlantic Alliance: Realities and Prospects' to discuss some new dimensions which have arisen in the fields of strategic study, such as the growth of Soviet sea power which threatens increasingly our lines of communications across the Atlantic, or the threat against the oilfields via the Indian Ocean. For me, as the planner responsible for the military security of Central Europe, neither of these threats warrants any weakening of the Alliance's efforts to ensure the defence of what will be the enemy's, and therefore our own, point of main effort, the Central Region. It might be tempting as well to speak about new dimensions of air operations in depth against the enemy's follow-up forces, contributing thereby to the continuing discussion on how to afford the sophisticated weaponry needed to improve our capability for that purpose. That, however, is not so much an operational, let alone a strategic, problem, but rather one of cost or cost-effectiveness.

Having limited myself in this way, therefore, I intend to discuss certain new dimensions of operational planning, which seem to me not to have been given the timely and energetic attention they deserve within our introspective Central European nations, with the exception – I must say – of the French, whose Minister of Defence has recently highlighted them with splendid clarity. These new dimensions appear to me to present us allies with growing demands and challenges for the future in the context of the development of operational concepts which lead to force requirements.

Military history records many examples in which the possession by one side of either superior mobility, or superior fire power, has been the cause of its successful operations, if not victory, in war. However, cases when both these two factors of superiority have been combined are indeed relatively rare and when it has happened an overwhelming victory has usually been the result. But all too often in history we find examples where developments in the military application of advancing technology were not transferred into tactical or operational concepts by the military leaders of that time. One famous example which comes to mind was the improvement in fire power which had taken place up to 1905, and which was demonstrated in that year in the Russo-Japanese war, when the infantry on both sides became bogged down in trench warfare. In spite of that evidence, European military leaders in 1914 let their infantry and cavalry march and ride into rapid fire from well-protected positions with devastating results.

Another example from recent history was the failure of many Western nations to make the most of the enormous quantum leap in combat power which was available through the mechanisation of large land force formations in the armies of the 1920s and 1930s, a mechanisation which offered a five-fold increase in mobility combined with advances in technology which had substantially increased fire power and extended it further by the application of tactical air power in direct support of ground operations.

In 1930, General Summerall, the US Army Chief of Staff, said and I quote:

> The extreme progressives foresee the Army of the future composed solely of air forces of much greater power than those heretofore known and ground forces endowed with high mobility by automotive means, capable of rapid movement both on road and cross-country under armoured protection, and equipped with high-powered automatic weapons including chemical warfare appliances.... A more moderate view concedes the value of a mechanised force as a powerful mobile auxiliary, but maintains that mobility and shock action have never been the sole qualities sought in a military force and that

a force endowed with high mobility must necessarily make a great sacrifice of fire power in favour of rapidity of movement. As in the past we did not have armies composed exclusively of cavalry, so for the future we do not foresee a completely mechanised army.

My point in giving you this quotation is not so much to draw attention to Summerall's failure to endorse a completely mechanised army, but rather to illustrate an example of an inability to perceive an opportunity to combine fire power and mobility in a decisive and battle-winning way. I should also say, in defence of General Summerall, that his views were shared at that time by many of his contemporaries in other leading countries.

In the USSR also at the beginning of the 1930s, the Soviets had formed numerous large motorised corps comprising all arms which could be employed not only tactically but also operationally, and independently from the rest of the conventional army of those days. They had produced a large fleet of combat vehicles, with which they held division and corps-size field training exercises on such a scale that Western observers could hardly believe their eyes – to the extent that they believed they were being deliberately deceived like Catherine the Great when she was being shown 'Potemkin villages'. But by the year 1937 the Russians had broken up, dispersed, and disbanded the majority of these large motorised formations and distributed the remainder piecemeal amongst their army, which consisted mainly of infantry *en masse*. The reason for this suicidal action was a wrong appreciation of the lessons to be learned from minor wars which had just taken place at that time, such as the campaign in Abyssinia, and the Spanish Civil War. In the second of these, the major military powers had only been involved with experimental task forces and, due to its political, financial, geographical and technological circumstances, it was a war of limited scale. The lessons learned from such limited size, predominantly infantry actions – in support of which the majority of tanks in Spain had been employed – were wrongly projected to the tactical and higher operational levels.

Through erroneous evaluations such as these, those responsible for military planning failed to give their armies that deterrent value they could have had against the aggressive intentions of Hitler's Germany.

That is enough of a historical reminder of the effects that a right or wrong appreciation of changing technological possibilities can have on an Army's mobility and fire power. However, such examples do help to focus our attention on a similar situation which is becoming apparent in the West today. Applying very simple, perhaps over-simplified, criteria, it could be said that most armies worthy of consideration have now reached a stage of full mechanisation, following the evolutionary stage of motorisation. Certainly that is true of the opposing ground combat forces in Central Europe, the area with which we are concerned today. The battlefield mobility of these ground forces has increased from 4 to let us say 20km per hour. Rather a modest figure in this advanced age of space travel. And yet at the same time fire power has increased enormously. But, as I pointed out in my introduction, superiority in one factor has seldom guaranteed decisive success and only the combination of superior mobility and superior fire power have provided the military leader with the means for decisive operations.

We are faced, in the Central European theatre, with a numerically superior adversary. An adversary who is likely to try to achieve rapid penetrations in our long defensive line. An adversary, who, in pursuit of this aim is apparently developing the concept of operational manoeuvre groups and air assault troops and, in so doing, combining mobility with fire power. How can we in NATO with our numerically limited resources best meet this threat? The answer lies in matching our increased fire power with a significant increase in mobility, perceiving now the possibilities for tomorrow offered by technology today.

It is my contention that it is an air vehicle which offers us such possibilities, whereas a vehicle tied to the ground does not. Here I must stop to make it clear that I do not mean the transport aircraft in the conventional sense, nor do I mean the transport helicopter, both of which are certainly useful means of increasing operational mobility. Troops similar to those from yesterday's armies, that is before the era of full ground mechanisation, can indeed very quickly be transported by such air transport. However, once such a move has ended, these troops are still of limited tactical capability. They are much less mobile and protected than mechanised forces. A combined arms battle cannot be brought to a new tactical dimension by this admittedly speedy, but still limited mobility. Operations against a fully mechanised enemy by unsupported light air transported formations should not even be considered. We should not be misled either by some of the lessons learned from the Vietnam War, a war which was limited from a political and military point of view as well as being unusual with regard to terrain and opposing forces.

The fixed-wing transport aircraft and the transport helicopter therefore are not the technological means we are looking for. What we are looking for rather is some way to make it possible to step from the intermediate stage of 'airmobility' to what I call 'air-mechanisation'. The means of transport must become a means of combat.

The US Army was among the first to pursue this idea and they developed the attack helicopter. Today's technology offers possibilities which obviously reach far beyond the present type of attack helicopter. We can assume that, in the medium term future, an air vehicle is technically feasible, which could have the necessary characteristics we are looking for. Many variations are possible. In simplified terms it could have:

Maximum speed about 300km per hour.
Cruising range about 600km.
Payload about 2 tons; primarily weapons systems.
Continuous hover capability.
Take-off/landing capability in any terrain.
IFR very low level flight and night combat capability.

The main disadvantages of helicopters or their successors are often stated as being the high logistic penalty and their vulnerability to attack from the air and from the ground. With regard to vulnerability, fast helicopters with a high climb, dive, and turn capability are a very difficult target for most modern jet fighters. In conditions where air defence systems have reached a high stage of development, as is the case in the Central European theatre, it is thought that modern air vehicles of the type I have described could have a good chance of survival when operating using ground cover and within the protection of these air defence systems. There would, however, be a clear need to provide air cover for these air vehicles whenever they were manoeuvring *en masse* in the positioning phase of an operation. There should be no need to subject them to the real danger of the enemy's forward ground-based air defence weapons since there does not appear to be any necessity to commit them over enemy-held territory.

The high logistic effort that would be required is not unlike the situation with developing ground mechanised forces. All technological progress has to be paid for by a higher logistic effort. This has to be off-set against the substantial increase in combat effectiveness which such progress affords.

The many advantages offered by this new dimension would include a ten-fold increase in deployment speed compared with any given land weapon system or formation. There would also be an almost unlimited capability to disperse, in the depth of a theatre or region, whilst on the move, and on the battlefield itself. Compared with land mechanised forces, there would be a superiority in the capability to concentrate fire power quickly. Furthermore, great flexibility could exist in the choice of weapons to be attached to the system. Our air vehicle could be armed with all sorts of armament, whether for area saturation or for precision attack against small, even protected targets. A suitable name for this air vehicle might be the Main Battle Air Vehicle (MBAV), and that is how I will refer to it during the rest of my talk.

A word now about the general concept. If the potential of the new dimension I have alluded to is to be fully exploited it will depend on finding a general concept of employment and organisation for a new type of formation. Many attempts have been made in the recent past to achieve viable concepts since the days of the Howze Board with the Tricap Trials in Fort Hood. Currently the American forces include the 101st Air Assault Division, which consists mainly of light airmobile infantry – some nine battalions – and its own integral combat support including a substantial helicopter component: it is also planned that US armoured divisions Type 86 are to have one attack helicopter brigade each; also of considerable interest to us is the 6th Combat Brigade Air Cavalry, which as many of you will know is a highly mobile armour defeating manoeuvre force. It is a powerful formation consisting of 2500 men and over 150 helicopters including large numbers of attack helicopters, but primarily it has an anti-tank role operating in support of conventional ground forces. In addition I should mention that the French also are progressing with their current ideas on the *Force d'action et d'assistance rapide (FAAR)*. These then seem to be the significant attack and assault helicopter concepts amongst Western countries. The general picture is, however, one of separate national development and my idea is that we should take these concepts a stage further as an integrated effort, a pooling of resources, by NATO and its main allies, in order to exploit fully the new dimension.

Learning from the lessons of history we need for our general concept to establish two general principles: one for organisation and the other for employment. The first general principle with regard to organisation should be not to scatter the new forces amongst the old but rather to concentrate them in independent large formations. The basic formation should be tactically and logistically autonomous, and, as a truly Airmechanised Force, use the MBAV as its main weapon system.

With regard to the second general principle, that of employment of the force, the ten-fold increase in mobility, coupled with the multi-role fire power capability, demands that the new doctrine for the tactical and operational employment of these new forces should be separated from the tactics and operations prescribed for the old conventional land mechanised army. This new doctrine should encompass fighting under all conditions of weather and terrain in all types of war, nuclear and conventional, and all types of combat, attack as well as defence and delay. I will deal in more detail with concepts of employment later, but first a few words on the detailed concept of organisation for our Airmechanised Force.

The basic formation should be the tactically and logistically autonomous Airmechanised Brigade (Figure 1). Organic specialist company-size units within the brigade are to provide intelligence and reconnaissance, anti-aircraft protection, and an anti-helicopter capability. The basic combat units should be two attack battalions each of about 24–28 Main Battle Air Vehicles, grouped in companies of some six to seven MBAVs each plus the necessary headquarters command and observation air vehicles. The tactical autonomy of the Airmechanised Brigade is to be achieved by it being independent from any ground forces which do not belong organically to the brigade. The Airmechanised Brigade may, however, need to have supporting infantry elements within the foreseeable medium term future so as to overcome as far as possible the existing limitations of helicopters, especially in night fighting and in the ability to hold ground for longer periods of time. These infantry elements would need to have an abundance of long-range anti-tank guided missile weapon systems of

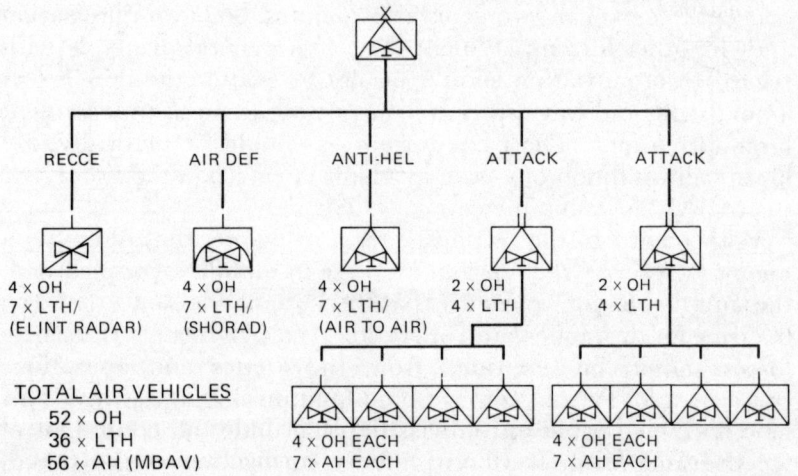

The symbols do not necessarily conform to any standardised NATO or nationally agreed system.

the TOW or HOT vintage with a night fighting capability, and should be grouped into Airmobile Brigades. The lack of armoured protection, and the resulting vulnerability, of these airmobile brigades must be counter-balanced by a high degree of mobility using organic transportation helicopters. The necessary airlift for the airmobile brigades, and for the logistic support needed by both types of brigade, would be provided by a helicopter Airtransport Brigade, consisting of about 60 transport helicopters, with the capability of lifting one battalion in one lift. In summary, therefore, of the organisational concept, these three types of brigade, the Airmechanised, the Airmobile, and the Airtransport, should, as a logical step then be grouped into logistically and tactically autonomous Airmechanised Divisions (Figure 2).

Returning now to the employment concept in more detail, I must first explain that the force organised and employed according to the two general principles I have already mentioned should have the following detailed tactical characteristics. The Air-

New Operational Dimensions

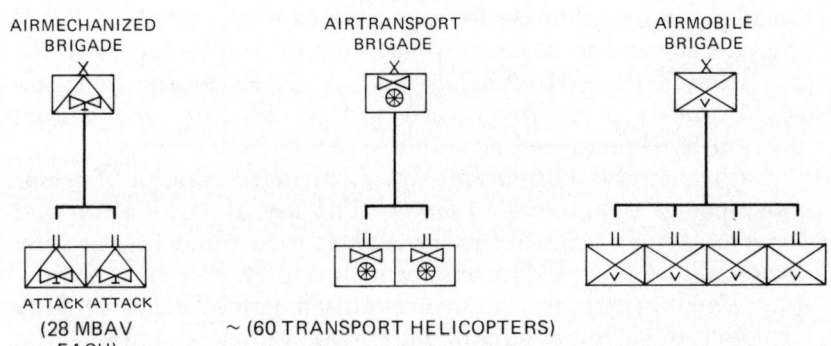

The symbols do not necessarily conform to any standardised NATO or nationally agreed system.

mechanised Forces must be capable of fighting against strong mechanised land forces and enemy Airmechanised Forces. Its wide range of weapons is intended to make it capable of fighting against all types of enemy ground and airmechanised weapons systems. The Airmechanised Force is to take no account of terrain obstacles, completely devastated areas and areas in which there is a highly dangerous amount of radioactivity must be of no significance. The vulnerability of the Airmechanised Force on the move and in the assembly areas is to be reduced by dispersal and its own air defence units to such an extent that it will be considerably less vulnerable than large land-bound columns and conglomerations of vehicles on roads.

So much for general characteristics. Let me now turn more specifically to my ideas on employment. The Airmechanised Formation will be launched into the attack from assembly areas some 200–300km distant from the tactical battle. Shortly before the attack, some forward elements will fly into forward positions and Forward Supply Points will be set up. In defence, the Airmechanised Formation will be prepared to dominate its defensive area with fire and destroy any enemy which penetrates the area. However, the defensive area will only be occupied on the ground by small strongholds and observation elements to deny chosen key terrain by day and by night. This tactic is to be based on the classical principle of area defence; forward elements secure ground and control the counter-attack forces of the formation. Because of its great mobility, the Airmechanised Formation is especially suitable for the delaying battle and MBAVs could hold up advancing land forces for a long time on natural obstacles. If the enemy were to deploy stronger forces in order to force the obstacles, further MBAVs, held back in reserve for that purpose, could quickly be flown forward and brought into action from previously reconnoitred positions.

Airmechanised Formations are particularly suitable for employment as operational reserves. The use of regional ground force reserves in Central Europe is likely to be much impaired by the devastation caused by enemy air interdiction or by a nuclear war, but the mobility of Airmechanised Forces could be fully exploited in such a situation. Their wide radius of action allows them to be launched to practically any point in the sector of an Army Group or even within a theatre of operations. They could also provide the main weight of a counter-attack, as a conventional operation, or in preparation or exploitation of nuclear employment.

Having given a few of my ideas on this future concept, I wish to emphasise at this stage that formations having a high degree of the required capabilities could, even now, be formed and employed, along the lines I have described, from those forces in place in the Central Region. The Airmechanised Brigades could be formed out of existing, but scattered, divisional – and corps – army aviation anti-tank helicopter units and in the case of the French, from the *Force d'Hélicoptère Anti-chars (FHAC)*. Apart from the French, it is my estimation that we could form half a dozen Airmechanised Brigades such as I have described.

With regard to the infantry elements for the operational support of the Airmechanised Brigades, the Airmobile Infantry Brigades, these could be found from existing light infantry formations such as the French *Division d'Infantry*, the German airborne brigades, the British 24th Infantry Brigade, and the units of a US light infantry division. As for the transportation requirement, such a capability exists even now in the Central Region with a lift for half a dozen battalions. German light and medium army aviation transport regiments, US transport and utility helicopter units, and British army and RAF helicopter units, could be grouped to form the Airtransport Brigades I have described. We would even be able to form Airmechanised Divisions, again half a dozen or so, which could in turn be grouped together under command of higher headquarters, as appropriate.

You may have noticed that in my discussion of this new dimension I have made only passing reference to the employment of Airmechanised Forces in nuclear warfare. The reason is that the time available simply does not permit it, but I have no doubt that you, like me, can supply your own ideas on that aspect since the forces I have proposed have an inherent flexibility.

In summary, therefore, let me emphasise my view that it is within such a new dimension that improvements for land armies are to be found. The step into the future must aim at integrating air mobility with the modern technology available for applying superior fire power, so as to create a new arm from this combination. A new arm which is to be utilised, not for improving the combat effectiveness of existing arms but which is to be used independently in the new operational dimension I have discussed. If the potential of Airmechanised Forces is not brought to bear independently, but instead is coupled to the forces of the conventional armies with their limited mobility and fire power, the same mistake will be made as that which our grandfathers made in exposing old-fashioned infantry to entrenched machine-gun fire in Flanders, or which our fathers made in the 1930s when they tied the battle tank to the infantry on foot.

The attack helicopter is the forerunner of the future Airmechanised Main Battle Air Vehicle. Already now, care should be taken to ensure that these assets are not used 'in dribs and drabs'. They should rather be exploited to test the airmechanised concept of operations and organisation which I have outlined. The fact that our forces may be involved in a nuclear warfare only emphasises the advantages in those circumstances of the very type of force I have advocated. Political difficulties should not prevent us either from using our imagination to test new organisations and tactics. The difficulties that we in the Army have had over the years in coping mentally with the problems of tactical doctrine in a nuclear environment, difficulties which still exist, should be overcome by a determined exploitation by us of the possibilities which technology offers to improve mobility. We can be sure that the Warsaw Pact will be doing so. A new combined autonomous all-arms group is required, a sort of state within the state, in which the new dimensions of airmobility and fire power are integrated.

Vigilia pretium libertatis! Vigilia means anticipation, but it does not mean taking a 'wait-and-see attitude'.

(*Address given to the RUSI on 2 February 1983*)

16 Dynamic Defence: The Northern Flank

GENERAL SIR ANTHONY FARRAR-HOCKLEY, KCB, DSO, MBE, MC

Formerly Commander-in-Chief Allied Forces Northern Europe

Every now and again the Northern Flank is rediscovered, rather like an ageing Hollywood star. I guess this is due principally when, from time to time, the appetite of strategists becomes sated with the problems of the Central Region: not least the appetites of those, like the British, whose professional land and air forces tend to be preoccupied with what is, after all, their major theatre of operations on mobilisation. Yet it is also rediscovered now and again, I suspect, when the eye of the strategist, professional or amateur, wanders northward across the Elbe river. There is sometimes a shock of discovery: why, here is a piece of West German territory which is not in the fief of the Commander-in-Chief of the Central Region! Astonishing, too, it is an area across which Russian tanks and aircraft might travel in an enveloping movement in the onrush of an offensive. I am speaking of Hamburg and Schleswig-Holstein, the northern-most and populous *länder* of the Federal Republic of Germany. These lie in the area of Allied Forces Northern Europe, the Northern Region.

Struck by these facts, the observer begins to take an interest in the Baltic Approches and finds these interdependent with Norway. So maybe this is the moment to look at the Northern Region comprehensively to determine just where it begins and ends and its relationship *inter alia* to the Central Region.

Like Caesar's Gaul, CINCNORTH's territory is divided into three parts: North Norway, South Norway and the Baltic

Approaches. The first two are clearly of a piece; the last was included on the well-tried principle that both sides of an important water gap should be within a common command. The Baltic Approaches comprise Hamburg, Schleswig-Holstein, Jutland – the Danish mainland, the Danish islands great and small, though Bornholm, 200 miles to the east in the Baltic is excluded in peacetime. Northwards across the Kattegat and Skagerrak we come to Norway, an extensive country with a coastline running up into the Arctic Circle to a border with the Soviet Union. Of course that border area of Russia belonged earlier to the Finns but, unlucky chaps, they found themselves on the wrong side at the end of the war in 1945 and had that taken from them as one of the several consequences. So that area now belongs to the Soviet Union, providing a useful extension for the defence of Murmansk. It is, may I remind you, one of the only two land areas of a NATO nation actually abutting Russian soil, the other, of course, being down in Turkey.

Now, if the Soviet Union projects the Warsaw Pact into an offensive, the general expectation in the West is of an onrush of massed armoured forces in close association with large conventional air forces: welling into the Federal Republic, making, as destruction of the defence progresses, for the Low Countries and, perhaps, the Channel coast of northern France. In such circumstances, what happens on the Central Region's flank on the river Elbe?

We may be sure that it is a question of considerable interest to CINCENT, but I suggest it is of no less interest to a Soviet commander directing an offensive immediately south of the Elbe. For if he is unwise he will have an open flank on the south bank of that river. Can he afford this, not least when it is apparent to him that east of Hamburg his open flank will rest on the narrow waters of the Travemunde canal and, in places, open country? Can he afford to disregard this area or perhaps just to mask it? I guess not. The consequences of an envelopment of his advancing units in the incipient stage of the offensive would be very serious, perhaps crippling. Quite apart from allied forces known to mobilise in Schleswig-Holstein and Jutland, he must take account of the possibility that SACEUR may decide to reinforce substantially the resident land force from elsewhere on mobilisation. A Warsaw Pact masking operation would not guarantee a safe flank. The only sure option is all-out conquest of Schleswig-Holstein,

Jutland and a range of the Danish islands. And the Russians seem to hold that view as they have dispersed forces along the land frontier there and an amphibious force to carry out such a conquest.

Beyond attaining the objective of flank security, they would gain important advantages from such an operation. They would obtain the well-found airfields of Hamburg, Schleswig-Holstein and Jutland. They would have broken through the Hawk/Patriot belt. No ground-based air defences would lie between the Baltic airfields and the United Kingdom or the ports of western Germany and the Low Countries. Taking the over sea route, air attack from the Baltic airfields could be made upon the airfields of 2nd Allied Tactical Air Force from the rear. And, concomitantly, they would deepen the air defence zone of East Germany and Poland. By this they would also deprive the Federal German and Royal Danish navies of all their bases. They would have overrun the passage through the Baltic narrows as far as the eastern edge of the Skagerrak. No mean advantages, these, protecting securely the right ground and air flanks of their campaign into the Central Region.

Now, they would open the narrows as far as the eastern edge of the Skagerrak because, of course, they have got to knock out south Norway before they have completely opened the waterway into the North Sea for their warships, their surface vessels and to an extent their submarines – to an extent because one might assume that a number of submarines would be out before war began.

South Norway has excellent port facilities including naval support facilities there and good airfields although unless we spend more money out of the NATO works pool on their infrastructure and maintenance some of those advantages could slip away. The problem of the commander of south Norway is that he is living in a big country which has a population of only four million, and the majority of them happen to live in his area, the southern half of Norway. Many of those mobilised have to go up to the north because the population up there is fragmentary, so his ability on his own to carry out tasks of shutting – as I would put it – the western gate of the narrows on the Baltic is difficult unless he has assistance in the air or on the sea, though air is the key factor in his task. But wait a bit, you may say: why is he sending all these people up to the north? Whatever is the object of fighting for Norwegian real estate except in our duty to try to protect the territories of one or another's membership of the Alliance? North Norway lies mostly inside the Arctic Circle, and seems to consist of mountains, or boulder-strewn plains of peat and moss, with a scant population decreasing to one person per 32 miles when you get up to Finnmark. What is it all about? Well, what it is about is that there is where the Northern Fleet lies. And of all the Soviet fleets – excluding the Far East Fleet which is a body apart – it is the only one of the three, Black Sea, Baltic and Northern Fleets, which has ready access to open water without having to pass through very narrow land areas, i.e. the Black Sea Fleet with the Turkish narrows and the Baltic Fleet through the Danish narrows.

Yet the problem for the Northern Fleet is that is has not got a major carrier potential and in any case the approach to its home waters is bordered by Norway as it enters or exits from the Barents Sea on which its complex of bases lie in the Murmansk area. It can never pass on the surface and for the most part below the surface without being observed by forces in Norway. If it wants to have free operation for war, sending ships out to refuel, replenish and the like, bringing damaged vessels back for repair and so on, it really cannot do that freely if that northern coast of Norway is not in its possession. So the Soviet Union needs to capture that area, beginning at H-hour on D-Day.

For NATO, the problem is how to defend that big area with such few numbers available and how Norway can make an effective contribution with such a relatively small intake of taxes available for its defence budget. Clearly it cannot carry out that task with its own manpower. It must be reinforced. Clearly also it cannot afford to procure and dispose an ocean-going navy which can sally out and take on the Northern Fleet at short notice. So what it does and what it is encouraged by NATO to do is to look after its coastal waters to ensure that they are not used by unfriendly forces and that the waters are kept clear and available for the reinforcements coming in. That means also preventing amphibious landings.

The Norwegian Navy is, therefore, a navy of small submarines, of a few frigates, the long-term future of which must always be in question due to pressure on budgets, and coastal craft such as fast patrol boats of which there are some excellently trained squadrons in Norwegian hands armed with their own missile, the Penguin, now in service. But overall, the Norwegians must be reinforced with men and aircraft at a very early stage in order to ensure that they are not overwhelmed. To that end – as the late Commander-in-Chief – I welcome very much SACEUR's rapid reinforcement plan which for the first time has set out in a coherent fashion where named formations and units are to go on mobilisation. It involves SACEUR – if I may make a general observation – in sometimes reminding national ministries of defence that they do not in war exercise direct command of the forces that they have promised to NATO in operations. They promised them to General Rogers or whoever is the incumbent of that office in the Allied Command of Europe. Only SACEUR can decide at the end of the day where reinforcements shall go. But a reinforced American Marine Brigade is going to Norway with its large air component and the Canadians are sending an air and ground force there – the combined Air and Sea Task Force. The British send to North Norway an air component plus the Royal Marine amphibious brigade. Like the United State Marines, this formation has the capability to land at difficult places on the coast if ports are knocked out, whether on first arrival or in subsequent contingency operations.

Still, the Norwegians are not altogether lacking in manpower. Their standing forces, part of a conscript army, cannot be much more than a brigade and a half at any one time. They have, however, a very full mobilisation capability. That fleshes out their forces. They have in addition a strong and very able Home Guard.

If I may just bang that last drum for a moment, if the Home Guard looks like Dad's Army, this scattered force providing a sub-structure to defence, those who have been there to exercise against them, will agree that they are not an easy force to get past in terms of moving down a village street if they do not want you to, or of passing across country unobserved. They know the countryside. They guard the key static places, such as the many ferry crossing points, bridges, tunnels and so on, and man certain static defences. If you had some member of a Russian sabotage team dressed as a Norwegian officer who appears before a Home Guard force guarding a key point and says, 'Well, men, that's enough. I've just come from the higher headquarters to tell you to pack up and go home', they are a very obstinate lot of men who say, 'Who are you Captain? We don't know your face. You come from Stavanger? Right, we'll ring up Stavanger and find out about you.' They are not a force you can just brush aside by bluff. They provide a military presence in every town and hamlet throughout Norway. Their obligations are few but many of them do it as a great hobby. Fornebu, the airfield at Oslo, is guarded by a force under a distinguished officer, Major Hauge, who obtained, by lobbying the Minister of Defence in the past, by virtually sleeping across his office door, agreement to transport under a private arrangement all the residual American White half-tracks and Chafee light tanks after the sale of World War II weapons, items that the United States was about to scrap. He had a relative in the Pentagon. They came free except for the freight across the Atlantic. They had 30 years of spares with them. They spent their whole time keeping those vehicles up to scratch. And although now the Norwegian Ministry of Defence have moved these vehicles to another body, Major Hauge has been round the military museums of Europe and has now collected a squadron of armoured jeeps. But he has put civil number plates on so they cannot take them away from him. That is the sort of Home Guard they have in Norway and it certainly has something to offer.

North Norway has a tough task. Its prospects are improved by the introduction of the F-16 into the Royal Norwegian Air Force, so that if it is thrown out of the very northernmost airfields in the early stages, there is an aircraft for fighter defence that can come up from the mid-Norwegian area and have an hour over Bodø or even further north Tromsø to fight there before it has to go back. With the F-5s and the F-4s we could not do that. The same applies, of course, to the advantage derived from the introduction of the E3A which is gradually coming into NATO service. All the Norwegian early warning air defence systems on the ground are likely to be shot out in the first eight hours of war. Stand-off weapons, homing on those radars, will knock them out. And CINCNORTH then has the problem of *ad hoc* arrangements for early warning. With the E3A standing off miles out over the Norwegian Sea protected by the air defences up there, there is a capability to look 100 miles or more into the Kola Peninsula at the Soviet airfields; airfields which I may say to those who believe that the Soviet Union have no intentions of doing anything unpleasant up there, that have grown in the last 10 years from nine rather backward airfields to 19 mostly advanced airfields which, though not financed by a budget going through a tough and critical legislature in Moscow, none the less cost roubles and kopecks which had to be found from somewhere. There they are in ferro-concrete: the majority deserted at this moment, yet ready to serve squadrons which practise deployment to them regularly from the hinterland of Russia.

Turning to Southern Norway, I would describe it as the heart of the Northern Region's defence. If one lost north Norway or the Baltic Approaches, a counter-attack can be launched into either from the ports or the airfields of south Norway. It is weak unhappily in sea, land and air units. Its claim for a share of reinforcement is strong, but it is likely to have to wait for that share as, evidently, all steps must be taken to prevent the loss of north Norway or the Baltic Approaches. You may recall that in General John Hackett's view of World War III, the Baltic Approaches were lost at the outset: nerve droplets disposed of them. Just as I do not believe that north Norway will fall, given its share of reinforcement, I believe that Denmark and the two northern *länder* of Germany will hold if their reinforcement needs are met – as they are being with United States aircraft and a British brigade group. Some here wonder whether the Danes have the tradition for fighting, perhaps because they did nothing in April 1940 to resist the Nazi invasion for reasons which are not difficult to comprehend and may – they will be the first to admit – have been inadequate. But Denmark is not a country that is ready to give up its territory easily to an invader. It may be very democratic; it may expect to enjoy a very high standard of living. Yet it has clear ideas about liberty. It has survived on that ideal of liberty for many hundreds of years as an independent kingdom.

Denmark has part regular, part conscript forces. There is no difficulty in finding conscripts for service. Men offer themselves for it. It has – it is true – all too short a period of conscription. It has had difficulty in meeting its 3 per cent increase in real terms in its defence budget. But as a matter of fact only tact prevents me from saying that at least two other nations in NATO have done much worse and avoided any odium whatsoever. Denmark has at least managed to get 2 per cent and has received scant praise for that. It is able to put into the field one division and half another. It cannot, out of five million, having also to provide for a strong air defence and quite a strong navy, do more than that. So reinforcement is essential to it as to Norway.

It too has a marvellous Home Guard, entirely voluntary, entirely unpaid. It keeps its weapons at home, surely dangerous in a civil community! I enquired how many murders were directly attributable since 1947 – the date of the introduction of the Home Guard service – to keeping weapons at home. The answer was three. People turn out far beyond the seven days that they are required *in toto* a year to appear. They, like the Norwegians, are not easily bluffed. They guard all key points. They appear in all the villages and towns. They observe strangers. They provide information by civil telephone to the regular military as well as to one another. Like the Norwegians their naval component mans the minefield exits and entrances. They have an air observation corps which works very well and does all sorts of extraordinary things I would not have believed possible, sometimes providing a better service than electronic air observation does.

In Schleswig-Holstein, the Federal Republic keeps a division with an excellent set of reserve and home defence forces which are under CINCNORTH as an exception to the system which operates in the rest of the Federal Republic. The whole of the Navy of the Federal Republic, much of it based in this area, is dedicated to the Northern Region and, launched by shore-based maritime air strike squadrons, disposes formidable strength in the North and Baltic Seas.

I would like to raise a couple of other points. First of all the Scandinavians – in particular Norway and Denmark – have problems with their own form of CND. But they have not taken root in quite the way that they have here. Perhaps that is because they live a little closer to the eastern bloc, though there are hard-core CND elements. At the same time neither Norway nor Denmark will permit in present circumstances – such is the phrase in the protocol – nuclear weapons to be based on their soil, nor will they have them themselves. The CND pressure groups operating in Scandinavia are attempting to get the governments to say 'in any circumstances whatsoever'. They are trying to get Sweden and Iceland to do the same thing, and Finland, which has more or less already agreed to do so. Then, they say, we shall have the best of all possible worlds – a Nordic nuclear-weapons-free zone. But one has to ask our friends there who have this sort of idea, who is it in the north who has nuclear weapons? Sweden ? No. Finland? Certainly not. Iceland? No. Norway, Denmark? No. Only the Soviet Union. What did Mr Brezhnev in his lifetime latterly say, and later Mr Andropov, about the Nordic nuclear-weapons-free zone? It is a good thing they said. 'You will not of course when you rightly carry this through expect us to give up our nuclear weapons. We're in a different ball park. But we'll make one big concession to you. We promise you that if there's a war we'll never use nuclear weapons against you.' A very sporting concession!

The second thing I must say is that budgetary problems will continue to make life difficult for Norway and Denmark in playing their part in NATO, though they play very readily and wholeheartedly a full part otherwise. Until and unless the bigger powers – the United Kingdom for example or the United States on yet a bigger scale – are willing to give wholeheartedly a greater element of defence contracts to those small countries they are always going to be strapped for cash. You might say that it is for America alone to do this; the United Kingdom is a victim in this field, as an exemplar in contract sharing. Well, I recall the days when I sat in the Ministry of Defence building and we inveighed against the Americans for not buying, for example, the latest British 81mm mortar, which they thought was so marvellous. They made promises. They said how good it was. They never bought it. Faithless Americans, we said. But meantime we had promised to buy the excellent 81mm mortar sight from the Kongsberg Våpens Fabrik in Norway. Have any crossed the North sea? Not one, because when we allowed RARDE to hear about it they said, 'Oh, we can make a better and cheaper sight than that'. They have not done so but they naturally thought they could and were able to persuade those concerned in Whitehall. The same situation now applies to the 81mm mortar fuse. Until we begin to shift the log jam in this way we are not going to get out of this problem of being strapped for cash as our costs rise in real terms.

Well, that is a brief look at the Northern Region. The people there are wholeheartedly behind NATO. Do not believe what you read in the press when you hear that some of the responsible political parties within these states are threatening to secede. I do not believe they will every seriously consider such a thing. No doubt it is true that if war comes it will not be won in the Northern Region. But my belief is and my advice is it could equally be lost there.

(*Address given to the RUSI on 4 March 1983*)

17 The Southern Flank and Out of Area Operations

LIEUTENANT GENERAL JAMES M. THOMPSON

Chief of Staff, Headquarters Allied Forces Southern Europe

The North Atlantic Treaty Organisation has served long and well the interests of peace envisioned by its originators. Through more than 30 years of existence this commitment to the common defence has been integral to the preservation of world peace and security. But in recent years the dangers to world peace appear to be both more diverse and more subtle than the original NATO structure was designed to counter.

What should be the limits of NATO's interests today? Can the limits ever be so wide that they include the regional interests of every Alliance member or must they be confined to those areas where a consensus can be achieved? Is there not some middle ground which can profitably be ploughed to renew NATO's vitality in this fourth decade of its existence? It is my contention that to cope with the broader challenges of the 1980s, NATO must build on the long-range common goal of peace shared by all members and the mutual trust and confidence developed since its inception to create an understanding that majority concerns can and must be collectively pursued, one way or another. These are the main issues I will address from a Southern Region perspective.

The Southern Region Alliance members do not have a continuous land frontier and the intervening territories and seas strengthen the demarcations among nations. A wide spectrum of ethnic and religious persuasions exist both within and adjacent to our Alliance members. But in spite of some basic differences of view and occasional disagreement from some of our members, Italy, Greece and Turkey have continued to support the Alliance because it has been and continues to be in their national interest to do so.

In looking at the Southern Region, a bit of history helps lend perspective. The Alliance had its beginning in a war-torn Europe under Communist pressure which the United States felt morally obliged and economically and militarily able to confront. Having come late into two world wars, it behoved the US to forestall a third one if possible and, if unsuccessful, not to forfeit the first lines of defence beyond its shores. The Alliance, therefore, made sense from the point of view of American self-interest.

The fact that Moscow did not demobilise its large armies while others did caused the Soviets to gain a sharp superiority in conventional military terms, but the American nuclear monopoly and industrial supremacy were sufficient to deter the Russians, once a line had been drawn and intentions clearly stated to defend it. This resolve was negotiated with the members of the Brussels Pact in 1948 and 1949 and the North Atlantic Treaty resulted. At that time Greece and Turkey were thought to be too far removed from the important centres of Europe and were excluded to prevent a dilution of emphasis and strength. The western Mediterranean countries were given little more consideration. Then fascist Spain was easy to exclude and Italy was viewed as an economic drain and a dilution of the Atlantic emphasis of the Alliance. But France argued persuasively that if Denmark and Norway on the northern flank could be part of NATO, so could Italy. Thus in 1949 Alliance members agreed in Article 6 that the NATO area of response would be their collective national territory.

Soon after the Treaty entered into force there were some significant events which fundamentally changed the orientation of the nations of the new organisation. First was the disquieting news that the USSR had exploded an atomic device, thus forever eradicating the nuclear monopoly of the United States. Second was the attack of 25 June 1950 by North Korean forces on the Republic of South Korea. There was considerable opinion that the Communist offensive would be widened to the European front and this inevitably changed Western thinking about the needs of the Alliance and about the countries surrounding the Soviet Union and its satellites.

Greece and Turkey had never abandoned their desire to join the new Western Alliance; now, in view of this new situation, their contribution in manpower and geography were viewed quite differently. Immediately, bids for membership from Greece and Turkey were encouraged. Even though membership was debated at length, principally due to concerns that this extension might involve the Alliance in operations too far from Central Europe, by February 1952 this 'out of area' problem was solved through expansion of the Alliance to include both Greece and Turkey.

The protocol of the North Atlantic Treaty on the accession of Greece and Turkey modified Article 6 to include '. . . the territory of Turkey' and '. . . the Mediterranean Sea'. So now the *Mare Nostrum* which has played such a central role in the development of Western civilisation, both as a crucial highway for commerce and a recurring battle site, was included in the NATO area.

In 1956 the North Atlantic Council noted in its report that:

> NATO should not forget that the influence and interests of its members are not confined to the area covered by the Treaty and that common interests of the Atlantic Community can be seriously affected by developments outside the Treaty area. Therefore, while striving to improve their relations with each other, and to strengthen and deepen their own unity, they should also be concerned with harmonising their policies in relation to other areas, taking into account the broader interests of the whole international community.

In fact, during this period there were considerable differences of view concerning the pace of change in the former colonial empires and, more particularly, in the Middle East. These differences came to a head in the well-known Suez affair when the US forced a withdrawal from the Canal area by Britain, France and Israel. Few recognised at the time the magnitude of the problems being stored up in what we now know as the Third World – and which we in NATO frequently describe as 'out of area' concerns.

The launching of the first Soviet Sputnik in October 1957 marked the beginning of a new competition between the Soviets and the US. At the same time, the European allies, which were mainly concentrating on their own economic recovery, had become less concerned about world events far from their region. There were by now clear indications of a shift in European thinking about the dominant role of the United States.

The most striking example of this shift in perception was in the contrasting European responses to out of area conflicts in Korea and Vietnam. It begs the point to assert that these two out of area conflicts were perceived quite differently by Europeans. In both instances the United States addressed basically what it believed to be the same threat in the same fashion for the same motives; the differences in European perceptions tells us perhaps more about changes in Europe during this period than it does about any intrinsic differences between the conflicts. We also learned that our enemies, even though stubborn, were certainly not stupid. They showed great sophistication by shifting the threat from the brazen starkness of the Korean invasion to the ambiguity which clothed a 'People's Liberation' of Vietnam. They realised they could exploit ambiguity to help reluctant Westerners find reasons to avoid involvement and used a subtle and effective public relations effort to erode Western solidarity. In retrospect, and at the risk of getting ahead of my thesis, this experience formed a solid basis for the much more sophisticated and widespread public relations capability the Soviets display today.

In 1967 the mood was such that the only mention in the final communique of the ministerial meeting concerning out of area interests was that:

> The North Atlantic Treaty area cannot be treated in isolation from the rest of the world. Crisis and conflicts arising outside the area may impair its security either directly or by affecting the global balance. Allied countries contribute individually within the United Nations and other international organizations to the maintenance of international peace and security and to the solution of important international problems. In accordance with established usage the allies, or such of them as wish to do so, will also continue to consult on such problems without commitment and as the case may demand.

This, of course, was rather tepid support for a country which was now heavily embroiled in a conflict on the Asian mainland that was creating a serious drain on treasury and manpower. But there was little reaction at this early stage to lack of support as a feeling of omnipotence still heavily dominated American thinking.

By 1974 the United States' failure in Vietnam had been displayed by the media in excruciating detail. Alliance members were constantly reminded of the negative aspects and costs of anyone's taking on the role of world policeman. Concurrently, the emergence of oil as an economic weapon helped develop a sense of impotence, leading to a general preference for isolationism and inactivity; world events were perhaps too complex and explosive to be influenced positively and might better be just observed from afar. In the Declaration on Atlantic Relations issued from Brussels in 1974 the only reference to out of area problems was:

> ... (the nations) are firmly resolved to keep each other fully informed and to strengthen the practice of frank and timely consultations by all means which may be appropriate on matters relating to their common interests as member of the Alliance, bearing in mind that these interests can be affected by events in other areas of the world.

The other nations of the Alliance were not at all satisfied with the level of consultation and clarity of intention displayed by the US Government during the Vietnam War. There was also no hint of the reality that without the energy resources of the Middle East, the economic fruits of almost three decades of post-World War II reconstruction could wither and die. Here, there were two very sensitive out of area problems that the Alliance *per se* seemed unable to cope with. In reality, the Treaty's major significance lay in its commitment of the full might of the US to the defence of Western Europe against a Soviet invasion, not to support global interests as seen by a major member of the Alliance.

Now I propose that with this historical perspective we should look critically at those areas of change in the world and assess their impact on the future direction of NATO and the pivotal question of NATO's area of interest or role in out of area operations.

Firstly, the Warsaw Pact threat has changed. The increase in Soviet offensive systems over the long term has been steady and single minded. To doubt that world domination is not still an underlying motivation for the Soviets is to be convinced that their 15 per cent GNP yearly military expenditures are necessary only for defence. We are all very familiar with the Soviet build-up: from strategic inferiority the Soviets have progressed to rough parity by building six times more ICBMs than the US during the past decade. Their theatre nuclear deployment has exceeded our most pessimistic estimation. The conventional force imbalance has also grown as they developed new systems across the entire spectrum of warfare. Expansion and modernisation of their chemical warfare capability has been particularly disquieting.

The second change is the nature of the world economy. Europe is no longer a collection of struggling nations economically subservient to the United States. It is now a thriving economic confederation whose increasing interdependence is leading discernibly to more formal ties of economic federalism. Not surprisingly, once Western Europe's internal recovery was at full steam, its resurgent industry began to redirect attention eastward, to what had been lucrative pre-war markets for Western producers. For quite a while the Coordinating Committee (COCOM) mechanism (designed to deny the Soviets strategic materials or know-how) kept this trade to a modest level, but eventually political interests and economic necessity prevailed and sales to the East climbed. Concurrently, supplies from the Middle East and Africa increased in volume and importance. During the 1960s and 1970s, the steadily expanding East–West trade and mutual dependence were fostered by and became closely identified with *détente*, an 'agree to disagree' approach made more palatable by the economic benefits of doing business with otherwise unfriendly nations. The United States, of course, also profited from this increased trade, but for them it was more of a luxury than a necessity. The fact remains, however, that the area of economic interest for industrialised nations is the whole world: there are no out of area places. The dependence of Europe on imported energy and the competition which has resulted from increased relative economic strength *vis-à-vis* America have resulted in less and less transatlantic cooperation in addressing world economic problems and East–West trade.

The third area of change I find is the broad spectrum of challenges to the Alliance from sources other than the Warsaw Pact. There have been marked changes in European security perceptions since World War II. Ironically, it is NATO's very success which has been the major factor. In the early days of the Alliance. Western Europeans remembered well the Soviet war machine at work and had witnessed its post-war repression of Eastern Europe. They genuinely wanted and encouraged a sizeable US military presence on their soil and did their level best to buttress it with credible domestic forces. But, over time, the evident success of deterrence, developing problems in Eastern Europe, the emergence of *détente*, and a growing taste for the good life have all combined to erode enthusiasm for NATO and to re-arrange European priorities in expenditure. Commitment to sacrifice for the common good seems to have faded. Today, many Europeans, and even some Americans, have chosen to convince themselves that the Soviets do not want war and therefore will not start one. Moscow's still-evident ambitions, its record for using force, and its awesome and steady pace of weapons modernisation are often ignored or repressed from consciousness.

Wars are fought by young men and, as a consequence, a long post-war period follows every war in which national character and policies are affected by wartime experiences. But it is now 38 years since Europeans – with some exceptions – have known war. Horrible as World War II was for Europe, those who fought and endured it are now becoming the grandparent generation, and men and women born after the war already have children of military age. Admittedly, they have all lived in the shadow of potential conflict, but with NATO's success and an era of *détente* that shadow has steadily lightened.

In contrast, every generation of Americans now living has had its war, and each of those war experiences continues in its own way to affect national attitudes and policies. Moreover, those wars have reinforced an American tendency to think globally. Perhaps this is why it is the United States that is willing to take the lead on the new challenges to the West posed by Afghanistan, Iran and Middle East instability, but with the burden being shared by its allies. For the past eight or nine years, the American population has been sorting out which of the various lessons of Vietnam are valid and which are spurious. A sense of national guilt seems to be yielding to a realisation that the US was simply unwise to invest so much blood and treasure in attempting more than it could reasonably attain. An acceptance is growing that Americans cannot, and in their own interests need not, be the world's policeman – at least not in every precinct. Americans seem more disposed to cooperative involvement and to look for burden-sharing with their allies. But the basic question remains: 'Who leads?' And a second would be: 'Who comes along?'

It is evident that America is still positively inclined to protect its own interests abroad. Major help in recovering from post-Vietnam self-doubt was supplied by the oil embargo and oil price hikes of the 1970s. These events angered Americans and, as the Japanese learned after Pearl Harbor, righteous anger can be a strong motivator to national character. But Americans now seem disposed to intervene more selectively and cautiously, weighing both costs and goals with greater care than was their experience from the 1940s to the 1960s.

Another non-traditional threat to NATO's security is the emergence of the nations of North Africa and the Middle East which geographically, economically and militarily affect both our daily lives and the strategic balance in the Southern Region. The only constants in this area are instability and unpredictability. The various forces of dissidence which afflict this array of young nations are predominantly indigenous and relate to rapid population growth, desire for social change and ideology. The Soviets seek to exploit these forces for change but do not create and can seldom completely control them. But after pushing and pressing unsuccessfully on Western Europe's front door, Moscow may have come to realise that Europe's greatest vulnerability lies elsewhere. Moscow apparently sees what many in the West still do not: that in this highly industrialised age, Persian Gulf and Middle East petroleum and various strategic metals of Africa hold the key to Western Europe's future prosperity and defence.

Severely complicating the strategic picture and simultaneously elevating the potential for conflicts have been the sweeping political changes of the last 30 years around the eastern and southern shores of the Mediterranean. Regimes range from authoritarian to genuinely representative; from assumedly Marxist to staunchly traditionalist; from pro-West to Soviet supported. Relationships between many of these countries are often severely strained and open hostilities are the norm, often in several places simultaneously. Today, for instance, conflicts between Iran and Iraq, between Morocco and the Polisario, Lebanon and various Libyan adventures are in progress. Some countries are acquiring impressive arms inventories which make a small population much more capable of force projection than it otherwise might be. I suggest that not even Lloyd's would insure against the certainty that the entire eastern and southern littoral of the Mediterranean will undergo major and frequent violent political changes before the 1980s run out.

A good example of Southern Region concerns about littoral nations can be seen when examining the current status of Libya. A nation of only three million people, Libya possesses more military aircraft than trained aviators and more tanks than any European NATO country except the Federal Republic of Germany. Libyan capability for mischief with naval forces within and beyond their excessive claim to the Gulf of Sirte is disquieting. Soviet-supplied Foxtrot class submarines and fast patrol boats equipped with both Soviet and Western-supplied sophisticated guided missiles are capable of offensive action. Their capability against unarmed merchant ships or to deliver a terrorist-type attack is unquestioned; only a lack of training and experience limit their potential threat. In any case, the types of weapons systems they have purchased are in no way optimised for defensive missions. Their offensive capability creates very visible pressure on Libya's neighbours. A country primarily concerned about defence of a thin coastal plain, where the majority of Libyans reside, would have concentrated more on static naval forces such as minelayers, but such has not been the direction of the mercurial Colonel Qadhafi.

However, Libya's military and anti-social behaviour has to be balanced against economic realities. As a major oil exporting nation, Libya has influence due to the energy dependence of other Southern Region nations and its own requirement and ability to employ foreign workers. Large numbers of Turkish and Italian workers are provided employment and, through remittances home, provide a major source of 'invisible earnings' for troubled balance of payments. For example, existing Turkish contracts in Libya amount to more than $9bn (some £5½bn) and the estimated yearly remittances of $800m (some £500m) are on a par with the entire US military and economic aid programmes for Turkey. It is little wonder, for example, that US exercises in the Gulf of Sirte are watched with high interest by Southern Region nations. But Libya is only the best example of the diversity of factors influencing Southern Region Alliance members. Soviet influence in Syria and Soviet potential for gains resulting from the

Iran–Iraq war place danger directly on the borders of Turkey, and thus, on NATO.

It is certainly true that the largest force concentrations in NATO and the Warsaw Pact face each other in Central Europe. As SACEUR so clearly points out, we need to provide sufficient conventional forces to ensure a reasonable level of deterrence and defence. This is essential. But, the vital natural resources that lie just beyond NATO's borders to the south and east, taken in conjunction with the diversity and number of non-traditional threats to the Alliance, leads me to the judgment that the centre of NATO's strategic concern has shifted towards the Southern Region. Although we lack the capability to do much about them by ourselves, we in the Southern Region are in the forefront of these new challenges. In this regard, the term 'flank' is appropriate to an area not principally threatened, and with the variety and magnitude of the challenges ahead, the Southern Region promises to be a 'front' for the foreseeable future. As we know from our studies of military history, a flank in the process of being turned becomes the main front – the area of central strategic importance to the defender.

What about the Southern Region nations? How have they come through the intervening years and what can they contribute to NATO and to this out of area question? The answer is mixed and complicated by long-standing regional differences. With the only economy in the Southern Region possessing the vitality to support an adequate defence, Italy finds itself as a natural leader. Italy has made some important moves to widen its horizons. The Italian/Maltese Treaty of 1981, which guaranteed the neutrality of Malta and excluded the superpowers, was followed by force commitments to the Sinai and Lebanese peace keeping forces, all positive steps toward regional stability. The Comiso deployment for Ground-Launched Cruise Missiles (GLCMs) was a courageous and pivotal decision for Italy and the Alliance.

Greece re-entered the Integrated Military Structure following a 1974 to 1980 absence; additionally in 1981 Greece became the tenth member of the European Economic Community. Greece has a small population and a fragile economy which has been severely hampered by the world economic slow down following the oil price shocks. Greece has been pursuing a comprehensive programme to revitalise its economy. Foreign investment has been encouraged as Greece strives to attract the external investment necessary for regional development, employment, and the introduction of advanced technology. Greece has been actively cooperating within the EEC to stimulate some of its new industries while simultaneously devaluing the drachma. Greece obviously looks forward to assuming the EEC presidency and understands the value and importance of such economic cooperation. With over 6 per cent of its population under arms, by far the largest percentage contribution among NATO nations, coupled with its economic problems, Greece needs considerable assistance from its allies to fashion a coordinated defence.

Turkey has recently emerged in a new strategic light. With neighbours Iran and Iraq locked in an apparently interminable struggle and with Syria involved in the Arab–Israel dispute, Turkey's only stable non-NATO neighbours are Bulgaria and the Soviet Union – not an optimistic situation. Internal order has been restored in Turkey and its leaders are slowly but resolutely leading her back to parliamentary processes. The economic situation is vastly better than during the chaos preceding the military takeover, but it must become a more efficient producer to remain self-sufficient in food stuffs. The requirement to feed its rapidly growing population is an imperative; the population will increase 43 per cent from the present 49m to about 70m by the year 2000. Turkish workers in the Middle East now remit $1.3bn annually, exceeding the $1.2bn from Turkish workers in Europe. These facts illustrate Turkish needs to balance competing external pressures and the terrific daily internal strains which influence her policies. The potential for economic pressure on Turkey by suppliers of critical commodities and those who provide markets for her goods must be recognised and addressed.

What can we make out of all this? In the Southern Region, nations on the northern littoral of Africa and in the Middle East will be key factors in the event of a NATO/WP conflict just as they are now in the daily affairs of the area. A NATO official such as myself cannot, of course, speak definitively for nations, but clearly it is Europe, not America, which is most endangered by these various developments just beyond NATO's borders. Rather than leave the leadership in coping with out of area problems to the US logic should impel Europeans to take the lead – or at least join in an equal partnership – in forging new, enlarged concepts for ensuring NATO and Western security. Ideally, we should seek to expand the scope of the Alliance to defend jointly each other's national territory into a joint commitment to protect vital – and carefully defined – Western interests beyond national borders. However, the consensus appears to be that such an attempt would be disastrous. It is just not politically feasible to make major changes in the structure of the Alliance. Whatever we do, the basic NATO policy of deterrence and defence, employing the strategy of flexible response, should remain the core of Alliance strategy. No useful purpose would be served by challenging the strategy as embodied in MC 14/3.

What factors, then, should a new concept – if any – embody? First there must be an explicit acknowledgment of the severity and relevance to NATO of the new dangers and a resolve to do something about them as we did the more direct Soviet threat of 1948 and 1949. The Southern Region is the area most directly affected by the multiplicity and magnitude of these new troubles. However, the economic dependence of Western Europe on Mediterranean trade routes and Middle Eastern resources argues persuasively to make it the concern of all NATO. Recognising the present dangers inherent in Soviet military support for Syria and possible future Soviet adventurism in the Gulf area are essential steps in NATO's addressing security concerns out of area. If we wait until something happens, it will be too late.

Second, an extension of the area of NATO concern has to be a joint acknowledgment to prevent the more vulnerable members of the Alliance from receiving undue pressure from the opposition, from whatever direction. Speaking plainly, vulnerable Southern Region allies need the full support of a united NATO to prevent economic and political blackmail. Without a NATO endorsement of some sort I am sure that nations in our part of the world will be reluctant to get deeply involved, or to make support facilities available. Life is just too tenuous already.

Third, in light of the new dangers, the richer nations of the Alliance must help those who cannot adequately provide the forces to protect themselves, or who, by taking a stand on behalf of the Alliance, find themselves cut off from oil and markets for their goods. Support by the wealthier nations could be an avenue to develop a greater commitment to sacrifice for the common good. The nations of the Alliance could be pulled together by an even-handed commitment, patiently and consistently applied, serving as a cornerstone of each nation's policy. The needs of the weaker nations, especially those in the Southern Region, transcend what the US or the FRG, the other major provider of assistance, seems to be prepared to make available. The cornerstone of an effective alliance is that every country that can help must do so, either in direct defence or in support of each other. There is no doubt in my mind that improvement in the defensive capabilities of the Southern Region would be a prudent move in bolstering NATO's ability to deter threats to security in areas beyond NATO's boundaries.

Additionally, the much heralded US initiative labelled the Rapid Deployment Force (RDF) – now embodied in the US Central Command – must be clearly incorporated into NATO planning. This US force is an acknowledgment of the importance of Middle East oil to the economic stability of the Western world. It is a commitment by the US to lead in at least one out of area region. Neither NATO nor NATO nations appear to have sufficiently acknowledged the nature of the problem or to make appropriate and feasible responses. The challenges in the Persian Gulf have been recognised by a few allies, but not by the Alliance as a whole.

When we think about the Rapid Deployment Force we must recognise that some of the long sought and recently won reinforcements slated to bolster the SR are undoubtedly the same flexible forces which would be most suitable for a force capable of rapid deployment. Such a dual responsibility for committed forces can be viewed as a dilution of support for SR nations which count on external reinforcement for critical political and military support. This difficult problem must be addressed thoroughly and frankly among the allies.

Without the use of support facilities of NATO and non-NATO countries in the area, the US could not effectively sustain operations in South-West Asia. Without the power projection capability of US assets, the Alliance cannot protect its interests in the area, should military force ever be required. This situation seems to be an ideal prescription for cooperation. Whether we are prepared to admit it or not, in times of crisis, NATO, or nations in NATO, are likely to have facilities available in friendly littoral states. It might be politically difficult but certainly rational to factor such considerations into NATO's thinking. Why not encourage contingency planning to facilitate such cooperation? Such an action seems necessary to update NATO's relevance and to continue its record of preserving the peace and providing for security in its broadest sense.

Alliances, like nations and businesses, must re-examine and revitalise their goals and their means of achieving them with each successive generation. NATO has been doing some of these things. I have noted in the rather lengthy list of recent pronouncements – such as the DPC statements of 1982 – an indication of a desire to move toward a more expanded concept of security; however, words without much commitment to substantive action are all that has seemingly evolved so far. I would suggest that we should take a broader view of security challenges to be met by NATO, or by members of the Alliance working together in what one might call a 'coalition of the willing'.

What we need is a 'call to action' by NATO. Perhaps the NAC or DPC can 'invite' members to do something about a threat to the collective interest. Those nations who disagree or who are reluctant to go along can register their views in a footnote, but they should not block the call to action. We need more than moral support for action, for example, by the Americans. We need to recognise that Alliance interests are at stake. For the challenges have that same duty today as informed citizens had after World War II.

If it seems that I have strayed a bit from the Southern Region you are correct, but the drift was intentional. The concern of the Southern Region to address adequately these new challenges will involve the entire Alliance, just as the contribution of the Southern Region directly supports the whole Alliance and not just itself.

(*Address given to the RUSI on 13 June 1983*)

Notes and References

1. INTRODUCTION

1. Both comments are cited in Michael Harrison, 'Our Atlantic Quagmire', *The Washington Quarterly*, 5:3 Summer 1982.
2. Irving Kristol, 'Does NATO Exist?', *The Washington Quarterly*, Autumn 1979.
3. Eugene MacCarthy, 'Look, No Allies', *Foreign Policy* 30, Spring 1978.
4. Earl Ravenal, *NATO's Unremarked Demise* (Berkley: University of California, 1979) p. 40. In a more recent piece Ravenal estimated that US forces in Europe would cost $115bn in 1984. A gradual withdrawal of those forces over a ten year period (plus the withdrawal of US forces from bases outside Europe) would reduce the number of US servicemen from 2 165 000 to 1 850 000 in 1994. Ravenal went on to argue 'Containment without tears is no longer possible. Better to accept some losses overseas than to wreck our economy and warp our society'. 'The case for a withdrawal of our forces', *New York Times Magazine*, 6 March 1983.
5. Eliot Cohen, 'The Long Term Crisis of the Alliance', *Foreign Affairs*, 61:2 Winter 1982/3.
6. Maxwell Taylor, *Precarious security* (New York: Norton, 1976).
7. Melvyn Kraus, 'It's Time to Change the Atlantic Alliance', *The Wall St Journal*, 3 March 1983.
8. Hedley Bull, 'European Self-reliance and the Reform of NATO', *Atlantic Quarterly*, 1:1 1983.
9. Jonathan Alford, 'European Security: The Military Aspect', *Thinking about European defence* (London: European Democratic Group, 1982).
10. See *Assignment of Ground Forces of the US to Duty in the European Area*. Hearings before the Senate Committee on Foreign Relations and the Armed Services Committee 82nd Congress 1st Session 1951.

2. STATE OF NATO DEFENCES AND WARSAW PACT THREAT

1. Ian Bellany, *Conventional Forces and the European Balance* (Lancaster University: Centre for the Study of Arms Control, 1981).
2. *NATO and the Warsaw Pact: Force Comparisons* (Brussels: NATO, 1982).
3. Waldo Freeman, *NATO Central Region Forward Defence: Correcting the Strategy/Force Mismatch* (Washington DC: National Defence University, 1981).
4. Ibid.
5. *NATO and the Warsaw Pact: Force Comparisons* provides one of the most up to date discussions.
6. *The Military Balance 1982–3* (London: International Institute for Strategic Studies, 1983).
7. Ibid.
8. Cited in Dean Acheson, 'The Practise of Partnership', *Foreign Affairs*, 41:2 January 1963, pp. 252–3.
9. Cited William Kaufman, *The McNamara Strategy* (New York: Harper and Row, 1964) pp. 59–60.
10. Jurgen Arbeiter, *NATO Strategy: Strengths and Weaknesses* (Kingston, Ontario: Center for International Studies, 1980).
11. Ibid.
12. *US Airlift Forces: Enhancement Alternatives for NATO and non-NATO Contingencies* (Washington DC: Congressional Budget Office, 1979). This subject is discussed more fully in Christopher Coker, *US Military Power in the 1980s* (London: RUSI/Macmillan, 1983).
13. Ibid.
14. *The Times*, 17 November 1978.
15. Kenneth Coffey, *The Strategic Implications of the All-Volunteer Force* (Chapel Hill: University of North Carolina Press, 1979).
16. For a good discussion of the new options provided by PGMs see 'Contributions of Advanced Technology' in *Strengthening Conventional Deterrence in Europe: Proposals for the 1980s*. Report of the European Security Study (London: Macmillan, 1983) pp. 197–209.
17. Cited in C. Coker, *The Future of the Atlantic Alliance* (London: RUSI/Macmillan, 1984) pp. 131–40.
18. *Strengthening Conventional Deterrence in Europe: Proposals for the*

1980s (Report of the European Security Study (ESECS): Macmillan, 1983).
19. Ibid., pp. 232–3 (Donald Cotter, 'Potential Future Roles for Conventional and Nuclear Forces in defence of Western Europe').

3. THE NUCLEAR DIMENSION

1. Christopher Coker, *US Military Power in the 1980s* (London: RUSI/Macmillan, 1984) pp. 38–39, 104.
2. Alastair Buchan, *The Multilateral force: a historical perspective* (London: International Institute for Strategic Studies) Adelphi Paper No. 13, 1964.
3. Richard Burt, 'Washington and the Atlantic Alliance', *Strength to weakness: national security in the 1980's* (Institute for Contemporary Studies, 1980).
4. Ibid.
5. David Yost (ed.), *NATO's strategic option: arms control and defence* (New York: Pergamon Press, 1981).
6. Fritz Stern, 'Germany in a semi-Gaullist Europe', *Foreign Affairs* 58, Spring 1980, p. 884.
7. Cited Coral Bell, *Negotiating from strength* (London: Chatto and Windus, 1962) p. 173.
8. Dean Acheson, 'The illusion of disengagement', *Foreign Affairs* 36, April 1958, p. 376.
9. Cited Bell, *Negotiating from strength*, op. cit., p. 172.
10. See Albert Wohlstetter, 'Is there a strategic arms race?', *Foreign Policy* 15 (Summer 1974); 'Rivals but no race', ibid. 16 (Fall 1974).
11. Statement to Senate Foreign Relations Committee reprinted Henry A. Kissinger, *American foreign policy* (New York: 1977), p. 160.
12. *The Washington Post*, 21 December 1981.
13. Richard Burt, 'The hidden nuclear crisis in the Atlantic Alliance' in David Yost (ed.), *NATO's strategic options: arms control and defence* (New York: Pergamon Press, 1981), pp. 56–7.
14. William Kaufmann, *The McNamara strategy* (New York: Harper and Row, 1964) pp. 59–60.

4. THE LILLIPUTIAN SENATE: THE FAILURE OF EUROPEAN COOPERATION

1. Henry Kissinger, *Foreign Affairs*, January 1963, p. 284.
2. Bull, 'European Self-reliance', op. cit.
3. Cohen, 'The Long Term Crisis of the Alliance', op. cit.
4. Henry Kissinger, *The White House Years* (London: Weidenfeld and Nicolson, 1979) p. 400.
5. Stanley Hoffmann, 'Fragments floating in the here and now', *Daedalus*, Winter 1979, pp. 1–26.
6. *The Times*, (London) 5 May 1982.
7. Cited William Cromwell, *The Eurogroup and NATO* (Lexington: Heath and Co., 1974) p. 54.
8. P. H. Scott, 'Beyond the Eurogroup: New developments in European Defence', *The World Today*, January 1976.
9. For a brief moment in 1963 after de Gaulle had vetoed Britain's application to join the European Community, the British entertained the idea of using the WEU as a vehicle for closer European defence cooperation. One recommendation which was not acted upon was broadening the terms of reference of the Secretary-General (R. Dobblestein, 'Britain's European policy and the WEU', *Revue de droit international de sciences diplomatiques et politiques*, 1976, p. 182).
10. The main developments between 1969–76 were the Hague summit (2 December 1969) and the summits at Paris (21 October 1971) and Copenhagen (14/15 December 1973); the publication of the Luxembourg report (20 July 1970); the Declaration on European unity (15 December 1973) and the Report on European union by the European Commission (25 June 1975).
11. For the Council's replies to Assembly questions see *European Yearbook*, xxii (1974) (The Hague: Martinus Nijhoff, 1974) p. 24.
12. Uwe Nerlich, 'West European Defence Identity: The French Paradox', *The World Today*, May 1974.
13. *The Times*, 19 June 1974.
14. Nerlich, 'West European Identity', op. cit., p. 197.
15. *Political Activities of the WEU Council: Reply to the 27th Annual Report of the Council* (Assembly of the WEU: 28th Ordinary Session (First Part) Documents 913, 18 May 1982).
16. See Anthony Eden, *Full Circle* (London: Cassell, 1960) p. 174.

17. Cited William Cromwell, *The Eurogroup and NATO* (Lexington: Heath and Co., 1974) p. 54, n. 99.
18. Except for a few cases provided for in Article 8:4 of the modified Brussels Treaty and specified in Protocols II, III and IV relating to force levels, the Council always reaches decisions unanimously.
19. *WEU Contribution to the Development of European Union* (Assembly of WEU: 23rd Ordinary Session (2nd Part) Document 756, 4 November 1977).
20. Paul Borcier, *The Political Role of the Assembly of the WEU* (Paris: Western European Union, 1963) p. 6.
21. See A. Glenn Mower, 'The importance of the North Atlantic Assembly', *Orbis*, 21:4 Winter 1978.
22. *Political activities of the Council: Reply to the 22nd Annual report of the Council* (Assembly of the WEU: 23rd Session (1st Part) Document 733, 9 May 1977) p. 3.
23. Cited, *The future of European security* (Assembly of the WEU: 26th Session (2nd Part) Document 854, 6 October 1980), para. 131.
24. WEU Assembly proceedings 11th Session 1st Part Official Report of debates, 31 May 1965.
25. Cited Colin Gordon, 'The WEU and European Defence Cooperation', *Orbis*, 17:1 Spring 1973, p. 250.
26. *The Times*, 19 June 1974.
27. *The future of European security* (Assembly of WEU: 26th Session, 6 October 1980).
28. See WEU Assembly Official Report of the 9th Sitting, 30 November 1981, 27th Ordinary Session (2nd Part) A/WEU (27) CR9.
29. John Wilkinson, Parliamentary Secretary to the Secretary of Defence 1979–82; Geoffrey Pattie, Minister of State 1983 for Procurement; formerly Minister for Air 1979–82.
30. Lawrence Freedman, 'British defence policy after the Falklands', *The World Today*, September 1982.
31. Michael Chichester/John Wilkinson, *The Uncertain Ally: British Defence Policy 1960–90* (London: Gower, 1982) p. 92.
32. Andre Beaufre, *NATO and Europe* (New York: 1966) pp. 37–8.
33. *The Guardian*, 24 November 1982.
34. Michael Chichester, 'Britain and NATO: The Case for Revision', *The World Today*, November 1982, pp. 415–22.

35. James Bellini/Geoffrey Pattie, *A New World Role for the Medium Power: The British Opportunity* (London: RUSI, 1977) p. 114.
36. Ibid.
37. *The Times*, 1 December 1982.
38. Ben Moore, *NATO and the Future of Europe* (New York: Harper and Row, 1958).
39. Dominique Moisi, 'The limits of consensus', *The Atlantic Quarterly* 1:2, Summer 1982.
40. *Non! Reperes pour le socialisme* No. 14 July–August, 1982, p. 48.
41. Cited in George Thomson, 'The Politics of Anglo–French Nuclear Weapons', *The Round Table*, April 1972, p. 158.
42. Pierre Gallois, 'The raison d'etre of French defence policy', *International Affairs*, October 1963, p. 501.
43. Testimony of H. A. Kissinger, *US policy towards Europe*. Hearings before the Committee on Foreign Relations US Senate June–July 1966 (Washington DC: 1966) p. 161.
44. Press Conference given by Giscard D'Estaing, 21 May 1975 (French Embassy Information Service, 75/78).
45. Cited David Calleo, *The Atlantic Fantasy: The United States, NATO and Europe* (Baltimore: Johns Hopkins University Press, 1970) p. 137.
46. Michael Harrison, 'Our Atlantic Quagmire', *The Washington Quarterly* 5:3, Summer 1982.

5. ATLANTIC ALLIANCE MANAGEMENT

1. Cited Gerald Ford, *A Time to Heal* (New York: 1979) p. 373.
2. Henry Kissinger, *The White House Years* (Boston: 1979) p. 215.
3. John Gaddis, *Strategies of Containment* (New York: Oxford University Press, 1982) p. 323.
4. *World Military Expenditures and Arms Transfers 1967–76* (Washington DC: US Arms Control and Disarmament Agency, 1978).
5. *Report on Allied contributions to the Common Defence*. A Report to the US Congress by Caspar W. Weinberger, Secretary of Defence, March 1982.
6. There are of course, many other ways of assessing defence burdens including payment in proportion to benefits and in the ability to pay with financing averages similar to a

progressive income tax system. See G. Kennedy, *Burden Sharing in NATO* (London: Duckworth, 1979).
7. See in particular Rae Angus, *Collaborative weapons acquisition: the MRCS (Tornado) Paravia Project* (Aberdeen University: Centre for Defence Studies, 1979).
8. *Political activities of the WEU Council* (Assembly of the WEU: 28th Ordinary Session Document 913, 18 May 1982).
9. *A European armaments programme*. Symposium held in Brussels, 15–17 October 1979 (WEU Office of the Clerk) pp. 53–4.
10. Ibid.
11. For a discussion of the European Parliament's competence to discuss defence matters see *European Parliament: Working Documents 1979–80*, Documentary No. 1 357/79, September 1979.
12. 'Arms Industry: How Much Is It a Community Matter?', *Europe*, 3063, 24 January 1981.
13. *International Aeronautical Consortia*, Colloquy held in London 9–10 February 1982 (WEU: Office of the Clerk: Committee on Scientific, Technological and Aerospace Questions, 1982) p. 62.
14. David Greenwood, 'Economic and social conditions of defence procurement'. Paper submitted at a Symposium in Brussels, *A European armaments policy*, op. cit., pp. 67–8.
15. See, 'Qualifications on Military Benefits of Standardisation' in *NATO Standardisation: political, economic and military issues*, Report to the House Committee on International Relations (Library of Congress: Congressional Research Service, 1977) pp. 29–31.
16. Speech by Malcolm Currie, Assistant Secretary of Defense (Public Affairs) in Detroit, 12 May 1975.
17. For further discussion see Davey Bartlett/James Polk. *NATO arms standardisation: two views* (Washington DC: AGI Defence Review, 1977).

6. OUT OF AREA OPERATIONS

1. Cited Stewart Menaul, 'NATO in the 1980's: a war winning strategy', *Conflict Studies*, April 1980, pp. 8–9.

2. Remarks by the Secretary of State for Defence to the Royal Institute for International Affairs, 22 October 1981. For a discussion on the RDF, see Christopher Coker, *US Military Power in the 1980s* (London: RUSI/Macmillan, 1983).
3. *The New York Times*, 18 January 1980.
4. *Defence in the 1980's: Statement on the Defence Estimates*, Cmnd. 7826, p. 39, para. 404.
5. For Geoffrey Pattie's speech see *Europaische Wehrkunde* 4, 1981, p. 156. At the same conference the American Deputy Assistant Secretary for Defence warned the allies that NATO could only become 'a mature alliance' if the Europeans were prepared to embrace 'an expanded concept of European security' by building up forces beyond the North Atlantic area.
6. Jeffrey Record, *The Rapid Deployment Force and US military intervention in the Persian Gulf* (Washington DC: Institute for Foreign Policy Analysis, 1981) p. 64.
7. Dov Zackheim, 'Of allies and access', *The Washington Quarterly*, Winter 1981.
8. For a general discussion see Frank Uhlig, 'A Western force for East of Suez', *Armed Forces Journal International*, August 1980.
9. *General Report on Alliance Security Issues* (North Atlantic Assembly: Military Committee 1980, X200 MC(80) 8, para. 13).
10. Michael Chichester, 'Whitehall cover-up, Westminster exposure', *Navy International*, July 1976, p. 8.
11. Cited Noel Salter, 'Western European Union: the Role of the Assembly 1954–63', *International Affairs*, 40:1 1964, p. 14.
12. See for example Admiral H. Train (SACLANT), 'NATO: global outlook', *Navy International* 86 (January 1981) p. 11, and see also Admiral Trains contribution to *US Military Power in the 1980s* (London: RUSI/Macmillan, 1984) pp. 107–114.
13. For a discussion of SACLANT planning see Christopher Coker, 'South Africa and NATO: a history of illusions', *RUSI Journal* June 1982.
14. Ibid.
15. Cited *European security and the South Atlantic* (Assembly of WEU: 27th Ordinary Session (2nd Part) Document 888, 26 October 1981, p. 16).
16. See Chistopher Coker, 'The Western Alliance and Africa 1949–81', *African Affairs*, July 1982, p. 334.

17. *Reappraisal of global dangers to Western peace and security* (Assembly of WEU: 27th Ordinary Session (2nd Part) Document 887, 26 October 1981, p. 17).
18. *The Times*, 5 May 1982.
19. For a discussion of the French role overseas in the light of possible WEU and Eurogroup initiatives see Christopher Coker/Heinz Schulte, 'A European option in the Indian Ocean', *International Defence Review*, 15:1 1982, pp. 27–34.
20. 'Protecting the West's Persian Gulf oil supply'. Remarks by the US ambassador to NATO at Hanns-Seidel Stiftung, 4 November 1981.
21. Alastair Buchan, *Crisis management, new diplomacy* (Paris: Atlantic Institute, 1964) p. 353.
22. George Kennan, *Memoirs* (Boston: Little and Brown, 1967) pp. 406–9.
23. Zbigniew Brzezinski, *The alternative to partition* (New York: McGraw Hill, 1965) p. 175.
24. Jeffrey Record, 'Beyond NATO: new military directions for the US' in Record/Hanks, *US strategy at the crossroads* (Cambridge, Mass.: Institute of Foreign Policy Analysis, 1982) p. 5.
25. Cited William Reitzel, *US foreign policy 1945–55* (Washington DC: Brookings Institution, 1956) p. 279.
26. Cited John Baylis, *Anglo-American defence relations 1939–80* (London: Macmillan, 1981) p. 13.
27. Cited David Reynolds, 'The US and European security from Wilson to Kennedy 1913–63': a reappraisal of the 'isolationist' tradition *RUSI Journal*, June 1983, p. 19.
28. Cited Peter Foot, *Defence burden sharing in the Atlantic Community 1945–55* (Aberdeen: Institute of Defence Economics, 1981) p. 41.
29. George Ball, *The past has another pattern* (New York: Norton and Co., 1982) p. 574.
30. See for example Alan Sabrovsky, 'Allies, clients and encumbrances', *International Security Review*, 5:2 Summer 1980; Kenneth Adelman, 'Revitalising alliances' in Scott Thompson (ed.) *National security in the 1980's: from weakness to strength* (San Francisco: Institute for Contemporary Studies, 1980).
31. See in particular Andrew Hurrell, 'The politics of South Atlantic security: a survey of proposals for a South Atlantic Treaty Organisation', *International Affairs*, 59:2 1983.

7. CONCLUSION: THE NEED FOR AN ATLANTIC COMMUNITY

1. Klaus Knorr, 'The strained alliance' in Knorr (ed.) *NATO and American Security* (New Jersey: Princeton University Press, 1959) p. 3.
2. See for example the collection of essays in Myers (ed.) *NATO: The Next Thirty Years* (Boulder: Colorado, 1980).
3. Lloyd Ambrosius, 'Wilson, The Republicans and French Security', *Journal of American History* 59 (1972) pp. 341–52.
4. Cited David Reynolds, 'The US and European Security from Wilson to Kennedy 1913–63', *RUSI Journal*, June 1983, p. 19.
5. Richard Burt, 'NATO: The New Challenge Ahead' address at the Copenhagen regional seminar, 5 February 1982.

Index

Air-land Battle, 20–4, 188–94
Air power, 147, 149–53, 158–9
Arms control negotiations, 34–7, 144–6, 165–74
   non-ratification of treaties, 37
Atlantic Policy Advisory Group, 113

Battlefield Nuclear Weaons, 31–4
Blitzkrieg, 8–9, 17, 19, 34
British Army of the Rhine (BAOR), 45, 64–8, 150, 183–6

Campaign for Nuclear Disarmament (CND), 38–9, 48, 141–3
Central European theatre, 196–206

Debré, 71
Defence expenditure, 79–82, 136, 156

European Economic Community, 53, 55, 59, 62, 74, 90–1
European Defence Community, 5, 51–4
Eurogroup, 52–4, 57, 72, 110–12
   and out of area operations, 111–13, 144

Falklands War (1982), 69, 95, 119, 144
Federal Republic, 13, 24
Flexible response, 12–13, 132–3
Force de Frappe, 69–71

Genscher–Colombo Plan, 52, 58, 61

Jobert, 53, 56, 72, 89

Kissinger, 40, 41, 48, 50, 69, 72
Korean War, 115–17
Kristol, 4

Labour Party (UK), 42–3, 45–7, 65, 103
Lisbon Conference, 20, 120
Long Term Defence Programme (LTDP), 77, 82, 114

Macarthy, 4
McNamara, 12
Mèndes-France, 58, 61
MLF, 51
Moynihan, 49

Index

NATO
  air forces, 9–10
  burden-sharing, 76–83
  comparisons with Warsaw Pact, 10–11, 134–5, 157–8
  main battle tactics, 12–14
  Northern Flank, 207–15
  out of area operations, 108–10, 144, 178, 180, 217–19, 220, 227–8
  Southern Flank, 216, 223–7
Neutron bomb, 42
Nuclear Forces
  force assymetries, 26–7
  modernisation programmes, 25–7, 30
Nuclear Planning Group (NPG), 29, 44

Peace Movement, 38, 124–6, 138–9, 177
Polaris, 27
Political bi-partisanship, 44–8
POMCUS, 15–16, 50
Precision Guided Munitions (PGMs), 17–18, 81
Public opinion, 23–4, 37–49
Pyrrhic defence, 19–20

Radford Plan, 5
Rapid Deployment Force, 278
  European contribution, 96, 97–101

Reagan Administration, 4, 95
Reinforcement (VS), 7, 14–16

SACEUR, 21, 23, 181
SACLANT, 1, 2–3, 108
SALT, 25–7, 145, 166, 167
Social Democratic Parties, 44–6
Soviet Forces
  air power, 9, 22
  comparison (with NATO), 10–11
STANAVFORLANT, 105
Standardisation
  CNAD, 85–7
  IEPG, 87–8
  WEU, 89–93
Stevens Amendment, 4

Taylor, M., 5
Theatre Nuclear Forces, 20, 21, 28–9
Trident, 27, 67, 144

United States, 15–16, 114–20

Vietnam War, 78, 219, 220

Warsaw Pact, 7–8, 14, 19
Western European Union (WEU)
  Assembly, 61–4
  Council, 58–61
  history of, 55–7
  out of area operations, 108, 110–11
  future, 72–5